EVERY LAST DROP

How the Blood Industry Betrayed the Public Trust

George T. Baxter, Esq.

Order this book online at www.trafford.com
or email orders@trafford.com
See actual court exhibits, Newspaper articles, gripping book trailer and
more on the book website. Visit www.Everylastdropbook.com

Most Trafford titles are also available at major online book retailers.

© Copyright 2013 George T. Baxter, Esq.
All rights reserved. No part of this publication may be reproduced, stored in a
retrieval system, or transmitted, in any form or by any means, electronic, mechanical,
photocopying, recording, or otherwise, without the written prior permission of the author.

Printed in the United States of America.

ISBN: 978-1-4907-1840-8 (sc)
ISBN: 978-1-4907-1841-5 (hc)
ISBN: 978-1-4907-1839-2 (e)

Library of Congress Control Number: 2013919522

Because of the dynamic nature of the Internet, any web addresses or links contained in
this book may have changed since publication and may no longer be valid. The views
expressed in this work are solely those of the author and do not necessarily reflect the
views of the publisher, and the publisher hereby disclaims any responsibility for them.

Any people depicted in stock imagery provided by Thinkstock are models,
and such images are being used for illustrative purposes only.
Certain stock imagery © Thinkstock.

Trafford rev. 10/29/2013

 www.trafford.com

North America & international
toll-free: 1 888 232 4444 (USA & Canada)
fax: 812 355 4082

In the early to mid-1980's, the blood industry refused to test blood donors at risk for transmitting AIDS and 29,000 people were given AIDS contaminated blood. U.S. Congressional Committee, Oversight and Investigations, Blood Supply Safety.

Nearly ninety-percent of those in New Jersey diagnosed with AIDS in 1985 were not alive four years later. Snyder v. Mekhijan, 126 N.J. 328 (1991) Justice Garibadi, dissenting, citing New Jersey State Department of Health, AIDS Data Analysis (as of April 30, 1991.)

"All that is required for evil to prevail is for good men to do nothing." Edmund Burke.

FOREWORD

By

Marcus Conant, M.D.

Human societies are based on trust. We trust our fellow citizens not to stab us in a crowd. We trust our physicians to tell us the truth about treatments we may or may not need. We have special places that we believe to be safe. As children, we climb into our parents' beds when we have nightmares. As adults, we flee to churches or embassies when we feel attacked. Everyone turns to hospitals and physicians when they need medical attention.

Events such as the Aurora movie theater shooting, the massacre at Newtown and the Boston Marathon bombings challenge this trust we are supposed to have in our fellow citizens, but victims of these horrific events found refuge and compensation from religious or medical authorities. The families of Newtown victims gathered at church while authorities scoured the elementary school; medical authorities provided amputated marathon runners in Boston with free prosthetic limbs. It would never occur to us that the priest in the church where we sought refuge was secretly plotting to turn us over to the enemy, or that someone in the health care system would knowingly provide products that could kill us.

Unfortunately, it is exactly the story of physicians who betrayed the trust of their patients, their colleagues, and their profession that George Baxter recounts in this true account of how the American blood banking industry knowingly conspired to sell blood contaminated with the HIV/AIDS virus and, as a result, infected at least 29,000 people with AIDS in the United States alone.

Every Last Drop details how blood bankers from the American Association of Blood Banks (AABB) and the Red Cross first denied and then concealed overwhelming evidence that asymptomatic individuals infected with HIV were donating blood, and the blood banks injected that blood into patients.

Every blood bank in America had a paid, certified medical director with a valid medical license. Only three or four of these physicians stood up to their trade organization, the AABB, and said that they felt further steps were necessary to protect the nation's blood supply. We see the same behavior in politicians who are unwilling to break with their party or their financial backers, even though they have sworn to do what is best for the people who elected them.

In addition to naming names and telling the sordid stories of the crimes perpetrated by the blood banking industry, Baxter's book picks up where Randy Shilts' book, "And The Band Played On," ends. Baxter highlights many flaws in the American legal system. He points out the Herculean task that a single individual faces when fighting a giant industry like the AABB or the Red Cross. His personal story of a young, inexperienced attorney fighting a billion-dollar industry is a refreshing reminder that tenacity and hours of study are two ingredients essential for success. Hollywood would have us believe that success comes from a momentary inspiration to a hero while he's playing baseball. *Every Last Drop* reminds us that success requires exhaustive preparation and restless nights of contemplation and reflection. It is the creeping fear that our efforts are getting us nowhere, but the faith that they will.

Finally, *Every Last Drop* reminds us of an essential lesson that Americans appear reluctant to learn: society cannot protect us without regulations. Alan Greenspan, former chairman of the Federal Reserve Bank, believed that financial institutions would not betray the public for fear that they would injure their institutions. It apparently did not occur to him that short-term profits to an individual are always more attractive than the long-term repercussions to an institution.

In the early 1980s, when the AIDS epidemic began, blood banks were not really regulated. Blood bankers were writing the regulations and passing them on to the Food and Drug Administration (FDA), who adopted them. This is as clear an example of the fox watching the henhouse as one can imagine. Government regulations are intrusive and annoying. Unfortunately, without effective regulations, tragedies similar to the ones you will encounter in this story are all too common.

In France, the blood bankers responsible for infecting patients with the AIDS virus were sent to prison. In the United States, the blood bankers were defended by prestigious legal firms employed by the AABB and the Red Cross. The blood bankers responsible for these crimes were not charged, and the cost of paying settlements was borne by the American people who were forced to pay more for blood products.

As usual, we did not learn from this tragedy. Instead of realizing that all institutions that directly affect our lives need to be regulated, we have continued to deregulate essential industries such as banking and real estate, and we have repealed laws that prior generations learned were needed to ensure trust in these industries. The sad truth is that we cannot always trust

George T. Baxter, Esq.

our fellow citizens not to open fire at a Mother's Day parade or movie theater or elementary school, but we should always be able to trust our hospitals and medical specialists—and the government we expect to protect us from harm if greed and laziness overcome these large, regulatory industries.

Every Last Drop is more than one man's journey to find justice for his clients. It is a cautionary tale of the terrible price we pay when we allow complacency and greed to destroy trust.

Marcus Conant, M.D.
The Conant Foundation
San Francisco, California

FOREWORD

By

Donald P. Francis, M.D., D.Sc.

During my twenty-one years at the Centers for Disease Control, working in the United States as well as in many underdeveloped countries, I confronted a number of deadly diseases and worked with responsible authorities to combat their spread. I had worked with medical teams in the jungles and deserts of Africa and with similar teams on the vast, crowded Ganges' plains of India and Bangladesh. But never had I come up against a group like the blood bankers in the United States of America.

The height of frustration for those of us working on the Centers for Disease Control AIDS Task Force to prevent the contamination of America's blood supply came when the blood bankers refused to begin testing blood donors who were at risk for transmitting the deadly AIDS virus through blood products.

It's a matter of record now that the blood bankers' failure to take action to prevent the contamination of the blood supply resulted in tens of thousands of people being given

George T. Baxter, Esq.

AIDS-contaminated blood and hundreds of thousands being infected with hepatitis C. It is the largest single catastrophic event in the history of American health care. The conflicts that occurred among the Centers for Disease Control AIDS Task Force members, who were working to prevent the epidemic; the American blood bankers, who refused to test donors; and the Federal Food and Drug Administration Blood Products Advisory Committee, which aligned itself with the blood industry, had devastating consequences for the American public.

To compound this disaster, American blood bankers exported contaminated blood products around the world, infecting other populations. Most interesting to me has been the lack of remorse from the blood bank leaders themselves. Even in the face of historic evidence of their stupidity and negligence, they continue to defend their lack of action with such statements as: we did everything we could, we did everything the FDA required, there was insufficient evidence, and a new test would soon be available. Each of these is untrue.

We at the Centers for Disease Control outlined exactly what needed to be done. We provided all the evidence to support the need for action. The tests we recommended were already commercially available, and the testing equipment was being used daily in blood banks. All they had to do was implement the test, and thousands of lives would have been saved. What follows is the untold story of how American blood bankers fanned the AIDS epidemic here and abroad.

Only a few transfusion AIDS victims, like attorney George Baxter's clients, attempted to take legal action. The vast majority of patients just suffered and died without anyone being held responsible or paying compensation. The blood industry expected the people they infected to simply go away and die quietly, which is, unfortunately, exactly what they did.

Every Last Drop

Now, in a story that is as enlightening as it is frustrating, George Baxter's story provides a shrewd look into the legal brouhaha surrounding this darkest hour in American health care.

Donald P. Francis, M.D., D.Sc.
Formerly: Centers for Disease Control AIDS Task Force
Currently: Executive Director
Global Solutions for Infectious Diseases
South San Francisco, California

For Janet and Bill

PART 1

CHAPTER ONE

My office is across the street from the side entrance of the Bergen County Superior Court, within eyeshot of the county jail. "George T. Baxter, Attorney At Law" is freshly painted on the front window facing Hudson Street. I rubbed the "G" with my thumb vigorously, just to see if the friction would erode it. My thumb never quite stopped smelling of varnish. Hudson Street begins where Main Street ends, just past Callahan's bail bondsmen office, the bus stop, a World War I memorial and a few public benches. The benches are usually occupied with jurors and courthouse staff having their lunches. The doors of the nearby grocery store are covered almost entirely in lottery posters with curling edges.

I check my watch and hasten my pace up the stairs, skipping two steps at a time. The fabric of my pants tightened around my knees with each step. The mailman left the mail wrapped in a rubber band on the floor, since I have no receptionist. The florescent ceiling light flickers with a clucking noise before it begrudgingly agrees to stay on. The two rear windows have one-inch thick iron bars on them, and face a neighbor's undernourished backyard and pigeon coop. I head straight for the coffee maker, which sits like a rooster on top of a re-painted teal filing cabinet.

George T. Baxter, Esq.

    I rinse out the glass coffee pot and fill it with water in the men's room sink down the hall. It's an old, pre-war building with boxy sinks that are almost a prank on my large, awkward hands. The coffee pot clanks against the sides of the sink and I have to maneuver it under the water tap. I check the time again, look around and clear the files from the two chairs in front of my desk. I'm 32, a couple of years out of law school, and building a personal injury law practice. I sit back in my chair with my hands on my desk, the way I saw presidents sit in photos of the oval office. Except my office is quiet. There have not been any clients.

    "Mr. Baxter?" A woman calls from the front door. I break out of my reverie to walk out to the reception area. It's Roslyn Snyder, the noon appointment. We spoke on the phone the day before.

    "Mr. Baxter?" She repeats my name, looking around, as though wondering if she is in the right place. Roslyn is about 5' 5", late-fifties, wears no makeup and does not color her gray hair. Her eyes scan past where I'm standing but she keeps looking around the room anyway, as though she is expecting the real George Baxter to jump up from behind a filing cabinet and yell "surprise!"

    "Hi, I'm George Baxter."

    "I'm Roslyn Snyder, and this is my husband Bill." Bill is smaller than Roslyn. The skin on his face droops from its pronounced bone structure and he looks painfully tired. He is wearing an Anheuser-Busch work jacket and wrinkled khaki pants that obscure all but the pointed tips of his shoes. The pants are too loose for him, and I can hear them trail on the floor as we walk to my office.

    "It's a pleasure to meet you." Roslyn and I shake hands. Her hand is thick and rough, like someone who works with them. "Come inside and have a seat." I offer them the chairs I had just cleared off. I notice a stray paper clip in one of the chairs and quickly flick it away before anybody could notice.

"Mr. Baxter, you said on the phone you do not charge for consultations."

"That is right—and please, call me George."

"Because we do not have money to pay a lawyer."

"I understand. Don't worry. Personal injury lawyers don't charge for consultations."

"So we will not be billed for this meeting then?"

"No. There is no fee unless I win you a settlement. Then, I take a percentage."

"All right."

I glance over to the top of the filing cabinet. "That is fresh coffee brewing." The smell of fresh coffee makes the frail office feel more comfortable. "Would you like a cup?"

"Bill, do you want some coffee?" Roslyn asks Bill, as though she is interpreting for me. He nods yes.

I reach for the package of Styrofoam cups behind the coffeemaker, but it is empty. "I forgot to pickup cups." On the desk is a ceramic Marine Corps mug, with the emblem of the Third Marine Amphibious Division proudly displayed on its facade. It is the only memento I have of my time in—shortly after I had dropped out of high school at age sixteen, until my twentieth birthday. It is an ornament that has never been used. I fill the mug with Maxwell House coffee and hand it to Bill. "Be careful, the mug is hot."

"Thank you." Bill takes a few sips then puts the mug down on the desk. I realize I forgot to offer the powdered creamer I had bought earlier just for this meeting.

"What is that noise?" Roslyn looks around the office, trying to pinpoint the sound.

"The pigeon coop." I try to be nonchalant, but the pigeons are cooing louder than usual. Bill and Roslyn look at each other, then me.

"Lets start from the beginning and see how I can help you."

"Well, Bill had shortness of breath that started after he retired from Anheuser-Busch, so we saw this cardiologist."

"What did he tell you?"

"That Bill had this blockage of his arteries. He sent us to see a surgeon at St. Joseph's—"

"What did the surgeon tell you?" Quit sounding so eager, I scolded myself.

"He says the reason Bill is tired all the time is because of the blockage. He says that bypass surgery will make Bill feel better and that it is routine these days. So we trusted him and went ahead. Then we moved down to Florida with the twins. We planned to enjoy what were supposed to be our golden years."

"Twins?" They look too old to have young children.

"Bill and I adopted twin boys when they were babies, and it turned out they have brain damage."

"You didn't know they were brain damaged when they were adopted?"

"No, but we love them. They're twelve now." Bill and Roslyn were in their mid-forties when they adopted the boys.

"Bill, what happened after the heart surgery?"

"I got this letter here from the hospital telling me to be tested for AIDS, because the donor whose blood they gave me was infected." Bill takes out the tattered letter that he must have shown to a dozen lawyers. "So I got tested at Halifax down in Florida." Bill looks scared and ashamed, and cannot talk about it. Instead he slides it down the table towards me. I read the letter.

"I'm sorry, Bill." There's a silence, filled in by the pigeons.

"We can't tell anyone," Bill hisses.

"Nobody can know, not even our family." Roslyn says, almost as a condition.

"We have to protect our boys." Bill is adamant about this.

"What do you mean, Bill?"

"Are you kidding? Look what they did to those boys in the next county over from us."

Bill is referring to the August 29, 1987 burning of the Ray family home in Arcadia, Florida. The Arcadia school board voted to keep three hemophiliac brothers—Richard, 10; Robert 9; and Randy, 8—from attending school because they were infected with AIDS from contaminated blood products. Arcadia's mayor, George Smith, and other parents had taken their children out of school and enrolled them in private school to keep them away from the Ray boys. Clifford and Louise Ray, the boys' parents, challenged the DeSoto County School Board's ruling in Federal Court. The federal judge ordered the school board to allow the Ray boys back into classes. This ignited hysteria in Arcadia against the Ray family that included bomb and death threats.

One evening, while the family was away, an arsonist set fire to their home. The fire started in the boys' bedroom and their uncle, who was in charge of them for the weekend, was pulled from the burning house and almost died from smoke inhalation. When Clifford and Louise looked over the charred remains of their home, they were driven away by shouts: "Next time they won't be so lucky," and "Get out of Arcadia! Get out of town!" At a news conference, Clifford and Louise announced it was time give up the fight and leave Arcadia.

The Rays held the politicians and school board responsible for the panic that overtook the town and drove them out. Other Arcadia residents told reporters that homosexuals brought this "plague" about: "They should quarantine everyone one of 'em, isolate them just like they would do with measles or chicken pox." The same board of education committee that kicked the Ray boys out of school offered the family donations of food and clothing. People wanted to be charitable, but charity stopped at the point of fear about their own personal safety. They provided support at an arm's length, helping victims with what looked like charity on camera but treating them like animals that would bite them if they got too close.

This new, mysterious disease that killed everyone who contracted it revealed ugly social prejudices. Emergency room physicians in New York who saw gay men come in with skin lesions and die soon thereafter referred to it as W.O.G. ("Wrath of God") syndrome. AIDS was a queer's disease, God's retribution against them for deviant life-styles. The Reverend Jerry Falwell and his Moral Majority, a new political force in American politics at the time, proclaimed AIDS had been prophesied as the precursor of the last days. National figures like Patrick Buchanan, a Republican presidential candidate, proclaimed, "The poor homosexuals—they have declared war upon nature, and now nature is exacting an awful retribution."

The nightly network news frightened people with images of emaciated gay men who were dying, their bodies covered oozing lesions and skin tumors. The demands to quarantine AIDS patients from society by rounding "them" up and shipping them off to some remote Pacific island were real. AIDS had a social stigma worse than leprosy when Bill came to see me. It was a time when legislatures had to enact laws to protect AIDS patients from discrimination. I knew that if people found out I was fighting an AIDS case, that somebody with AIDS sat in my office, nobody except other AIDS patients would come to see me. I had to ask myself the question: "Do I really want to be known as an AIDS lawyer?"

"Do you have to disclose Bill's name?" Roslyn asks. "We're afraid that if we sue, it'll come out about Bill."

"I can use a 'John Doe' for Bill's name in the complaint, but I can't promise your identity won't come out. It'll be news, and people will be interested because it's a new AIDS case." Bill's case would be the first AIDS-transfusion lawsuit in New Jersey filed by a patient, and it is bound to create a stir.

"We can't risk it," Roslyn insists. "I just don't want anyone to take it out on my boys. They have the bodies of young men, but they have the minds of children. They wouldn't understand."

After a minute of silence, all I can say is: "It is something you need to consider."

"They lied." Bill said, breaking his stupor of silence. "They just lie to you and get away with it."

"Who lied, Bill?"

"They told me the blood was safe, that I would feel better after the surgery."

"Who told you this?"

"All of them: my doctors, the hospital, and the blood bank." Bill's anger fades to fatigue before my eyes at an alarming speed, like a deflating beach ball. Within minutes the blood drains from his face, his body shrinks inward, and his complexion turns ashen.

"You spoke with people at the blood bank?" I thought it was unusual.

"Yes." Roslyn jumps in.

"Tell me what the blood center said and how it came up?"

"We were starting to hear things."

"What kinds of things?"

"You know, things about blood not being safe."

"What did you say to the blood bank?"

"Bill has friends at the brewery who were willing to donate blood for him if he needed it. We didn't want blood from strangers. I asked if Bill could use his own donors."

"What did the blood bank say to that?"

"They told me that there was nothing to worry about, that blood is safe. They wouldn't allow us to use our own blood donors."

This is called designated donors. It's common practice today for family members to donate blood for each other in elective surgeries. The blood industry was against it then because it was an inconvenience. It messed with their procedural flow and overall control of the blood system.

"Everyone kept saying that there was nothing to worry about." Roslyn looks at Bill like she let him down.

"Look at me now." Bill had punched new holes into his belt to hold up his khaki pants. "I have diarrhea all the time, and my medications make me sick."

"Bill, are you all right?" Roslyn tries to calm him.

"I have to use the men's room." Bill tries to hold back tears, but can't.

"Here, you'll need the key." I hand Bill the key and he leaves for the men's room. Roslyn watches Bill until the door shuts behind him, and quickly turns to me.

"If something happens to Bill, I won't be able to handle the boys alone. I'd have to institutionalize them."

"How is Bill with the boys now?"

"They love him. He makes their lunches with them; he's better at helping them with schoolwork; and when Bill tells them to go to sleep at night, they listen. Even though Bill is tired most of the time, the boys still listen to him."

After a few minutes, Bill returns and I grab the legal pad from my desk and begin taking notes. "When did you have the surgery, Bill?"

"Four years ago, on August 23, 1984." My pen screeches to a halt.

"Bill, New Jersey has a two year statute of limitations for personal injury law suits. It begins to run from when you find out you are injured. You didn't know you were infected from the transfusion until the blood bank sent the letter to you, right?"

"I got the letter six months ago."

"All right." A narrow miss.

"It's about the boys," Roslyn adds.

"Roslyn, if blood banks weren't testing for AIDS when Bill was transfused because there was no AIDS test yet, then there isn't a case." I want to stay detached, as I was told to do by so many professors and law textbooks, and did not want to be distracted by emotions. A lawyer should never let his clients believe they are going to win. The best way to make sure clients don't get their hopes up is to bore them with terminology. "I know what's happened to you is awful, but there are two aspects to a personal injury case: Damages and liability. Liability is like fault. I have to prove it is the blood bank's fault that Bill got infected. Even though the blood infected him with AIDS, I am not sure the legal system can help you."

"You mean they can just get away with it?" Bill says.

"I can get your hospital records and see what I can find?" I don't expect more than a settlement, at best.

"What's your fee for taking the case?" Roslyn asks, looking around the office.

"I would take your case on a contingency. If I win, I would retain one-third. That is the standard contingency fee."

"Will you take less?" It is a surprise that Roslyn negotiates the fee. Clients never try to negotiate me down on a contingency fee.

"One-third is standard."

"Yes, but this happened to Bill and me."

"This is a difficult case. It will take a lot of time and I will have to advance the expenses too. And, if I don't win, then there is no fee. It is a big risk for me, Roslyn." I stop short of telling her it may not be a case at all. Bill and Roslyn stand up to leave. Roslyn wants a reduced contingency fee. They don't take me up on the offer and decide to shop around for another lawyer. Roslyn and I are indifferent and noncommittal. I am not sure it is a bad thing, because I am queasy over shaking Bill's hand.

Bill leaves my battalion coffee mug on the edge of the desk. I throw it into the metal wastepaper basket. It makes a load clank and dents the inside of the can. The nightly news has shown too many of those frightening, scarecrow-like images of emaciated gay men dying from AIDS. The alarming body count and new theories of person-to-person transmission dominate the airwaves. I think about my wife and daughter, and decide I can't risk it.

I realize I am late for a court settlement conference again. I grab an overstuffed red expandable legal file from the floor, turn off the lights, and lock the door from the outside. I make a quick pit stop in men's room on the way out, like I have done dozens of times. This time I remember Bill used it earlier. I roll out a few feet of tissue paper and cover the toilet seat, but then decide that is not safe enough and leave. People still wonder if the AIDS virus can survive on a toilet seat.

CHAPTER TWO

Before moving into the office across the street, I practiced law from a silver 1975 Oldsmobile Starfire. I ricocheted from court to court taking per diem work from any lawyer who would give it to me. Finally, I met Joe Buttafucco, a Jersey-born lawyer who gives work out to a few tyros, like me, that show up every day.

Joe was corpulent, with a thick, billowy neck that probably deterred him from owning any neckties. "Money and a good cigar," he smacked his lips. "I love 'em." Joe's office is a converted trucking garage in the ironbound, industrialized section of Kearny, just off the Jersey turnpike. A full-sized brass replica of a medieval knight in antique armor stands at the doorway of his office, more or less in the center. Visitors must squeeze around it to get into the reception area. Its pointy elbow always scratches me I squeeze past, leaving sharp lines on my starched button-downs. Buttafucco pays per court appearance so I try to do multiple in a day, which means I come home looking like a cat clawed at my chest. There is no medical plan or sick days, and by the time I pay for the gas to get from court to court, it works out to a screech more than minimum wage.

Everyday, I get on the Jersey turnpike at Exit 16 towards Secuacus/Meadowlands and drive south, past the landfills and high feather reed grass and towering power lines. The schedule never varies: Exit 15, Jersey City court, 9:00 a.m.; Exit 14, Newark courthouse, 11:00 a.m.; Exit 13, Elizabeth, 2:00 p.m.; and on down to Exit 9, New Brunswick. There is a four-story building just before exit 14 which was once the old water repellant plant, but is now a crumbling brick monstrosity with so many broken windows and structural cracks that you can almost see through it. Driving past Newark Airport and the Elizabeth Seaport, the turnpike turns into a cacophony of noise and fast energy. It is twelve, fast-moving lanes of cars whizzing north and south; low-flying jumbo jetliners descending overhead from the east and west; yards of cargo containers, tall cranes, fuel storage tanks, towering smoke stacks, colossal recycling plants. I circle the crank handle away from me to close the window and turn the radio up.

The cases have to move so fast that I develop a few key tactics. For example, if my witness gets into trouble during a tough deposition, I yank him from the conference room because "he has to go to the bathroom," and coach him in the hallway. Court rules require a witness's deposition to be continuous and ongoing until finished, so over the strenuous objections of the defense counsel I reaffirm, "I'm sorry, Counselor, but nature calls. There is no rule against that, is there?"

I also perfect the art of inserting ambiguity into every little nook of a scenario. "Objection, please rephrase the question. Are you asking whether the light was red when my client approached the intersection or when he proceeded? There is a difference." When it gets really ugly, I slam the conference table with the palm of my hand, saying something like, "Objection. That question has been asked and answered. You are badgering my witness." In the end, it is not about justice, but about winning a settlement.

I find the courtroom I am looking for. "Honorable James Cassidy" is written on the top of the door. I walk into the courtroom and am stopped by the bailiff. "Counselor, are you here from Buttafucco's office?" Judge Cassidy asks, without even looking up from his coffee-stained *Daily News*.

I know what he is thinking. There is a stigma that comes with covering Buttafucco's cases, because his lawyers are in and out of courtrooms all over Jersey. It is like wearing a badge that says you are the lawyer just for the day, not unlike a soap opera actor who has to learn his lines the moment he steps into the studio. It is not a great feeling, but I swallow my pride. I am just waiting for that big case to come my way. Besides, it is how I keep the lights on and pay for the groceries. Right now, this is the best I can do.

Judge Cassidy is near retirement. His black robe, a powerful symbol of judicial authority, is thrown over the back of his chair. I can tell by the disinterested gaze that he has checked out; he still comes to work, but his days of caring have long passed. Cassidy's agenda is to clear his docket. He does not care what a case settles for, so long as it goes away.

Judge Cassidy looks at me with a condescending smirk. "You here from Buttafucco's office?" He asks again.

"Yes, Your Honor—"

"This is Frank." He points to a slightly overweight, middle-aged lawyer sitting at a small table in the corner. The table is one of those scrimpy ones with desktops attached to it, like one you'd find in a school. I'm not sure why such a large man elected to sit in the smallest seat available, nor what a school desk was doing in the courtroom. "He has been writing out checks all morning. Right, Frank?" Cassidy chuckles.

"That's right, Judge." Frank leans back in his chair. His checkbook sits in his lap. He taps the back of his pen on the checkbook's leather protector in swift, axe-like motions. He is ready to screw me.

George T. Baxter, Esq.

"Mr. Baxter, you can leave here with a check in your hand this morning if you like. Let's make this easy for all of us. What is it going to take?" The judge asks.

They think I will roll over on the case because I am inexperienced and hungry. There is an art to handling a settlement conference; it is no different than a street hustle. I reach into Buttafucco's file for the medical report. As I pull it out, I smell Joe's cigar smoke on the file. Cassidy puts up his hand, a signal to stop what I am doing.

"Mr. Baxter, I don't want to see that. Just give us your number."

I try to ignore his patronizing tone and push forward. I put the file on the table.

"Judge, just allow me to show you the medical report—"

He gets annoyed. "Mr. Baxter, let me be clear. I do not need to see it. When you have seen one Buttafucco medical report, you have seen them all, from that stable of whores he keeps." In Legalese, a whore is a physician, or any other expert witness, who has become a full-time expert witness and will say almost anything for a retainer check.

He is trying to rattle me. "Judge, the client has twenty-five in medical treatment and another seven hundred in damage to the rear bumper of his car. I need seventy-five." There it is, the first rule of negotiating. Put out the demand, and wait. The demand is always three times the client's medical bills in these soft tissue cases.

Frank cuts me off, "Seventy-five what? Dollars?"

"That is funny, Frank." I retort.

The second rule: do not bid against yourself, wait for the counteroffer. Otherwise, they have you lowering your figure without them coming up with counter-offer money. This is how the wheels turn in the gristmill of justice.

Cassidy's tone changes. He tries a different approach with me now. "Look, George, I can show you how to make money around here. Listen to me. Let me tell you how it works." He leans forward, speaking more softly. "I want to move cases. And Frank, here, he wants to settle them. You work with us and you will make money."

It is an invitation in, and I am curious about how much they think they can buy me for. "How much?" I ask.

There is a glimmer in Frank's eyes, and his mouth relaxes into a smile he is too old for. He thinks I caved in. "I will give you five thousand on it." Frank offers. "That is a sixteen hundred dollar fee for a morning's work. You can go home and watch TV for the rest of the day." Maybe it is a sixteen hundred dollar fee for Buttafucco, but I am paid the same sixty-five bucks for each case.

Frank is holding back. Defense lawyers always hold back the reserve money the insurance companies put on the case. It makes them look good to their carriers to settle under the reserve.

"Am I the only one around here who cares about justice for my client?"

Cassidy and Frank eye each other across the table. Even I was surprised by what I said.

"My, my Mr. Baxter. You are a young tiger. I am going to call Buttafucco and tell him how you handled this case for him."

Frank folds. "Sixty-five. Good only for this morning. Take it or leave it."

"Take the money" is what I always say. Sign up the client, work up their case and settle it. It keeps everyone happy. Leaving money on the table is like letting a roulette wheel ride in Atlantic City. One should never leave the money to chance. A jury may give you less—or nothing at all. The deal is done. I have to remind myself of these rules constantly, like a commentator at a football game. It helps prevent me from getting too emotionally involved in the clients' case. While personal injury is emotionally tense,

George T. Baxter, Esq.

personal injury law is not more than a numbers game. Empathy fogs judgment. Bring in new clients, work up their cases and take the money. Getting emotionally involved is bad business. It is like a surgeon getting too personally involved with patients. Fast settlements are what clients want and the quickest way to build my practice.

Frank stops me on the way out. "You are new around here, George. You should be concerned with making friends—not pissing people off."

CHAPTER THREE

Home is a cramped two-room apartment above my in-laws' garage. The shower is in a closet, and we duct-taped winter insulation over the porch windows to keep the winter chill out. Call it the bedroom. Patti hung a fluffy curtain across the rectangular "bedroom," making an enclave for our four-year-old daughter Courtney. She has a knack for making things cozy.

Patti does not acknowledge that she grew up in the big house we share our driveway with. On the evenings I get home late, she eats dinner in her parents' luxurious kitchen, looking through their French windows at the backyard we have no way of entering directly from our home in their garage. Her parents' disapproval of me is not hushed in that eerie suburban way; it is obvious they expected a lawyer to own a house just like theirs in a town just like theirs. Patti defends me relentlessly, but I still worry that one day, over veal cacciatore and refilled glasses of Malbec, one of their flippant remarks will resonate with her.

Some mornings, I tease her before we get out of bed to start our day.

"Say it. Go ahead." I nudge her playfully.

"No!" She laughs.

"Come on, say it!"

She shakes her head. "No, I am not saying it!"

"Say it to me. Say, 'Come on, get out of bed, you bum, or you will end up like your father.'"

Patti blushes. The words are too hard for her.

"I am not leaving until you say it . . ."

She gives in. "All right. Get out of bed, or you will end up a bum."

"Close enough."

I kiss her. On my way out the door, I dig deep into my pocket for that last twenty bucks. I put it into the cookie jar on the kitchen counter. Groceries.

It is 10:00 a.m. on Sunday morning. I am in Jersey City, re-shifting my weight from one foot to the other to keep from falling off the rickety fire escape. The front door of the apartment building is locked and the person I am trying to contact does not answer the doorbell. I count the windows and floors from the first level and figure out which window is his, and hesitate for a fraction of a second before I climb. It is my first product liability case, and I do not want to screw it up.

A roofer I had worked with during my college summer job fell from a roof, breaking his hip and arm. He fell when construction equipment designed to remove tarred gravel from the roof propelled gravel at him and knocked him right off the roof like a bowling ball to a pin. I have to prove the machine was defective because its manufacturer did not design it safely for its anticipated use.

The company's lawyer is Buttafucco himself. Neither of us seem bothered by any conflict-of-interest in being adversaries on the case while also working together. I had deposed the company's engineer for two days. Finally, he produced a blue print of the machine with the draftsman's name at the bottom.

I hired a private investigator to locate the draftsman. He checks with the state's registry of licensed engineers and this is the current address listed on there.

I knock on the window more ferociously.

"Who the hell are you?" A young man, eyes still half-shut, wants to know. I worry for a moment that he might grab the potted cactus on his windowsill.

"It's okay," I assure the man. "I am a lawyer."

"What the hell are you talking about? Get off my fire escape before I call the police!"

"It is all right," I need to calm him for my own safety. "I am a lawyer. I just want to speak to you." I press the blueprint against the window and point to his signature.

He recognizes it and reluctantly agrees to come downstairs. We talk for a few minutes on the sidewalk outside his building.

"I don't work for them anymore," he says in between cigarette puffs.

"Do you remember working on the design of this machine?"

"Yeah, I remember." He scratches the back of his head with his cigarette hand.

"Just answer one question; did anyone ever suggest putting a guard on it to stop the gravel from shooting up like projectiles?"

"Yeah. The first design had a guard, but they took it off to save money."

It is over. Buttafucco settles the case and my turnpike lawyering days come to an end.

I scrap together a down payment toward our first house. It is nowhere near as robust as Patti's parents place, but a few fixes here and there and a new golden retriever puppy, Abby, make it home. I am not comfortable with a mortgage because the law practice is new and settlements are few and far in between, but we are a family with our first home, so running around to make the payments month after month is worth it. Patti borrows a sewing machine and makes curtains. She uses vine stencils to paint hydrangeas on the wall, and frames a couple of her watercolor landscapes in the living room.

On the nights I make it home on time, I look forward to dinner with just Patti and Courtney, occasionally with a candle on the table. When I can't make it, there is always a plate left in the refrigerator with a warm note in Patti's script. Upon first seeing the new house, her mother remarked that as a little girl, Patti would be the one to bring home the hungry stray cat. "Not much has changed," she mutters loud enough for my father-in-law to guffaw at. Patti laughs and puts her hand on my shoulder: "You're my diamond in the rough, honey."

On the weekends, Patti and I begin to decorate the new office. We borrow her father's truck to get an old oak conference table from a surplus warehouse. An extra five dollars got us the wooden chair to go with it. The used filing cabinet was twenty. But the real jewel is my "rebuilt" copy machine. It is beige and makes only a single copy at a time. It is temperamental and breaks down a lot. The room is not much—but it is my first law office.

"It is too bad you could not have helped them. I feel badly for them." Patti is talking about Bill and Roslyn.

"Yes, it is too bad."

Whenever the opportunity arose, Patti handed out my business card. "Oh, my husband is a very good lawyer. He can help you with that," Patti would tell the guy at the dry cleaners when she picked up my suits. I imagined her nodding attentively, tucking her strawberry blond hair behind her ear and holding Courtney's hand: "That is not right. You should call my husband."

When the butcher mentioned a tiff with his landlord, she slid my card across the counter: "Here's my husband's card. Call him." Her charisma muted her zealousness. She once marched into the women's bathroom at Red Lobster to take photos of a broken light fixture that fell on my client.

This evening, a few months after we moved, Patti tells me that she stopped at the video store to pick up *The Little Mermaid* for Courtney. She had given the clerk my card because he said he had a friend looking for a lawyer. That's how Bill and Roslyn Snyder found me.

A few weeks after the sounds of the rebuilt coffee machine joins the cooing pigeons, Bill and Roslyn come back to see me. There are no other takers for their case. It is a frightening decision for them to go forward with the lawsuit, for Bill may not even be alive by the time the case goes to court. After much soul searching, they consent to filing the case in their name, rather a fictitious "John Doe." Roslyn signs the retainer agreement and I send a request for Bill's hospital records, to sniff out any suspicious details. I take the case because my filing cabinet is empty, and fervently hope that smaller cases with easy settlements will come and go while Bill's file sits in there for what I expect will be a year, at least. I am not sure I can keep up with our new lifestyle without them.

CHAPTER FOUR

One evening, I get home late and Patti holds dinner for me. It is a chicken dish in a white sauce made with wine and flour, with mushrooms and grapes over rice, one of my favorites. The smell of her homemade rolls baking in the oven gives me a relaxed feeling. I was not used to home-cooked meals before marrying Patti, so every dinner is a feast. I take the serving spoon and pile it on my plate as the butter melts on the hot rolls.

"George, do not eat it all in one night." Patti is amazed, and slightly embarrassed, at how much I can eat.

"It is my favorite."

"They are all your favorite." Patti laughs. "So. Today, while I was ironing, I had the television on and they were talking about the Masters and Johnson report that just came out."

"Oh yeah," I mumble in between bites. I am not usually interested in those daytime talk shows.

"Yes. They said that the blood supply was unsafe in the early eighties." I nearly drop my fork.

The next morning, I walk down from my office to the Hackensack Johnson public library at the other end of Main Street. I sit at a reference table and look through the Masters and Johnson Report. Sure enough, there is a chapter about how blood was unsafe when Bill had his transfusion. I check out footnotes that lead me to Randy Shilts' book, *And the Band Played On*, which recently came out in paperback.

On my way home from work, I stop at the Riverside Square Mall bookstore. I scour the bookshelves for the book but do not see it. I do this a few times, reciting the alphabet over and over in my head and tracing my finger along book spines, hoping it would suddenly stand out. I do not want to ask the woman behind the counter because I worry that by just asking for this book about AIDS, she will wonder why I want it. Even the customers at the counter may wonder: "Is he gay?" "Does he have AIDS?" I pretend to look at other books, killing time, working up the nerve and waiting for the right moment to ask for the book. Finally, I walk up to the counter and ask for it. I pay for the book, cover it with two plastic bags, and get out of there.

And The Band Played On: Politics, People And The AIDS Epidemic by Randy Shilts provides me with my first account of the explosive politics of the epidemic. I cover the text with so much yellow highlighter that the pages resemble window blinds. On evenings, I bring it to the dinner table and read passages to Patti. I read how Dr. Marcus Conant, a San Francisco physician and AIDS pioneer, is among the first physicians in San Francisco to discover the early cases. As a dermatologist, he began to see legions and tumors on gay patients before there was a diagnosis of Kaposi Sarcoma. In the early days AIDS was called GRID, Gay Related Immune Deficiency, but it was later changed to Acquired Immune Deficiency Syndrome to de-politicalize it. The Regan administration refused funding for research and treatment.

"Wait, listen to this. It says that Dr. Marcus Conant coordinated a press release with University of California Hospital physicians to get a guy named Herbert Perkins, the director of

George T. Baxter, Esq.

Irwin Memorial Blood Center, the Bay Area's supplier of blood, to begin testing its donors for AIDS because the blood was infecting their patients." I tell Patti, wide-eyed with muckraking discovery.

"I thought there was no test?" Patti asks.

"So did I. But Dr. Edgar Engleman, the director of Stanford's Blood Center, started testing donors for AIDS in June 1983. That's eighteen months before Bill's transfusion."

"You have to get this before a jury." Patti smiles and arranges ingredients for a celebratory dinner. I don't stop her, but I know that a journalist writing about something is far different from a lawyer proving it in a court of law. Witnesses need to be located, convinced to testify, and grilled with vigorous cross-examination. There are no quick victories, just settlements.

Bill's records from St. Joseph's Hospital show that an anesthesiologist transfused Bill with a unit of platelets from donor #29F0784 during the bypass surgery. I track the blood donor by crosschecking the hospital blood bank record with its supplier. The origin of Bill's platelet is Bergen Community Blood Center, in Paramus, New Jersey, a ten minute drive from my office. My pen froze to a halt when I realized how close this disease was to me, to our suburban quietude. I thought of the manicured lawns in front of, almost safeguarding, the houses in affluent Ridgewood, on the border of Paramus. AIDS, like death—a jarring simile—could happen to anybody, regardless of how groomed their gardens. People talked about AIDS like it was the weird, inbred family on the other side of the tracks. Those poor San Francisco gays. But the gossip that colored in their silence only made it feel more pervasive.

I decide, not without naïveté, to track down all the sources in Randy Shilts' book and ask them if they would like to serve as witnesses and experts, anyone willing to testify. I spend the next few days getting acquainted with various voice mailboxes, especially Dr. Engleman at Stanford University, whom I called a few times every day. The book was on the *New York Times Bestseller List* for weeks, translated into several languages and even nominated for a National Book Award. Randy Shits is a celebrity, compared to revolutionaries like Thomas Paine. I am a Jersey lawyer with a shitty beige copier.

The quietness in the office and that hollow sound of the empty filing cabinet drawer closing is worrisome. I try calling a chiropractor friend for an accident referral, but he is not in. I glance over at a paper bag filled with unopened bills and wonder where the next settlement will come from. When the overwhelming florescence of the ceiling light forces me into further desperation, I pick up the phone once again and dial a number.

"Hello, Dr. Conant's office." I am caught off guard by the male voice on the other end.

"Hi." I pause. "May I speak with Dr. Conant, please?"

"Who is calling?" the male voice asks politely.

"My name is George Baxter. I am a lawyer from New Jersey."

"What are you calling about?" This is farther than I expected to get.

"I am looking into a AIDS-transfusion case."

"Just a minute, please." Guess he has another call.

"Hello, this is Dr. Conant." I nearly drop the receiver. Since when did doctors actually get on the phone?

"Hello, still there?"

"Yes, I'm here."

"And whom do I have the pleasure of speaking with?"

"I am George Baxter, a lawyer from New Jersey, and read about you."

"Your client is infected with AIDS from that transfusion, I presume?"

"Yes, that's right."

"When was your client's transfusion?"

"August 23, 1984."

"Then you have a case, Counselor."

"What do you mean?"

"The blood banks could have prevented your client from being infected with AIDS."

"You mean—"

Dr. Conant cuts to the point. "I mean, Counselor, you have a case." At this instant, I know I may have a credible witness and have to meet him.

"I would like to help you, Counselor, but I have an office filled with sick patients right now who need me more. Tell the receptionist that I said to give you an appointment." In the background, I hear pagers.

That night, I pack my travel carry-on for a weekend trip. Patti puts sliced carrot sticks, trail mix, and a few containers of Courtney's Juicy-Juice in a bag for me. I am uncomfortable with leaving home and flying, so I stay awake until 4:30 a.m. finally rolls around. I kiss Patti and Courtney good-bye before leaving for the airport in the dark. It is dawn as I drive down the Jersey Turnpike. Rail yards, industrial smoke stacks, and power lines silhouette the navy of just-before-dawn. As I get closer to exit 14, lights from the landing jumbo jetliners hover in the sky.

I park in the long-term parking lot to save some money. It is a couple of miles from the airport, connected by a shuttle bus. The sun, reflecting off the tops of cars, has a blood orange tinge. Purples and pinks always make their ways into Jersey sunrises. The lights on the passenger jets puncture the groggy air before they disappear in the distance. I was the only one in the parking lot, but I couldn't shake the inkling that other people were sleeping in cars.

CHAPTER FIVE

When the pilot's voice of the morning United flight comes through the speaker to tell us that we are beginning the descent into San Francisco, I watch with apprehension at the bay water beneath us. The runway begins right at the edge of the water, and when the wheels touch down, I exhale. For most of the trip, I stared out the window at the sheet metal rivets holding the wing together. When I was sixteen, I worked in a sheet metal plant and operated a riveting gun that put metal skins on the Disney Land monorail. While taking off from Newark, I scrutinized every rivet in the wing for flaws through the plastic of my oval window. I wondered how cold the water beneath us would be if we missed the runway.

The airport tarmac shines from early morning rain showers. There is even a rainbow in the distant mountains. The peaceful, wide-open terrain of mountains and sea are a world away from the old infrastructure and bustling commerce along the Jersey turnpike. The strong aroma of San Francisco French roast coffee from one of the concession stands catches my attention. Newark didn't even have a Dunkin' Donuts back then. On the way to the hotel, I cannot peel my nose away from the side window. The bungalows built on the sides of mountains look like they had grown there organically.

George T. Baxter, Esq.

At the Sheraton at Fisherman's Wharf, the plastic door key is alien to me. On the first try, it doesn't work. I reverse the plastic card and slide it through again. This time yellow and green lights go off, but I fail to turn the doorknob on the green in time and it locks again. I wonder who thought of this complex system and what was so wrong with metal keys. I try once more before going down to the reception desk to tell them its not working. With one hand on the door knob ready to turn it on the green light, I swipe the new plastic card they gave me. It is me against this magnetic strip. The green light comes on: I push the knob down, and I am in. I victoriously toss the plastic key onto the dresser as though saying, "take that!" I open the drapes to let light into the room and sit on the edge of the bed and take in my new surroundings: the Monet-ish prints of gardens on the wall, desk, chair, and single cup coffeemaker.

As I unpack my carry-on and hang up the clothes, I find a small yellow Post-it note that says, "Someone in New Jersey misses you. Love, Patti." I stick it on the mirror. I unpack a little more, and find a second note. This one says, "Come home soon," signed with X's and O's. I stick the second note on the armoire door.

The next morning, I take a cab to Dr. Conant's office, which is across from the University of California San Francisco Medical Center. I walk into the reception area, startled by the presence of so many men and no women. I had never been in a room filled with gay patients, or gay anything. I walk to the reception window. There is a flurry of patient and physician activity behind it.

"Excuse me, I am here to see Dr. Conant." As soon as I say it, I realize so is everyone else.

"What is your name?" a young male receptionist asks politely. I recognize his dulcet from the telephone.

"George Baxter."

He checks the appointment book. "I see you are down for lunch with the doctor. Have a seat; he is running late today."

The reception seats are filled with emaciated, sickly men that up until now I only saw on the nightly news. My initial reaction is to stand away from them, against the wall, rather than sit down. After a while, I decide to sit. I place my hands on my lap and keep my elbows at my side, careful not to rub against anyone. As time goes on, I reach for a magazine on the coffee table. Then I wonder about all the sick people who must have held it.

"Mr. Baxter." A slightly pudgy young man with a round face and a soft voice walks over to me. "I am Robin, Dr. Conant's assistant. Dr. Conant will see you now. Come with me." Robin leads me down the corridor, past small treatment rooms, to Dr. Conant's office.

"Wait here. Dr. Conant will be along in a few minutes." As Robin walks out, I check out Dr. Conant's accolade-filled wall. There are all kinds: humanitarian activism awards, the San Francisco Physician of the Year Award, photographs of him with political figures like Mayor Willie Brown. Dr. Conant is a public health celebrity and a San Francisco hero.

"So, Mr. Baxter, how was your trip?" I turn around and meet Dr. Conant. He is charismatic and handsome, with wavy brown hair, holding a patient's chart in his hand and a stethoscope hanging around his neck. We shake hands. He could be the cover of *GQ* magazine.

"Did you get settled in at the hotel all right?" Dr. Conant is from northern Florida, educated at Duke, and has charming, gentlemanly southern manner.

"Yes, thank you." He is slightly intimidating at a personal level, but immediately, the lawyer in me thinks that he will make a great witness.

"Have a seat." Dr. Conant sits behind his desk as I page through a few notes I made on a legal pad.

"I made reservations for us to have lunch at the physician's lounge across the street to talk, but as you see, I can spare only a few minutes."

I suspect Dr. Conant is canceling lunch because he was expecting a sharp east coast lawyer, and instead there is this unsophisticated guy trying to hide his Jersey drawl thumbing through notes.

"Tell me how I can help you."

"I read that in early '83, you led group of physicians at the University hospital to issue a press release to get Irwin Memorial Blood Center to begin testing it donors blood for AIDS. Is that true?"

Dr. Conant looks out the office window behind his desk at the hospital across the street, then back at me across his desk. I'm not sure I understand this brief silence.

"Yes, it is true. Irwin supplies all the blood to the university hospital. We began to see patients were being infected with AIDS from Irwin's blood."

"Well, that is my question. Was there a test to screen blood donors at risk for transmitting AIDS in August '84?" Bill was transfused with platelets on August 24, 1984.

"Yes, there was a test."

I flip through more notes and ask about a Centers for Disease Control meeting in Atlanta, which I had read about in *And the Band Played On*. I worry that I appear clumsy with my questions. Frankly, I am still in awe of just being in a San Francisco office. Until this day, my professional world has been between exits 16 to 9 of the Jersey turnpike.

"Was there a meeting in Atlanta, Georgia where the CDC and the newly formed AIDS Task Force recommended testing blood donors to the Public Health Services and Blood Banks?"

"That's right. But no one would take action."

"Who wouldn't take action?"

"The blood bankers. The American Red Cross, Irwin, New York Blood Center, no one."

"Wait. So you are saying that there was a test that the Bergen Community Blood Center, in Paramus, New Jersey, could have used that would have prevented Bill Snyder from being infected with AIDS?" This is it, maybe I can get Bill a settlement from the blood center. I squeeze the black felt-tip with my fingers ready to write his next words. Dr. Conant leans toward me.

"Mr. Baxter, you are not getting it. It is not just your client, but thousands of other people too who were transfused with contaminated blood and died."

"But, how?"

"Because the blood banks refused to test their donors' blood." I am silent for a moment while I process the word "thousands."

Robin pops into the room. "Dr. Conant, you are needed in the examination room."

"I am sorry Mr. Baxter. I know you have come a long way, but I have patients that require my attention right now. We are really backed up this morning."

"Dr. Conant, please. I need more time with you about my case." An expert report from him will surely get me a settlement.

"Spend the afternoon seeing our beautiful city, and then we will meet for dinner."

What a relief.

At the Zuni Café on Market Street, Marc Conant brings me up to speed. The waiter comes over to our table and opens a pressed white linen napkin to place on my lap. I awkwardly lean back in the chair to make it easier for him. I am not used to this kind of restaurant. Marc suggests the chicken dish and orders us a couple glasses of Napa Valley chardonnay. The waiter walks away and Marc starts at the beginning—before there was an AIDS epidemic.

"Patient Zero is a gay flight steward named Gaetan Dugas, who works out of the New York, Toronto and San Francisco. He had unexplainable swallow lymph nodes, and a year later, discovers purple blotches on his face. He sees his doctor because he wants the purple lump removed from his face. His doctor insists on doing a biopsy. It turns out that he has a rare skin cancer that no one gets, called Kaposi's sarcoma. And he infects his partners from New York, Toronto to San Francisco."

"When was this?"

"The summer of '80, the same time I began seeing patients show up in my office with the same purple skin blotches."

Dr. Conant's dermatology practice quickly turned into the largest AIDS practice in San Francisco. He treated more than 3000 patients. He explains how over the next 18 months, the disease spread through the gay community, eventually killing everyone who got it. He worked with the San Francisco Department of Health and a CDC physician named Don Francis to close down the San Francisco bathhouses. The etiology of AIDS was still uncertain, other than the knowledge that it was transmitted by semen among gay men, causing it to be identified by the acronym, GRID, Gay Related Immune Deficiency.

"By June '82, we noticed that three hemophiliacs who had no other risk factors than the blood products they used were infected with AIDS. This raised the question of whether AIDS is transmitted by blood and blood products."

I managed to get the copies of the Centers for Disease Control's 1982-1987 Morbidity and Mortality Weekly Reports, called MMWR's. The CDC puts them out weekly, to update the public health community. On December 10, 1982, the CDC reported a 20-month old infant from the San Francisco Area developed unexplained cellular immunodeficiency and opportunistic infection after being transfused with blood products, including platelets, derived from the blood of a man subsequently found to have AIDS. The baby was delivered on March 3, 1981 and appeared well. However, at 14 months of age the baby's skin became puckered; he was chronically sick. The CDC discovered the blood donor of the blood products given to the baby is a 48-year-old San Francisco male who appeared healthy when he donated blood but was later found to have AIDS. The CDC put the puzzle together and knew that although the etiology of AIDS was unknown, its infectious agent was transmitted sexually and by blood.

"The blood that infected this infant came from Irwin," Marc states.

It was an unimaginable public health crisis on its way. The evidence that AIDS was contaminating the national blood supply was so convincing that the CDC arranged an emergency public health meeting in Atlanta, on January 4, 1983. This was the point at which the legal liability clock began to tick on the blood industry.

"Marc, can you tell me about the CDC's Atlanta meeting?"

"Everyone from the blood industry and public health service was there."

"Like who? What do you mean everyone?"

"I mean everyone with the responsibility for protecting the blood supply of this country: Joseph Bove, American Association of Blood Banks; Gerald Sandler and Paul Cumming, American Red Cross; Dennis Donohue, FDA; Herbert Perkins, Irwin Memorial Blood Bank; Aaron Kellner, New York Blood Center; the CDC's AIDS Task Force, and the Pharmaceutical Manufacturers Association. They were all there—all the way up to the Office of the Surgeon General."

"What happened?"

"Six months earlier, the CDC had formed an AIDS task force made up of infectious disease specialists. And, they figured out two things: AIDS was one hundred percent fatal, and it was getting into the blood supply. So the task force invited the blood industry to Atlanta to look at the evidence that AIDS was contaminating the blood supply, and if the blood industry did not take action, an epidemic would hit this country like a tsunami."

Marc describes the historic clash between the CDC's public health experts and the blood bankers, and our food, which we had barely noticed the server place on the table, went as cold as the forks we did not touch. He condenses the energy of our discussion to one point: "The blood bankers cared more about saving money than they did about savings lives."

The minutes of the Atlanta meeting showed that the CDC's AIDS Task Force had collected AIDS-blood specimens and determined that over 90 percent of them were also positive for hepatitis B-core antibody. Gay men who were exposed to AIDS were also positive for hepatitis B core antibodies. The CDC AIDS Task Force members alerted the blood industry and public health services that the coming AIDS epidemic could be avoided by testing donors with the hepatitis B core test.

The blood bankers, largely led by the American Red Cross, the American Association of Blood Banks, the Infectious Diseases and Transfusion Committee, and the New York Blood Center, rebuffed the CDC's evidence of transfusion-AIDS as too weak to justify absorbing the cost of testing its donors. A line in the sand was drawn between the CDC's AIDS Task Force members and the blood bankers. The CDC Task Force members admonished the blood bankers about how their refusal to take action would kill thousands, and the blood bankers accused the CDC of prematurely overreacting to just a few transfusion-AIDS cases.

"Is it true that Don Francis, an assistant director of the CDC and member of the AIDS Task Force, pounded the conference table with his fists, demanding to know the threshold number of deaths needed before the blood bankers would do something?" I read this in Randy Shilts' book.

"It is true. You see, George, so long as the lazy media and politicians labeled it as a 'gay' problem, nothing got done."

I put the wine glass down on the table and notice sharp creases on the edges of the perfectly pressed tablecloth. The other tables, across the room, are empty and meticulously set with the same white linen and sparkling clean wine glasses. The restaurant was eerily quiet with not a person in sight. Marc and I say good-bye outside and he walks in another direction. Market Street is quiet, not a cab in sight. In a darkened doorstep a couple doors away, a homeless man fits a sheet of cardboard under himself, pulls an overstuffed plastic garbage bag with all his worldly belongings close to him, and drifts off to sleep. He covers himself with a makeshift cardboard sign that reads, "I have AIDS, please help." Whether it was true or just a gimmick, the disease was ubiquitous. There is a beat-up empty tin can at his feet.

CHAPTER SIX

Back at the office, I crank up a couple of space heaters next to my desk. The electrical smell means the winter chill will be gone soon. I hang a poster of the Golden Gate Bridge on the wall across from my desk.

Marc Conant gave me a lot to think about, but it is not enough to throw Bill's case into suit. I need to figure out who is responsible, and under what legal theory. These are uncharted waters, because the courts have not defined a patient's legal right to sue a blood bank over being infected with AIDS-contaminated blood. Most lawyers will not touch the case, as though the paperwork itself could be infectious. Day after day, for weeks, I pour over cases on the third floor of the old courthouse law library, searching for a legal precedent. Every morning, I sneak brown bag lunches pass the officious librarian with the "No Food Allowed" sign on her desk for the long day ahead.

Since blood is considered a biological "product" by the industry and government, I consider filing Bill's case under a product liability theory, like I did with the roofing machine. When I was in law school, I hustled my way into a large defense firm, where I wrote briefs on product liability, so I knew it well. After I graduated they offered me a job, but I was soon fired from that—my first and only law firm job. The managing partner called me to the carpet to explain why my weekly client billable hours where below the other associates. When I defended myself by arguing that there is no way they could legitimately bill sixty-hour weeks to clients unless they were double billing, he showed me the door. That was when I hit the road and began to work from my car.

Product liability works like this: The AIDS-contaminated platelet that infected Bill is a blood product derived from processing whole blood. The platelets are extracted from the whole blood, then sold to the hospital and transfused into the patient. Product liability theory holds the manufacturer who sells a defective product responsible for the injuries it causes to consumers. It's the same as an automobile manufacturer who refuses to move a fuel tank, despite knowing that upon certain rear-end impacts, the car would explode into an inferno.

The blood bank's defense, however, to a patient's product liability lawsuit is that the blood was unavoidably unsafe. The unavoidably unsafe doctrine protects manufacturers from product liability lawsuits, establishing that they made their products as safe as possible with the information known at the time. I figure that since the CDC showed that over ninety-five percent of the high-risk donors could have been eliminated with the hepatitis B core antibody test before Bill's transfusion, then the blood banks failed to make blood as safe as possible.

The American Association of Blood Banks has so much influence over the regulatory process, including courts and government, that much of the oversight is delegated to them. In New Jersey, for example, the state administrative code that regulates blood banks defers to the AABB's standards for blood banks to follow. The AABB inspects local blood banks and hospitals that rely on these inspections and screening standards when they decide to purchase blood. The AABB has achieved a quasi-governmental status. They had already successfully lobbied Capitol Hill and state legislatures for tort reform that included "Blood Shield Laws." Blood shield laws prevent patients' product liability lawsuits for contaminated blood. To my sheer luck, it turns out that New Jersey is one of three states that never adopted a Blood Shield Law. The courts follow them anyway.

I consider filing a negligence lawsuit against the Bergen Community Blood Center, because had they used hepatitis B core testing to screen donors, there was over a ninety percent probability that donor 29F0784 would have been rejected, and Bill not infected with AIDS. The problem with this, however, is that it penalizes the blood bank for following the industry standard of care set by the Red Cross and American Association of Blood Banks. Since their January 13, 1983 joint statement, blood banks followed the industry standard of care that rejected the CDC's recommendations to test donors. To put it succinctly, the blood industry created its own legal "standard of care," which the court will use to judge the practices of blood banks' lack of core testing. They couldn't break the law because they wrote it.

I consider suing the blood bank based on its own independent duty to safely screen blood, but even this theory will be dismissed as holding the blood bank to an unfair standard, as no blood bank at the time, except one across the country at Stanford University, screened donors for AIDS. I did not want to admit it, but I was hitting a wall.

All night, I watch the red digital numbers of the clock on the bedroom dresser change time into the early morning hours. The story of a sea captain and a tugboat sails through my thoughts in a dreamlike stupor. In 1932, two tugboats, one of which was the T.J. Hooper, were towing barges. During a storm, the barges sunk and their cargos were lost. The owners of the cargo sued the barge owners, who in turn sued the tugboat owners. They claimed that the owners of the T.J. Hooper were negligent because they failed to equip their tugboats with radios that would have warned them of the bad weather. The tugboat companies defended under the "prevailing practice" theory. They argued that because no other tugboats in the area were using radios, this constituted the standard of care for the industry.

I drink lots of coffee and wait for the sun to rise before heading to the courthouse law library. I go upstairs to the loft where they keep books no one uses anymore. I check the volume numbers of each binder and finally pull one from the shelf. I wipe off the dust and see that the binding is broken. I flick a calcified spider that's God knows how old off the page number mark. I turn a few pages, there it is: T.J. Hooper. Judge Learned Hand, a legal scholar of his time, found the tugboat companies liable because they did not use readily available technology, the radio receivers, to listen for broadcast weather reports, even though the use of radios was not yet standard industry practice. With complete disregard of library rules, I circle Judge Hands' words in pencil: "Indeed in most cases reasonable prudence is in fact common practice, but strictly it is never the measure. A whole calling may have unduly lagged in the adoption of new and available devices... Courts must in the end say what is required. There are precautions so imperative that even their universal disregard will not excuse their omission." This half century old, rarely used legal opinion about radios is my precedent to challenge the practices of the entire, gargantuan blood industry about AIDS. It is at this moment, holding this decrepit law book in my hand, that I realize the magnitude of Bill's case.

In the spring of '89, the media reports the first jury verdict in the country against a blood bank for infecting a patient with AIDS from contaminated blood. The case is *Osborn v. Irwin*

Memorial Blood Center. Like Bill, Baby Osborn was transfused with a unit of platelets during heart surgery and developed AIDS. Irwin is the same blood bank that Dr. Conant and other University of California Medical Center physicians issued a public press release about, to get them to begin testing their blood. Dr. Herbert Perkins, Irwin's director, refused to listen. Baby Osborn was the figure in the CDC's MMWR report that the blood bankers refused to listen to in Atlanta.

I decide to fly to San Francisco to meet the Osborn family lawyer, Michael Moriarty, who won the first AIDS-transfusion case against a blood bank in the country. This is great news, because it means that a court is willing to look beyond the industry standard and hold a blood bank responsible for not testing its donors. I wake up early at the Sheraton at Fisherman's Wharf, still on east coast time, fumbling through the lobby in search of coffee. The café has not open yet, but as usual, there's an early bird pot of strong coffee perched on a serving cart. I take an apple Danish and munch it down as I exit through the lobby doors.

I cab it over to Moriarty's office on Hyde Street and ring the doorbell of a Victorian villa with a heavy, metal gate and buzzer. I am taken aback when Michael Moriarty, a tall, slender guy with a full mustache, welcomes me inside with a hearty embrace. Lawyers are a competitive breed and do not easily help each other. The ones I encounter in New Jersey hide behind their lunches to avoid eye contact. I am relieved when Moriarty turns out to be that stereotypical, easygoing Californian out to save the world and lend a hand to anyone. He briefs me about how, nationally, defense firms and blood bankers have prepared to win patient lawsuits. "Getting a blood banker to break ranks to testify is an obstacle," he says.

Moriarty's office is charming but sparsely decorated. He did, however, spend money on a new copy machine, and shows it off to me. Mike, being a sole practitioner like me, really appreciates a good copy machine and is justifiably proud of it. When you are running a solo law practice, a reliable copier is your ally for keeping up with defense firms' barrage of paper intended to wear you down. Mike puts scrap paper into the copier tray for a demonstration. In a second, it copies, collates, and staples the colored paper. It is the Cadillac of copiers, more than I can afford.

By the time I meet Moriarty, Irwin Blood Center has already filed its appeal to the California Court of Appeals, and Mike is swamped with briefs piled from the floor to the window ledges.

"Irwin is appealing the jury verdict on the standard of care." He rolls his eyes. Mike is talking about the joint industry statement the American Red Cross and American Association of Blood Banks put out which refutes the CDC's recommendations. "Irwin says they can not be negligent when they did what everyone was doing, which was nothing."

I am worried that if the California Appellate Court reverses the Osborn verdict, that it will set a bad precedent for Bill's case in New Jersey.

"Who were your expert witnesses?"

"I used Tom Asher, from HemaCare, down in Sherman Oaks. You should talk to him."

"Thanks. I will. What about Ed Engleman? I read someplace that he tested donors at Stanford in June of '83."

"He did, but you will not get him to testify. I tried." Mike's mustache moves when he shakes his head. "He does not testify."

Mike and I are pioneers in this new legal frontier, trying to blaze the trail for AIDS patient rights against the blood industry. He invites me to join him and his family for dinner that night and picks me up at the Sheraton. It felt surreal to drive over the Golden Gate Bridge, like I had woken up inside the poster hanging across my desk in Hackensack. The San Francisco skyline is spectacular, unlike the Newark skyline, which somehow manages to look no less annoyed than a DMV clerk. The boats in the marina are all lit with Christmas lights.

Mike's wife slices a lime Mike picked from a tree in the backyard. She twists one of the slices through the neck of a cold bottle of Corona Light and hands it to me. This San Francisco lifestyle is incredible to me. We enjoy the view of the bay from his yard. Ever since that evening, Corona Light with a slice of lime has been my drink of choice. We watch a tugboat and tanker slowly pass through the bay below and continue our discussion about the trial.

"My client is this baby who has heart surgery and gets a platelet from Irwin. The family wanted to donate their own blood for the kid, but Irwin wouldn't allow it. So they give him AIDS, and we sue the bastards," he says offhandedly, while offering me another Corona.

"What can you tell me about Tom Asher? Since he testified for you, do you think he might testify for me?"

"He runs a small plasmapheresis center in Sherman Oaks. He has a Red Cross memo showing the bastards did a cost-benefit analysis and decided it was cheaper to defend a few lawsuits than to start testing donors in its blood centers."

"Really? I have to meet Dr. Asher."

"It's a hard case to sell to the jury." Mike warns me. "They will put up posters about saving lives in the court house during trial."

I already know it will be hard to convince most people that industry leaders who control our vital blood supply put profits before patient safety, but that is the way the case is shaping up.

"Yeah, it is a real fucking mess, and there is no money for your client unless you win." Mike's fury occasionally spills out of the pores in his surfer-dude-turned-savvy-lawyer persona.

"It's: 'Oh, we're sorry. We did the best we could. Now go away and die quietly.'"

I congratulate Mike for getting farther than any other lawyer has for his client and wish him luck with the appeal. We toast his work and watch the tugboat and tanker crawl through the bay below.

CHAPTER SEVEN

By the time I fly to Los Angeles to meet Tom Asher, the California Court of Appeals has reversed Moriarty's jury verdict; they reject penalizing Irwin Memorial Blood Center on the basis of following the industry standard.

The Osborn case affirms that I can't limit Bill's case to the blood bank. I have to sue the people in charge of the entire industry. Anything short of this will meet the same fate as Osborn. It is a setback for patient rights in California, for Tom Asher and Marc Conant who testified for the Osborn family, and especially for the parents who already suffered the tragic loss of an infant. It is also near financial ruin for Mike, who committed so much time and money to the case. Personal injury lawyers advance their own money for the client to pay litigation costs, and get paid only if they win. On the other hand, the firm-backed blood industry defense lawyers are paid by the hour, regardless of the outcome.

The cab driver drops me off at a small two-story strip mall on Sherman Way. I look at the Chinese buffet restaurant and Wells Fargo and think this must be a mistake. Then, I see a small, laminated sign on the second floor of the building exterior that reads "HemaCare, Upstairs." As Moriarty said, HemaCare is a small operation specializing in plasmapheresis. Tom Asher, a microbiologist, worked for the Centers for Disease Control before creating HemaCare and taking it public. It is not a blood center like Irwin, because it is limited to collecting plasma from paid donors. I follow the sign with a red arrow and walk into the small reception area. The receptionist offers me coffee. I stare at the clumps of powdered creamer floating near the rim as I wait.

Tom Asher comes out and shakes my hand. He's an older man, late sixties, but has one of those really firm handshakes that grabs your attention. He stands at about 6' 3" and begins each day with a 5:00 a.m. workout at the YMCA. I instantly like him. He leads me into his private office with photos of his wife, son, and grandchildren on the credenza. When we spoke on the phone, I asked him to catch me up to speed with how blood is processed in a lab. He agreed, and we begin my education.

"This is a plasmapheresis center, which is different from community blood centers. We take whole blood from the donor's arm, extract the plasma, then inject the rest back into the arm. This way, the donor is allowed to donate more often than other whole-blood donors."

"I understand your donors are paid. I have heard stories about people selling blood not being the most suitable donors."

"It's safer than the nonprofit blood banks because we know our donors personally, do complete exams, and follow their medical histories."

"So then, HemaCare is a 'for profit' unlike the rest of the industry?"

Dr. Asher sighs. "That's a distinction the industry lobbyists like the American Association of Blood Banks and the American Red Cross like to make about us. They have a business and geographical monopoly and want to keep it. I tried to sell blood products to Los Angeles hospitals, but the LA Red Cross undercut our prices to keep us out of their market. We have an antitrust suit against them." That sounds like the opposite of non-profit.

He suggests I contact Gil Gaul, a reporter at the *Philadelphia Enquirer*, who did a series of articles on the big business of blood bankers.

"Tom, what made you begin screening donors for AIDS when the rest of the industry still denied the link between AIDS and blood?"

"When I got back from the Atlanta meeting, I told my board of directors that we had to do something. The CDC's evidence of transfusion-AIDS was convincing and a blood bank could not legitimately deny that transfusion-AIDS was a serious threat."

"When did you begin screening donors for AIDS here at HemaCare?"

"By June '83, every donor was screened with the absolute lymphocyte test, and we never had a transfusion-AIDS case associated with our products."

"What about core antibody testing?"

"We considered it, but we are too small to afford it. So we chose another CDC recommended test."

"Why didn't the rest of the blood industry do something?"

"Greed."

"Greed?"

"The American Association of Blood Banks, the American Red Cross, pharmaceutical companies—all of them knew AIDS was contaminating their products but did nothing. You know, George," he continues in his professorial way, "surrogate testing isn't new in blood banking. When there isn't an actual test for the viral agent, we use a surrogate test that picks up markers associated with it. For example, there is no test for syphilis, but we use a surrogate test that detects markers associated with the infection."

I am clearly in the business world of biological products now.

"So long as they stuck together and denied the evidence, they got away with it and refused to test—just to save money."

I scribble notes on a legal pad. It is all about the timeline now. The blood industry's refusal to take precautions against distributing AIDS-contaminated blood products becomes less tenable the further away in time from the Atlanta meeting. Even if we were to give the blood bankers the benefit of doubt in January '83, the evidence was undeniable by the end of the year. And, by the time of Bill's transfusion, 18 months after Atlanta, it is arguably criminal to still distribute untested blood.

A young lab technician pops her head into his office.

"Dr. Asher, it's ready for you," she tells him.

"All right. Thank you."

This is what I was waiting for, to see how it is all done. I need to understand the whole system in order to hit the right notes in court.

Tom leads me towards the lab. "It is all about money to them ... profit," he grumbles as he opens the door. Once inside, he is more audible: "The United States blood industry is the largest exporter of blood products in the world. Blood is big business." I am astounded by what Tom is telling me. "The American blood industry is like the OPEC of blood. It's a billion-dollar-a-year cartel, a monopoly."

Tom takes me to a stainless steel table where gray Rubbermaid trays filled with red bags of blood had been placed. They look like red Christmas ornaments in dish trays—the big, gray kind I used to collect dirty dishes in one summer when I worked as a dishwasher.

"See this. This is how raw product, whole blood, looks when it comes into the lab from collection sites." Whole blood in this process is not unlike crude oil waiting to be refined.

We walk to the technician in a white lab coat, wearing surgical gloves, at a stainless steel centrifuge. She breaks her concentration for a second to half-smile, then goes on with her routine. "She is separating the whole blood into products, like platelets, red cells and plasma."

The technician places a bag of whole blood into each of the eight cups extended at the end of the mechanical arms. She turns on the centrifuge; the mechanical arms WHIRR faster and faster. Tom talks over the sound of the WHIRRING. "The centrifugal force forces the plasma to separate from the red cells." The centrifuge stops. The technician takes the bags from the cups, puts them on trays.

He points at the containers. "See that: the amber-colored plasma has risen to the top, and the red cells are left at the bottom."

Dr. Asher leads me to another table where a technician uses a V-Press to hand squeeze the amber plasma from the bag until it empties into the red cells. He explains, "Here, the plasma is separated from the red cells. A unit of plasma sells for $400, red cells $200, and platelets $35.

"This doesn't include the commercialization of the product, where it's freeze-dried and exported around the world for hemophiliacs." There are two industry sectors that make up this global business: whole blood and the commercial clotting factor used by hemophiliacs. I want to understand the entire business, so I'm not caught off guard by technical terms I know the blood industry's lawyers will use against me.

"Pharmaceutical companies like Baxter-Travenol and Cutter Biological Laboratories are able extend the shelf-life of their clotting factor and export it around the world." Bill's case is against the whole blood sector, as opposed to the pharmaceutical side. The importance to me, however, is how the entire industry, the commercial and the non-profit sides, worked together to reject the CDC's recommendations.

Tom knows I am staying alone at the L.A. Sportsmen's Lodge, so he invites me for dinner. I rent a car and get a street map to find my way to his home. I pull up to the curb of a small, modest ranch house. I check the address, but this is it. I just anticipated that a hero like Tom lived in a Hollywood villa.

Over dinner, Tom shows me a *Philadelphia Enquirer* article with a photo of the Atlanta clash between the CDC's AIDS Task Force members and the blood bankers. It's like looking at a grainy black-and-white photo of a crime scene. The major thrust of the article is about the showdown between the CDC investigators and the blood bankers. Most vociferous among the blood bankers were Dr. Joseph Bove, chairman of the American Association of Blood Banks' Transfusion and Transmissible Disease Committee, and Dr. Aaron Kellner, president of the large New York Blood Center. They insisted the CDC was overreacting and denounced the evidence of transfusion AIDS altogether. This led a frustrated Dr. Donald Francis, a CDC AIDS Task Force member, to pound the conference table, demanding to know how many people needed to die before the Blood Bankers would accept the evidence.

But the CDC has no regulatory authority over the blood bankers. That is the duty of the FDA, who has the final say on whether blood is safe to distribute. The FDA delegated that duty to its Blood Products Advisory Committee, which is controlled by blood bankers. Dr. Bove was a member and consultant of this committee. It is such a conflict-of-interest that even by the end of the year, on December 16-17, 1983, when the FDA finally proposes a regulation that would require core antibody testing, the Blood Products Advisory Committee shoots it down.

"The foxes were watching the hen house. The fix was in when blood and pharmaceutical committee members met the evening before in a Bethesda hotel to rehearse ignoring the CDC. Even though the blood bankers believe core testing is inevitable, six months later, the committee succeeds in killing the regulation," Tom explains. An internal memo from Cutter Biologicals, Inc., at the time the largest manufacturer of plasma in the United States, says, "This proposal was agreed upon by all the fractionators the previous evening. The general thrust is to provide a delaying tactic. It was generally agreed that core testing would eventually become required."

By April '84, a couple of blood bank medical directors began to break ranks with the industry. Presumably under pressure from Dr. Ed Engleman's decision to begin testing donors at Stanford in June '83, the Red Cross San Jose blood center and Irwin announced they were going to begin core antibody testing it donors. Furthermore, Dr. Engleman would not allow blood into the Stanford hospital community that had not been screened for AIDS.

The FDA quickly weighed in by announcing, "The recent decision by several blood banks and plasma organizations to use the antibody-core test was a voluntary decision on their part." The conclusion of the FDA's statement reads, "It would therefore be unwise to adopt core antibody testing to the exclusion of other screening tests." The blood and pharmaceutical industries had hijacked the FDA's Blood Products Advisory Committee.

After dinner, Tom digs deep into a box of papers. He hands me the internal Red Cross memo that Mike Moriarty had mentioned. I continue to piece the industry's actions in reference to the timeline like a sleuth in a detective novel.

Dr. Cumming's memo is a cost-benefit analysis of core testing donors. It places a dollar value of each transfusion-AIDS case, like Bill's. Then, it calculates that out of the total number of transfusion AIDS-infected patients, most will die from the reason they are in the hospital in the first place; others will die shortly after being discharged from the hospital; and of the relatively small percentage of patients who survive to bring a lawsuit, its value is outweighed by the cost of implementing national testing.

Every Last Drop

I catch the red eye back home. The cabin lights are off and I try to catch some sleep. But, instead, I think about Professor Chuck Jones, my criminal law professor at Rutgers law. He always wore a stylish suit with a handkerchief in its front pocket and explained criminal law in a knell-like baritone. He was also relaxed about me missing most of his classes because he knew that I took a job as a law clerk at a firm to support my family. But I did make it to class the week he covered conspiracies. He talked about hub conspiracies, chain conspiracies, and all kinds of complex criminal and civil conspiracies. All I took away from his classes was that when two or more people work together for an illicit purpose, it is a conspiracy, like corporations that engage in price fixing. The New Jersey criminal code defines a conspiracy as a combination of two or more persons acting in concert to commit an unlawful act, or an act that results in damages.

In the Red Cross internal memo dated February 5, 1983 that refers to the Red Cross's refusal to question donors about high risk behavior or do laboratory testing on their blood samples, marketing director Dr. Paul Cumming writes, "As time goes on we are liable to get more and more pressure to utilize these means. If AIDS continues to double every 6 months, the concentration in gay males continues, and there is absent evidence to the contrary, this pressure is likely to be overwhelming in 6 to 12 months. Even if the evolving evidence of an epidemic wanes, the CDC is likely to continue to play up AIDS—it has long been noted that the CDC increasingly needs a major epidemic to justify its existence."

Then, Dr. Cumming writes, "To the extent the [blood] industry . . . sticks together against the CDC, it will appear to some segments of the public, at least, that we have a self-interest which is in conflict with the public interest, unless we can clearly demonstrate that the CDC is wrong." The way they clearly demonstrated it was by not testing donors.

There is a nagging feeling in my gut about the way the blood bankers acted in concert against the CDC. It is no coincidence that after Atlanta, the American Red Cross, American Association of Blood Banks, and Counsel of Community Blood Centers, the three organizations that control blood banking, put out the January 13, 1983 Joint Industry Statement against the CDC's recommendations to implement testing—the one that reversed the jury's verdict on the Osborn case. That is followed by the American Red Cross internal memo, on February 5, 1983 by Dr. Cumming, stating that they (the industry) have to "stick together" against the CDC. Old Chuck Jones used to say, "If it walks like a duck and quacks like a duck, then it's probably a duck."

Back at the office, I brew a fresh pot of coffee over the filing cabinet, turn up the space heater, and hammer away on my word processor, putting the final touches on the complaint that will ignite the first AIDS-transfusion case in New Jersey—the first case ever against the AABB. Up until now, my practice has been the occasional rear-end whiplash or supermarket slip-and-fall cases.

It's late Friday afternoon, November 25, 1988. As I climb those courthouse steps in the shadow of the historic rotunda, something feels different. This case will expose a public health disaster that the AABB, the Public Health Services, and the FDA could have prevented. Both frightened and excited, I slide the complaint and filing fee under the glass partition. The court clerk looks it over, sees the word AIDS, and looks back at me. Then she takes her shiny, polished-metal hand stamp, pushes it down on the complaint, and I hear that distinctive sound of the stamp striking the top page: "Filed."

CHAPTER EIGHT

On Monday morning, Bill's case is the news story of the day. It is the front-page story in Bergen County's major newspaper, *The Record*: "Hospital Is Sued Over AIDS Virus." Bill's case catches the attention of Bill Sanderson, a staff reporter at *The Record*. Sanderson is a serious, young reporter that looks as though he is so busy tracking down stories and making deadlines that he sleeps in his clothes.

When Sanderson interviews the American Association of Blood Banks' spokesperson about Bill's lawsuit, their spokesperson proudly boasts, "No AIDS victim has yet won a damage award in a transfusion lawsuit." And then, sure enough, the blood bankers proclaim, ". . . its members have succeeded in arguing to judges and juries that before reliable testing became available . . . they had no way of testing their products."

By the time I pick Courtney up from school in the afternoon, the story is carried by TV and radio news organizations. The transfusion-AIDS case in New Jersey against the blood bankers is national news. The office phone, which up until now I had used as a paperweight, has a three-day burst of ringing off the hook with reporters calling for more details. Not all the attention to Bill's case is positive. There is anonymous hate mail sent to my office too. Some letters enclosed the newspaper clippings with the word "asshole" written across it. After all, I am suing their Community Blood Center, where bloodmobiles come to their jobs for donations and many people support their blood drives. Some people disliked me dragging their blood center into court over AIDS. "Just leave the AIDS cases alone, it nobody's fault," they'd say. The blood center is an American icon, as American as apple pie, and their only purpose is to save lives.

When Patti goes to the bank, the teller recognizes my name and questions her about the lawsuit. I left the office early to volunteer at one of Courtney's soccer games. As I walked across the field to talk to her coach, he busied himself with picking up equipment.

Patti and I enjoyed watching Courtney's Saturday morning soccer games. It is great being outside on the field on a cool Fall morning to watch your child run up and down the field, in a body he is she is clumsily growing into. She gets the ball and I can't refrain from voicing my excitement. A few parents inch further away from me every time they hear my voice. I never really fit in with them anyway, and my suing their blood bank gave them the excuse they were seeking to flat out ignore me. I remember just one father, a New York stockbroker who had a genuine, unbiased interest in Bill's case, who used to talk with me. The coaches stop including me in carpooling the kids for post-game ice cream.

Sanderson calls me at the office and wants to interview Bill and Roslyn. On the one hand, they fear Arcadia, Florida-type repercussions, but on the other, Roslyn wants the people to know what its like for them. We offer Sanderson a compromise. Roslyn will do the interview so long as the newspaper keeps her name out. It is one thing to file the complaint in their names, but another to reveal their identity to the thousands of Sanderson's readers. Roslyn and Bill just are not ready for that yet. Sanderson promises anonymity for Bill and Roslyn in exchange for an exclusive interview. Sanderson strikes me as being bigger than his job at the local newspaper. Behind his disheveled beard and clothes is a sharp journalist with integrity. I trust him.

I want Sanderson to do the interview because I know his readers will make up the jury pool. Bill and Roslyn tell Sanderson how they worry about reactions of relatives, friends, and neighbors. "We are two nervous wrecks. You just sit here and cry together." (*The Record*, November 28, 1988).

Sanderson's story in the *The Record* about Bill's fight gives other AIDS-transfusion victims the courage to come forward. Elery Fudge, a retired worker who was infected while having heart surgery, was already wasting away by the time his daughter brings him to meet me. Elery wants to fight back like Bill. Sanderson brings a newspaper photographer to my office to interview Elery Fudge and me. *"Infected and Out For Blood,"* is the headline with our photos in the article, *The Record, September 25, 1989, Bill Sanderson*. Elery isn't concerned about going public so Sanderson reveals his name. Elery passes away before the case is filed.

CHAPTER NINE

The first case management conference in Bill's case is before Judge Robert Hamer. When I walk into the courtroom, the defense counsel hushes.

"George," Judge Hamer smiles, "come over and join us." We have a history together, so him calling me by my first name feels like a wolf luring its prey into its den. Sanderson has already made me a local celebrity over Bill's case, a small-time lawyer representing transfusion-AIDS victims against the big bad industry lawyers. They don't like it. The hush means they were getting the scoop about me from Judge Hamer before I arrived.

"You know Ed Matthews, your adversary, who is defending the American Association of Blood Banks?" Hamer antagonizes. He knows we haven't met. Ed Matthews extends an obligatory handshake without a smile. He is 6' 2" and about 230 pounds, with a slicked back cloud of gray-hair and strong handshake. I am 33 and gangly, still inexperienced as a lawyer. Matthew's seniority makes me queasy. Roger Ellis, another senior partner with a firm named after him, represents the Bergen Community Blood Center. And Milton Gurney, a real old-timer (especially with a name like "Milton Gurney") is there for St. Joseph's Hospital. These guys wear dark pinstriped suits and carry those litigation bags with their names engraved in gold lettering. I never expected our paths to cross. There was no night school or state college for them. The silk handkerchief I occasionally tuck into the jacket pocket of my gabardine suit means I am on my way up. "But not quite there yet," the look in their eyes finished my sentence.

"All right, counsel, put your appearance on the record." The foreplay is over. Judge Hamer gets to business. One by one we state our names and clients for the court stenographer.

"George, how are you going to prove the defendants were negligent when no one was testing blood when your client was transfused?" Judge Hamer frames the question in a way that posits me to lose.

"Your Honor, there were tests available that they could have used—"

"How do you intend to get around that it was not the standard?" Matthews and Ellis just relax and watch Judge Hamer work me.

"Your Honor, it wasn't the standard because the American Association of Blood Banks orchestrated a conspiracy—"

Mathews jumps to his feet from behind the counsel table. "Your Honor, that's a slanderous and scurrilous allegation against my client." He rolls his r's impeccably, almost purring.

"They conspired to set the standard—"

Matthews interrupts again. "That is a false and libelous accusation."

"I see this case is about *bad blood*." There is a pause. Judge Hamer's joke is not funny.

"Your Honor, there was a test that the CDC told the American Association of Blood Banks and the American Red Cross to use, and they refused—"

"You can't prove that, George." Judge Hamer says.

"I need donor discovery—"

"What for, Mr. Baxter?"

"Your Honor, at a minimum, the blood center was supposed to give donor 29F0847 educational material to read about high risk behavior that put them at risk for AIDS. They were supposed to ask him if he used intravenous drugs or had sex with men. I need to know if the blood bankers checked for swollen lymph nodes, or recorded his responses to the medical questions. I can't know this unless I ask the donor."

Matthews argues that the blood donor's privacy is the pillar of the volunteer blood system. "If a blood donor thinks he can be exposed to litigation just by the act of donating blood, the entire system will collapse."

"But, your Honor, I don't need the donor's identity. I am not asking to know the name of donor 29F0847. He can be anonymously questioned through the court." Tom Asher had already tipped me off that the right to privacy would be the blood bankers' argument to prevent the discovery. I was not looking to sue the blood donor, but rather check to see if the blood bank screened him.

"It's a fishing expedition, Mr. Baxter," Judge Hamer argues.

"It's not a fishing expedition, your Honor." Judge Hamer knows that without the donor discovery, I cannot prove that the blood bankers failed to take the most basic precautions to protect Bill from AIDS-contaminated blood.

"You can take the depositions of the blood bank workers and ask them. Ask them what their normal routine was." The problem with Judge Hamer's argument is that their lawyers will prep the blood bank workers by the time I depose them, but Judge Hamer will not bend.

I tried and lost my first case before Judge Hamer. I am still not over it. Back when I was working from my car, a Hackensack lawyer named Bill Nunno gave me a rear-end collision case to try for him. Nunno's client was stopped in traffic when she was rear-ended by the defendant. I prepped the case like it was the Lindbergh trial. I met with witnesses in the evening, I subpoenaed the police officer on the scene, and I wrote out my direct examination questions for the treating physician and insisted on meeting with her beforehand to go through them. It was my first trial and I intend to score big. Judge Hamer had other plans. No ambulance chaser would score in his courtroom. Judge Hamer jumped on my awkwardness and rephrased my questions before the jury. In qualifying my client's doctor to testify, also known as voir dire, I asked, "So, what kind of doctor are you?" Judge Hamer quipped from the bench, "Why, she's a good one, of course." The jury laughed. I didn't know how to respond to a judge taking over my case and lost credibility with the jury. The case should have been a home run. Instead, the jury came back with nothing. Needless to say, I never got another referral from Billy Nunno. That's just another reason why you take the settlement money, because you never know how a case will go.

Judge Hamer is tall and thin, with brown hair. He resembles Jimmy Dean, the country-singer-turned-sausage-mogul, only with a worse sense of humor.

"Judge, if I don't get donor discovery, then I cannot establish negligence or the link between his blood and my client's infection."

"That's not my problem, Mr. Baxter. I am not allowing a fishing expedition."

"It's not a fishing expedition." I argued desperately, but it was no use.

In the prepared opinion, Judge Hammer states: "There is no basis to conclude or infer that they did something wrong; and therefore, I will deny any access to the donor's records or access to further interrogation or invasion of the right to privacy."

Judge Hamer's ruling for the blood bankers is sure death for Bill's case and patient rights. It defies logic because he says there is no evidence of wrong doing in screening the donor, but denies me the right to gather this evidence. It is also in line with the decisions of many other courts considering a patient's right to sue a blood bank for AIDS contaminated blood. Forcing me to trial without discovery from donor 29F0847 about the blood bank's screening measures will undoubtedly result in a dismissal of Bill's case. If I have to try the case, loose it and then go through the lengthy appeal process, Bill wouldn't survive for a retrial. And, everyone knows the chances of an appeal before the trial is over are slim. Trying to get an appellate court to intervene on what is known as an interlocutory appeal is like hitting all the rubber ducks with an air gun at the carnival. But I have no other choice. I file an appellate argument, and wait.

PART II

CHAPTER TEN

"Hello, Mr. Baxter," a tallish woman with a soft Scottish accent says as I enter the reception area. Janet is a twenty-eight-year old mother of two children, and was transfused on November 6, 1984. Janet's daughter, Naomi, is Courtney's age, and her son, Christian, is in preschool. We had made an appointment to meet while they were in school.

"Hi. Please come in. It's nice to meet you." I offer her the chair in front of my desk.

An older woman named Kay, from a local AIDS support group, read Sanderson's article and called me. AIDS support groups were becoming popular but had a clandestine feel to them. Members take oaths of confidentiality and swear to protect the anonymity of the other members. Any infraction of confidentiality meant expulsion from the group. She said there was a young woman in the group who needed help. I told Kay to have her friend call. Janet called, and we spoke a little on the telephone before our meeting.

"Can I get you coffee or anything?" Patti suggested I offer coffee to clients when they visit, so there is a fresh pot of coffee brewing on the filing cabinet.

"No thank you. I'm all right." Janet is attractive, with high cheekbones and a fair complexion. Her shoulder-length brown hair is parted to the side and still has the wind from outside in it. There is something about her that feels familiar.

"Did you find the office without too much trouble?" I want to give her a chance to settle into the chair.

"Yes, I took the Parkway from Millburn." Janet leans forward smiles with a puzzled expression. "What is that sound?"

I am not sure how to respond and sigh. "When I rented this office, I knew the front door would face the courthouse, but I didn't know my back window would overlook a yard with chicken wire and pigeon coops."

Janet chuckles. I see it was this, not small talk about the polysyllabic highway namedropping so common in Jersey directions, that made her comfortable. "Janet, why don't you start at the beginning to see if I can help you?"

Janet exhales. I can tell she is about to go into a difficult story, so I don't take notes but rather give her my full attention.

"When I delivered Christian, my son, the doctors gave me blood transfusions. I began to feel tired all the time. I would practically fall asleep on the side of the bathtub when I bathed Christian before bed. I went back to see my doctors for a checkup and told them how fatigued I felt all the time. But they said it was probably the new baby. Then after a while, I started getting these night sweats."

"What were the night sweats like?"

"I would just sweat so much in the middle of the night that I soaked the bed sheets. After a while, I double sheeted the bed and folded them so I could change my side of the bed without waking up my husband, Kyle. I told my doctors about the night sweats, but they said it was probably anxiety. They told me to try sleeping with the window slightly opened. Eventually, they dismissed it as being all in my head.

"I continued to feel sick all the time, and a couple of years later, I read in the newspaper that if you got a blood transfusion before 1986, you should be tested for AIDS. I got scared and called my doctors to ask them to test me. They didn't want to at first and thought I was just imagining it, but I knew something wasn't right."

Janet did not get the courtesy of a look-back letter like Bill did. A look-back letter is how the blood banks notified a transfusion recipient that a blood donor whose blood they got was later found to have AIDS. She had to figure things out for herself, like thousands of other unsuspecting people who were infected by transfusions during this time.

"One evening, a couple of weeks later, there's this message on my answering machine from the nurse at the doctor's office, requesting me to call him. I got scared because I knew that if everything was all right, they would have told me. I stayed up all night. The next morning, after I dropped Naomi and Christian off at school, I called the doctor but the nurse picked up. She said the doctor wanted me to come into his office to talk. I knew something was wrong and insisted on talking with him right then."

I hand Janet a glass of water. She takes a sip and continues.

"The doctor got on the phone, and said that he preferred to talk with me in person. I freaked out and demanded that he tell me right then. He told me that my AIDS test came back positive.

"I was home alone. Kyle was at work and the kids were in school. I just dropped the phone, fell on the floor and began to cry. I didn't know anything about AIDS except the pictures I saw of really sick people on television. I though I was going to die straightaway. I panicked about Christian, because I got the blood when I delivered him."

"Is he all right"?

"Yes, I had him tested three times to make sure."

"Thank God."

Janet looks away, down at the floor, then back at me. She is having difficulty continuing.

"Janet, are you all right?"

She shakes her head no, and that she wants a minute. She looks back at me after a long silence.

"I infected Kyle." Janet's eyes swell. I slide the blue Marcal tissue box across the desk toward her.

I feel badly for Janet, but her case presents a legal complication. Now, Kyle will have to be included as the possible source of Janet's infection. The blood bankers will use it to create uncertainty about how Janet was infected. I will have to find a way to establish that Janet was chronologically infected before Kyle to rule him out as the source. I respond like a lawyer, not as a human being, at that moment because it is easier than acknowledging the truth: thousands of individuals who never received transfusions—husbands, wives, lovers, children—fell into the quicksand of AIDS as collateral damage.

"I was pregnant with my Christian when we came to the States. Kyle wanted to come here for work. There was no work in Edinburgh, and he was feeling depressed all the time. I had a job and friends and didn't want to come, but he kept saying, 'Come on, let's go to the States.' He was excited about it so I gave in for him and we came here."

"So you had a job, friends, and didn't want to come here?"

"No, not really. I did it for Kyle. When I came here, to the States, I didn't know any doctors, so Kyle's aunt recommended this OB-GYN. The first time I saw him, I filled out this form that asked if I had any history of bruising or a bleeding disorder. I put down that as a child I bruised easily, and that they thought I had Von Willebrand's disease."

"What is that?"

"A bleeding disorder like hemophilia, but it is only in women."

"What happened?"

"My doctor sent me to see this hematologist for a consultation, who transfused me at the hospital."

"How is Kyle doing?"

"He's doing all right, but we haven't told Nicky yet."

Janet dabs her face with the tissue she keeps folding in half until its a tight, bulging cube. "We don't know how to break it to Naomi. I worry about what will happen to her and Christian if something happens. Kyle will never be able to handle it alone."

Janet is comfortable opening up to me because she has no one else to confide in. Here she sits on my rickety office chair, a mother and wife in a foreign country with no friends, desperate and afraid for her family. I recognize the same sense of desperation I saw in my own mother as a child.

"One afternoon, I came home for lunch from the third grade, and our kitchen table was repossessed because my dad was out of work. We ate peanut butter and jelly sandwiches off the silver ironing board for weeks."

Janet politely listens, but does not respond. There is an awkward silence.

"Go ahead Janet, it's all right." I wait for her to tell her story at her own pace as she chooses to unfold it. I wonder why she doesn't respond to the story I told her. Perhaps she can sense my discomfort with how much intimate knowledge I have, or my fear of not being able to help her. The word bank of my practiced, professional speech when talking to clients has not prepared me to respond to such raw anguish, so I responded with whatever stray thoughts were in my head, often the ones I didn't even know I had.

Janet puts down the glass of water and continues.

"Now they won't leave me alone."

"Who won't leave you alone?"

"The bill collectors. Even the hospital still calls me for the unpaid bills for the blood they gave me. I tell them that I'm sick and have no money, but they keep calling and told me I need to speak with a lawyer. I'm afraid to pick up the phone because it might be a bill collector."

"They want you to pay for the blood that gave you AIDS?" I have difficulty processing this audacity.

"Yes." Janet sighs. She takes a breath, and continues. "I'm afraid to go to the mailbox because there are always threatening letters in it."

She shifts in her seat. "You know, it's funny." She leans back. "I met Kyle after my mother passed on. I took care of my younger brother and sister by myself. When I met Kyle, he was kind to us and helped out. But my family, my aunts, didn't like him because he was poor. They wouldn't come to our wedding. But now look at what I've done." She looks out the window at the cooing pigeons and lets out a shrill, gutting laugh.

Looking over Janet's hospital records is like going back in time to the day of a crime scene. It starts on the day of Christian's delivery. I labor over admittance records, anesthesia charts, doctor's orders, and transfusion records, cross-referencing Janet's blood loss with the delivery and times of transfusions, as well as the source of the blood.

Janet was admitted to the hospital on November 6, 1984 to deliver Christian. Her records show that her physicians transfused her with cryoprecipitate on that day, and continued on November 8, 1984 for a total of twenty-one transfusions. I pause. Did she really need that many transfusions?

After hours of perusing hospital records, I discover the cryoprecipitate that infected Janet came from the New York Blood Center. I should have known. Aaron Kellner, the director of the New York Blood Center, was at the Atlanta meeting. He openly stated that the CDC's evidence was too soft for him to start testing donors with the added cost of millions of dollars. If he hadn't so doggedly denied the evidence, people like Janet would have at least gotten a look-back letter that would have prevented them from unknowingly passing the virus onto their loved ones.

Taking on Janet's case against her physicians and the New York Blood Center while fighting Bill's case against the American Association of Blood Banks is like fighting a war on two fronts. Bill's case is just beginning the appellate process and if he loses, it will deny the rights of all transfusion-AIDS patients to sue, including Janet. I am becoming the AIDS lawyer I initially feared I would become. Other kinds of clients no longer come to me.

The bank constantly calls about late mortgage payments. I intercept the mail at home so Patti doesn't get upset with the collection letters. One day, I came home from court and all my clothes were packed into large garbage bags and out on the sidewalk.

"You lied to me!" Patti shouted, her voice raspy. "Why didn't you tell me we are this bad off?" The pressure of trying to keep the bill collectors away is too much for her. It agitates her need for security—a need she never knew she had until she married me. Spending an extra minute deciding between store brand cola and Pepsi was something she never expected to do with a lawyer husband. "If I just get through this rough patch, things will get better," I tell her over and over again until she stops shaking her head. The friction from her hair rubbing against her sweater makes strands of her hair spurt in odd directions until she finally calms down.

CHAPTER ELEVEN

On October 2, 1990, I exit the third floor Hackensack courthouse elevators and detour to the men's room. I put the file I'm holding in my hand on the window ledge and slouch over the sink, eventually falling out of my stupor by putting water in the area around my eyes. I let the water drip down my face before I rip off paper from the dispenser on the wall without using the side lever and look into the mirror, taking deep, meditation tape-inspired breaths. I open the alarmingly wide window that lends itself to a vista of the gravel roof of the courthouse annex. It just glides open and pulleys with a slight lift of the hand. As a teenager, I appeared in that same juvenile court downstairs. My father was there, and we drove straight to his house in Long Island after the hearing. Before I had time to process that I'd moved away from my home in Jersey and into the house of a man I barely knew, he was introducing me to his friends at a bar and buying us all rounds. I look at the back of the men's room door as though waiting for it to open sesame. It's time to go.

Just down the hallway, there's a sign on the door of courtroom 310 that says "Appellate Arguments Today." I quietly enter the courtroom as Judge Sylvia Pressler, a shrewd older woman, barely 5' 2" and 100 pounds, finishes drilling the lawyers like an annoyed law school professor. As Judge Pressler excuses the other lawyers, she methodically slides their pile of briefs to her right and picks up the next case briefs from her left before the swoosh of the discarded pile even stops. She is the presiding judge of the New Jersey Superior Court Appellate Division.

"Counsel on Snyder v. American Association of Blood Banks?" Judge Pressler calls me up to the counsel table. Today will not only determine the fate of Bill and Janet's cases, but of every New Jersey patient infected with AIDS from contaminated blood. If I lose, it's back to the Oldsmobile—no one would want to be associated with me after all that AIDS-related press. They'd be scared to touch the doorknob of my office. My mouth is dry. I fill a paper cup that is too small for my hand with water from the pitcher on the counsel table.

Matthews places his leather litigation bag on the counsel table and takes out his copy of my appellate briefs. Small Post-its stick out the sides of all the pages he marked up, like a kiddish but nonetheless terrifying lion's mane. Many of those pages are further marked with yellow, pink and red highlighters. The highlights on his pages are far more vivid than the pale yellow lines that suffocated the text of my notes back when I was studying for my high school equivalency test, which I took in an old Quonset hut with a tin roof. I dropped out of high school to join the Marines, and tried assiduously to memorize an outdated textbook in the dark of an Okinawa bunker. I passed the test and they waived my SAT scores because of my service, but no benefits would help me now. I longed for the time when my biggest obstacle was the weight of a flashlight in my hand.

"Mr. Baxter." Judge Pressler turns to me first. I immediately stand.

"Yes, your Honor."

"Are you trying to hold the defendant to a higher standard of care with regard to donor screening than what the customary industry practice was at the time?" Why do they always poise the question in a way that makes me seem like a lunatic?

"Well, no, your Honor. There was a test they could have used—the hepatitis B Core antibody test—that the Centers for Disease Control showed would have identified high-risk blood donors." My office looked like Moriarty's office when he did the *Osborn* appeal, with drafts piled all over the room. Day and night I worked on the brief. I did it with the vigor of a lawyer fighting for a condemned man in need of an eleventh hour reprieve from a death sentence. I even included the Atlanta meeting minutes with copies of the slides the AIDS Task Force used for its presentation.

Judge Pressler asks me about the standard of care of the blood bank to screen its donors. "Your Honor, since there was a test that could have prevented my client from being infected by contaminated blood and the whole industry refused to use it, they should be judged by the "reasonable and prudent person standard," rather than the "industry standard of care." This is half the ball game. The other half is being allowed donor discovery.

Judge Pressler turns her attention to Matthews. I take a sip of water as soon as she turns her head. This woman is intimidating and I dared not sip water while she was drilling me.

"Mr. Matthews, why shouldn't the plaintiff have access to the blood bank's donor records?"

"Your Honor, they're confidential." Matthews just exudes confidence. I doubt he's perspiring under his jacket like I am. He has been doing this a long time. He is, after all, a decorated ex-Marine officer who served in Vietnam and was awarded a Purple Heart and a Bronze Star. I went to Japan and studied in a hut.

"The donor has a right to privacy. His confidential medical information cannot be waived by the mere altruistic act of donating blood."

No one has even bothered to ask donor 29F0284 if he will mind answering a few questions. Judge Pressler looks at me again.

"I am not asking for the donor's identity. He can be questioned anonymously through the court." I had played the scenarios of today over and over in my mind, and had already anticipated Matthew's response. I instinctively concede the need for the identity of donor 29F0847.

Matthews adamantly maintains the blood bankers' position that the donor's right to privacy is the pillar of the volunteer blood system. "If a blood donor risks being sued and hauled into court just by the charitable act of giving blood, they will stop giving and there will be blood shortages." He lifts his arms and lets them fall to his sides with a thud. "The whole system will collapse."

"Mr. Baxter isn't suing the blood donor, Mr. Matthews." Judge Pressler snaps. She has read the briefs, and seems to resent a lawyer employing theatrics on her. It is her tough Bronx upbringing. She looks at me again to reply.

"No, your Honor. I am not suing the donor." There's something about her gaze to the center of the room that indicates to me she's not yet decided on this question. I quickly speak up. "But, your Honor, I need donor discovery not just to prove negligence, but also to establish causation." Judge Pressler's eyes open wide, like that was something that did not occur to her before. She shifts back to Matthews and Ellis.

"Mr. Matthews, is your client denying that Mr. Snyder was infected from the transfusion in this case?"

Matthews' confidence seems to fade away and he wrestles with the answer.

"Mr. Matthews, is it the position of the American Association of Blood Banks that the plaintiff was not infected with AIDS by blood from donor 29F0784?" Judge Pressler presses for an answer.

Tactically, if Matthews and Ellis insist on denying that Bill was infected from the donor's blood, then they make it necessary for the court to grant my request for the donor discovery. On the other hand, if they agree that their blood products infected Bill, then they will make my need for discovery unnecessary and the court will deny my request. But they would look extremely guilty.

Matthews quickly recovers. "Your Honor, my client has no duty to Mr. Snyder. We did not collect the blood or test it." A trial lawyer has to think fast on his feet. It is the difference between dodging the bullet or getting hit between the eyes. "For the record, I have to deny it."

Matthews and Ellis went with the instinctual defense lawyer response to deny everything. The blood bankers would have given up nothing by conceding Bill was infected from the transfusion. It's a no-brainer that Bill got platelets from donor 29F0784. After all, the blood bank sent Bill the look-back letter. Matthews doubts my ability to prove the causation between the contaminated blood and Bill's infection at trial, so he decides to leave it on the table. I am an untested lawyer who has never won a major case, so they want to make it as confusing as possible.

Matthews veers the causation issue in another direction. "Your Honor, we didn't put AIDS into the blood, it was already there. We, personally, did not cause Mr. Snyder to be infected with AIDS." Matthews is a legal superstar who seems to actually believe in his case—the most dangerous kind of lawyer. These are all worrisome arguments and Judge Pressler may buy any one of them.

"You will be notified of our decision." Judge Pressler stands, collects her notes, and without the slightest sign of how she going to decide, leaves the bench, followed by the other judges. That is how appellate arguments end, without any indication of the outcome. There's nothing to do now but wait a few months.

I try to go on at home as though everything is normal, but it's not. I constantly pace around the kitchen and Patti asks me to sit down. Even Courtney says, "Dad, you're pacing again." Weeks later, on Halloween, I take Patti and Courtney to the Allendale nursery to get my mind off waiting. We pick out a large pumpkin to carve. We put newspaper over the kitchen table and make a mess, with pulpy stalagmites all over the kitchen, but even this does not take my mind off waiting for the decision. The automated "boo!" from the plastic scarecrow Patti hung outside our front door occasionally reacts to the teenagers trying to TP the neighborhood on Cabbage Night.

On Halloween day, Bill Sanderson writes an article: "AIDS Victim Can Question Blood Donor," The *Bergen Record*, Wednesday, October 31, 1990. My jaw drops and I cannot believe Judge Pressler took my side. Other newspapers continue to follow Sanderson's interest in the case: "Court Grants Couple Limited Right to Sue for AIDS-tainted Transfusion," *The Star-Ledger*, Wednesday, October 31, 1990.

In a landmark decision, Judge Pressler deals a blow to the blood bankers by reversing Judge Hamer's refusal of donor discovery. She also carves out a patient's right to sue for AIDS-contaminated blood. With regard to the causation issue, which the blood bankers refused to admit, she says they may be responsible for not taking precautions that ultimately enhanced the risk of being infected by contaminated blood. It's called the *"enhanced risk test."* In other words, the blood bankers' position that they didn't put AIDS into the blood supply is not tenable because Judge Pressler reasons that they had a duty to reduce, or eliminate, the risk. If their failure to implement tests increased the risk of Bill being infected with AIDS, then they may be liable to him. The enhanced risk test, new to me, is used in medical malpractice cases. It is like a radiologist who fails to see cancer on a patient's x-ray. He didn't put the cancer there, but the failure to detect the cancer enhances the likelihood of the patient going undiagnosed.

In the official opinion, Judge Pressler writes for the New Jersey Appellate Court:

> If it were determined that the conduct of either the American Association of Blood Banks or Bergen Community Blood Center, or both, unreasonably created an appreciable enhancement of plaintiff's risk and that the enhanced risk was a substantial factor in producing his injury, they would be liable to him in negligence even though he might have contracted AIDS even if they had taken every available precaution. *Snyder v. Mekhijan*, 244 N.J. Super. 281 (App. Div. 1990).

I call Bill and Roslyn in Florida to give them the news. "Thank God," Roslyn says. Even sincerity sounds like sarcasm on her.

After dealing with the blood bankers' causation arguments, Judge Pressler moves on to the donor's right to privacy issue. She grants court supervised discovery from donor 29F0784. In writing for the court, she states:

> Beyond the causation issue, plaintiff cogently asserts a need in respect of questions of Bergen Community Blood Center's negligence (App. Div. 1990).

Judge Pressler's opinion stirs the kettle, and the fact that she calls me "cogent" delights me. Her opinion becomes entrenched in the law of New Jersey and is instantly reported around the country. In resolving the AABB's argument that the volunteer blood industry will collapse if donor confidentially is breached, Judge Pressler writes:

> We are convinced that confidentiality of blood bank AIDS records rests upon significant public and private considerations and is ordinarily essential to assure the continued effectiveness of the screening process, the willingness of donors to continue to participate in blood collection efforts, and the general integrity of the nation's blood programs. Nevertheless, where, as here, a litigant's discovery need cannot otherwise be met and it is possible to accommodate that need with limited and controlled intrusion, some access under careful court supervision is appropriate and justifiable. *Snyder v. Makhijan*, 244 N.J. Super. 281, 295-296 (App. Div. 1990).

Judge Pressler, unknown to me at the time, was a progressive judge who gained national notoriety when she bucked the establishment's ban on girls playing Little League baseball, calling it unconstitutional. She is a champion of individual rights. She worked her way to being among one of the first women appointed to the New Jersey Appellate Court. Tort reformist state politicians, like Senator Gerald Cardinale, had unsuccessfully tried to block her reappointment to the bench.

Back at the office, there is a message from Janet. I call her house and Kyle tells me the ambulance took her to hospital last night, and she wants me to know. I ask for her phone number at the hospital and call her.

"Hello?" Janet was sleeping.

"Janet, it's George. How are you feeling?"

"They said I have pneumonia again. My T cell count is down too." Janet sounds half-awake. I don't want to keep her on the phone. "They're not bringing my food trays into the room."

"Why not?"

"There is a sign on the door that says 'AIDS.' The food service people just leave the trays outside."

"Are you getting them now?"

"Yes, the nurse brings them in to me. They gave me a transfusion to get my white cells up." Janet's voice is fading.

"All right, Janet. I'll call and check up on you tomorrow." I send flowers to Janet's hospital room so that people will see that she has friends, maybe treat her better.

While Judge Pressler's landmark decision clears the way for Bill and Janet's cases, the wheels of justice move slowly and are not equipped to handle their cases in the expeditious manner their conditions require. I am hopeful for settlements rather than long and risky trials that they may not live to see. As my office begins to fade behind towers of paperwork, Bill and Janet continue to deteriorate, lose weight, drop in their T-cell counts, and have bouts with phenomena.

CHAPTER TWELVE

The hopes of getting Bill and Janet settlements are quickly doused when the blood bankers appeal Judge Pressler's decision to the New Jersey Supreme Court. Once again, the AABB stands on the donor's right to privacy as a pillar of the volunteer blood system, and want to block the disclosure of donor records. They figure that the more conservative State Supreme court will reverse Judge Pressler's progressive decision.

It has been two years, several judges, and dozens of briefs since starting Bill's case, and we are still fighting over his right to sue them in the first place. The New Jersey Supreme Court agreeing to hear the blood bankers' appeal means it has an interest in their arguments. This is disconcerting to me, and means more delays for Bill and Janet.

This time, the New Jersey Attorney General weighs in and submits an "amicus curiae" brief. An "amicus curiae" is a non-party who submits a brief as a friend of the court. In this case, the New Jersey Attorney General and New Jersey Department of Health submit a brief aligned with the AABB's position against donor disclosure. I suspect the AABB or Mathews pulled some political strings behind the scene. "Oh brother, what a surprise. All we can do is wait again," Roslyn's voice creaks through the phone receiver.

George T. Baxter, Esq.

There are so many briefs that I had to hire a receptionist despite not having the money. The copier is on its last legs. Any day, I expect to be reprimanded by a judge for submitting grainy, illegible copies with lines running across each document. There is no money for a repairman to look at the copier, so I take the toner cartridge out and shake it daily, trying to squeeze out just few more copies. I pined for Moriarty's copier. The fate of Bill's case hinges on draft after draft that I hammer out over the next few months. Finally, the day before its deadline, my supreme court reply brief to the blood bankers and the State's Attorney General's office is ready. I hand it off to my cousin Lou Melucci, an independent courier, to hand deliver to the supreme court clerk.

Patti comes with me for my first Supreme Court argument. We park the car in the visitors' parking lot across from the Justice Hughes Court Complex. I get out from the driver's side and look up at the towering monstrosity of tainted glass and steel. Inside the lobby, I stare at the remarkably lifelike statues of Thomas Jefferson sitting on a bench, Benjamin Franklin reading a book, and John Hancock holding a document. They seem timeless in the middle of the hustle and bustle of this modern lobby, with its overhead announcements and faint odor of McDonalds emanating from the discarded packaging that was once lunch. Patti and I get visitors' badges at the security desk and head upstairs for the challenge ahead. I hardly imagined I would argue a case over patients' rights here.

As the elevator door opens, I catch a glimpse of a dozen dark suits at the supreme court's state police security check. Mathews is among them. My stomach feels queasy and I immediately detour to the men's room. Patti probably wondered why I suddenly vanished into thin air. I lean on the sink and see a small crack in the mirror. It has a yellowish tint around it and my reflection stops where it begins. I shut the water off, exhale, and head through the door.

The supreme court doors open to a large amphitheater court room. At the front is a podium facing seven empty wingback chairs where the justices will soon sit. There is a low buzz from the whispering of blood bankers, high-priced lawyers, reporters and spectators. I sit down at the respondent's table and unpack the briefs and notepads from my litigation bag. I notice the second hand on the clock over the door turns clockwise with a jerking mechanical action: turning, then turning back a fraction before locking into its place. It does this over and over again. I turn around, and there's Patti, the only person sitting in the section behind me. She gives me a confident smile. I wish I could smile back, but my face is frozen.

The clerk calls the court into session. There's a hush over the room except for the sound of everyone standing in unison. All seven justices file in to take their seats on the bench. Sometimes less than the full court hears an appeal, but today the presence of the full court is indicative of the seriousness of the issue before them. It may also mean there is a split in the court over the case and they need the full court to reach majority opinion. My mouth is dry; I constantly sip water from a small paper cup.

Matthews is the appellant so he goes first. In a dark pinstripe suit, starched white shirt and manicured nails, he stands straight at the court's lectern. He has reduced all his argument points to only a few index cards that he puts down so they are inconspicuous to the justices. He centers himself behind the podium. He looks like has done this before, many times. Matthews says good morning to the justices by name as though they are his colleagues. I am learning the routine from watching him, but I know I could never do that.

Matthews argues that donor confidentiality is protected with the same sanctity as the physician-patient relationship.

He also relies on a recently enacted New Jersey statute, *N.J.S.A.* 26:5C-9, that protects the confidentiality of a person who has or is suspected of having AIDS or HIV. The statute was enacted to protect people with AIDS or HIV from discrimination, to prevent Arcadia-like incidents. In fact, in 1987, the same year as Arcadia, the New Jersey supreme court backed the New Jersey Departments of Health and Education which promulgated regulations that the HIV status of children is confidential and children could not be kept out from school. Arcadia was not an isolated incident. This legal precedent, together with the brief from the New Jersey Attorney General's Office on behalf of the New Jersey Department of Health, leaves me threadbare.

Beyond the donor's right to privacy, Matthews argues that the social policy of a safe and adequate blood supply is predicated on the donor's confidentiality. As a skilled appellate advocate, Matthews knows that at this level of review, a case will turn on the social policy argument. Blood banks, like the Bergen Community Blood Center, are supposed to ask donors if they are sexually active gay or bisexual men with multiple partners. The blood bankers insisted that asking such screening questions was gay discrimination. Is asking somebody about their sexual orientation in relation to a medical procedure really discrimination? I thought to myself. It seems like inserting one's own opinions into how gay individuals might feel, assuming and other-izing, is far more discriminatory. I knew the blood bankers did not care a hoot about gay discrimination, because as transfusion-AIDS cases increased and the epidemic grew, they asked those screening questions anyway.

Matthews continues to argue that if donor privacy is breached, then they will not honestly answer these screening questions and stop donating blood altogether, which will result in national blood shortages. Matthews delivered his arguments, backed by New Jersey's Attorney General, against donor discovery for Bill with elan, ingeniously employing the homophobia so rampant at the time in his legal agenda.

Chief Justice Wilentz calls me up to the podium. In front of the podium are green, yellow and red lights about four inches in their diameters. They appear as harmless as small traffic lights, but will literally direct the unfortunately real narrative of the AIDS epidemic. The green light is on, which means I go, with twenty minutes to convince the Justices of my arguments.

Chief Justice Wilentz and Justice Pollack ask me to explain how Bill's need for donor discovery outweighs a donor's right to privacy. "Your Honors, I'm not asking to know the identity of donor 29F0784. Problem is, the defendants deny that Bill was infected by the platelets that came from this donor. And, they state they screened the donor by asking him the required high-risk behavior questions. I need the discovery to prove Bill was infected by this donor's platelet and to determine whether he was asked the required screening questions."

Justice Garibaldi begins to consume much of the time with questions about the chilling effect on the volunteer blood system if the court makes an exception to donor confidentiality, as Matthews and the AABB argue. "We must balance Mr. Snyder's need for information with donor 29F0784's right to privacy." It is clear that she weighs on the side of the blood bankers. I refuse to buckle under, but am distracted by the ominous yellow light. I wonder if the court will give me extra time, since it is being mostly taken up by answering rhetorical questions. Garibaldi was a partner at a large defense firm before being appointed to the supreme court, and does a poor job of showing impartiality: she is clearly aligned with the blood bankers. I remind Justice Garibaldi that the blood bankers have shown no evidence that a donor will not answer screening questions honestly, or that blood shortages will occur. The AABB had not offered a single credible study to support their position. The clock hand jerks in that maddeningly hesitant way.

"They're just scare tactics," I argue as the red light enforces silence. I turn around to Patti and she gives me an encouraging nod.

The ride home on the Jersey Turnpike is filled with radio commercials, neither of us bother changing the station. My thoughts are occupied with how good Mathews was, and the points I did not get to make. Matthews delivered his argument for the blood bankers with a controlled cadence, with changes in his infliction, volume and tone. I even noticed how he subtly flicked his gaze towards the clock to manage the pace of his delivery.

On the other hand, Justice Garibaldi's hard-hitting questions caused me to pause oafishly as I groped through my notes for answers. I am almost relieved Bill and Roslyn could not come to see me argue their case. I dread Roslyn's phone call, and having to tell her that she will have to wait a few months for the court's decision.

"It's out of your hands; no use in worrying anymore," Patti says.

That night, to relax, we make a homemade pizza. I break the canister of frozen pizza dough against the edge of the counter top because Courtney likes the sound of the air pop. We throw flour on the counter top and flatten the pizza dough with an old wooden rolling pin. What a mess—with flour marbling the counter, floor, and Courtney. We spread a package of PathMart shredded cheese and pizza sauce over the dough and stick it into the oven. For a few minutes, the smokescreen of flour and the smell of baking pizza dough takes my mind off the case. I feel in control of something, rather than helpless with events of such heavy consequence.

The summer after eight grade, I stole a car. It was serious this time. I tried to outrun the pursuing state police car and collided with the cement barrier. Then, injured and bleeding, I ran on foot. A warning shoot was fired, but I ran harder and faster. I am not sure what I was really running from; I knew they would find me. I outran the state trooper, but got caught later that night walking home, injured from the accident. I had just turned 15.

About a month later, I was home alone, sitting on the couch, when I realized that if I kept going as I was, I would end up in jail. When I appeared before the juvenile court judge with my father for the second time, I explained that I planned to join the Marines on my 17th birthday. It was agreed that I would permanently live with my father, this time in California, and work until that day came. He lined up jobs for us in a Glendale sheet metal factory, which provided material for the monorail at Disneyland. Every day, I'd wait for the 10:00 a.m. break bell to ring, go out to the parking lot with the other workers and grab something off the catering truck. Then I worked a sheet metal press until the 2:00 p.m. bell. Most of the workers seemed content to live bell-to-bell, but I already knew by then that I was not well-suited for routine.

Standing guard on the Cuban fence line in Guantanamo Bay one pre-dawn morning, I saw tracer-rounds being fired at me by Cuban soldiers. Tracer rounds glow in the darkness and look like fireflies. I chambered a round to return fire, fumbling because I had never done it before nor planned on doing it so soon into my time in. I soon realized that the Cuban centuries were not firing at me, but the fence jumpers trying to escape. I waited for the refugees to find their way to me for asylum, but I knew that wouldn't happen after one, two, three loud explosions of land mines. There was nothing I could do.

I decided to become a lawyer because it seemed like a way to change lives without those horrible detonation noises that reverberate in your bones years after the fact. It didn't strike me as routine because every case would indicate a different battle, a second chance to make things right that, hopefully, did not involve death. I had wild notions that law was a profession in which a single person can adjust an entire crooked system or, at the very least, have two lives: a work one that was a crusade for equality, and a comfortable home life that was richly funded by that crusade for equality. Did a person such as myself, who so narrowly missed a life in various juvenile penal institutions, even deserve to have such grandiose dreams? I think of Patti and the bills that keep piling higher due to my total lack of income at the moment. I wish I could afford the luxury of smaller dreams, but I am too far in and too many people are relying on the ambitious version of myself I presented before I realized exactly how difficult this legal foxtrot surrounding the AIDS epidemic would be.

CHAPTER THIRTEEN

Three months later, on August 1, 1991, I get up at sunrise and head straight to the newsstand. I glance at the headlines and scoop up an armful of newspapers. I hand them out to friends and relatives—my in-laws, first of all. "AIDS-Infected Can Question Blood Donor: New Jersey Supreme Court Backs Victims of Transfusion," reports the *New York Times*, August 1, 1991.

The New Jersey Supreme Court ruling makes national news with stories in the *New York Times*, *Associated Press*, *Bergen Record*, and on television news. The *New Jersey Law Journal*, Thursday, August 8, 1991, "AIDS Victim Wins Fight for Blood Bank Discovery." The story includes my photo.

The New Jersey Supreme Court affirms Judge Pressler's decision. Justice Pollack writes a concurring opinion to emphasize the court's reliance on the statutory balance of the donor's privacy interest, Bill's interest in full discovery and compensation for his injuries, and society's interest is a safe and adequate blood supply. He states:

> Confronted with defendants' denial, plaintiffs' need to question the donor is obvious. Judge Pressler's insightful opinion suggests the relevance of the discovery on the negligence issue: Beyond the

causation issue, plaintiff cogently asserts a need in respect of the question of Bergen Community Blood Center's negligence. Illustratively, it was known before August 1984 that early symptoms of AIDS infection include particular lymph-node swelling and skin disorders, and, in fact, by 1983 the commercial blood bankers were conducting routine physical examinations of donors to determine the presence of these symptoms. Did the donor here have those symptoms then? Was he asked about them? Was he physically examined in this respect? Was he given appropriate high-risk group self-exclusion information? Was a reasonable effort made to determine if he was in a high-risk category? Were the questions adequately explained to him? . . . All of this information is, in our view, highly pertinent to the issue of Bergen Community Blood Center and American Association of Blood Banks's negligence and is, moreover, to a large extent not available from any other resource other than the donor himself. *Snyder v. Mekhjian*, 125 N.J. 328, 341 (1991).

The supreme court balanced the donor's need for privacy with Bill's need for discovery and society's interest in a safe blood supply. I especially get a kick out of being referred to as "cogent" by both the appellate and supreme court. I tease Patti that now I am certified "Mr. Cogent." She rolls her eyes and responds with, "Okay, Mr. Cogent, take out that garbage."

Justice Garibaldi wrote a dissenting opinion, noting "Here, obvious considerations include the fact that if the donor is still alive (nearly 90% of those in New Jersey diagnosed with AIDS in 1985 are not alive), the donor may be very ill, and contact, even in the form of veiled deposition or written interrogatories, may be significantly burdensome." She wrote that the infected donor may not have revealed his or her AIDS to relatives and that his or her need for privacy outweighs a Bill's need for information. Of course, there was not a scintilla of evidence to support this. No one knew whether the donor was ill, alive or even willing to cooperate. It was all hypothetical argument to prevent the blood bankers from disclosing that Bill had in fact gotten AIDS as a result of their negligence.

After two and a half years, this is where we are—we now have the legitimacy to actually go forward. Now we have to begin the donor discovery we fought so hard for, and continue depositions of everybody involved in both Bill and Janet's cases.

The case is sent back to the trial court and Judge Anthony J. Sciuto is assigned the case. Judge Sciuto is also an ex-marine who keeps his battalion mug on the bookshelf. He once played drums in the old Joey Dee and the Starlighters Peppermint Twist Band back in the Sixties. He is from the working-class town of Garfield, which is where I lived as a child. But this does not mean he cuts me any slack. The AABB and I become even more entangled in combative litigation as they stonewall my efforts to get Bill's case to trial.

The first order of business is to determine whether donor 29F0784 is still alive. This becomes a frustrating ordeal. The Bergen Community Blood Center produces the donor's alleged last known address for the court. Judge Sciuto sends a certified letter to this address, and now we wait. Bill's case is once again placed on hold while we wait for a reply from the blood donor; statistics claim there is 90% chance he is dead.

CHAPTER FOURTEEN

I stop quickly at John's coffee shop across the street from the courthouse for a take-out coffee, small bottle of apple juice and egg sandwiches. John's is the local lawyers' hangout. Every county courthouse in every county up and down the Jersey turnpike has a small coffee shop across the street from the courthouse where you will find lawyers killing time. Many cases get settled in them. I stop in, but don't really fit in. I grab the bag and head for the office.

At the office, I take the rubber band off yesterday's mail and toss it into a garbage bag next to the filing cabinet. There is no money in the office checking account, so there is no use opening it and agonizing over the bills. In the bottom drawer of the filing cabinet are the paper plates. Janet called and said she needs to see me. She did not say much on the phone except it is about a parents' meeting at Naomi's school tonight. I put the paper plates on the desk for Janet and I to have some breakfast. The paper containers of my coffee and her tea have leaked in the bag. I clean it up with a paper towel from the men's room just as she walks in.

"Janet, how are you?"

"Sorry I'm late." She had just dropped Naomi and Christian at school.

"No problem. Here, have some breakfast."

"Thank you." She is always running on empty. I knew she would need something to eat.

"So tell me what's up."

"I may need you to write a letter to the principal at Naomi's school. The other parents found out about me and want Naomi tested for AIDS every couple of weeks, and her test results posted on the door of the school nurse's office. I don't want Naomi treated this way."

"They can't do that, so don't worry."

Janet had gotten on a free experimental AIDS program at New York University. Kyle doesn't have medical insurance, so Janet was relieved when she got into the program. She goes a couple of times a week into the city for treatment. On the days she went for treatment and could not get back in time to pick up Naomi from school, she asked another mother with whom she was friendly to get Naomi and take her to her house until Janet could pick her up.

"I remember you mentioned her to me. What happened?"

"After a while, she started to say things like, 'You don't look well.' She kept it up every time I picked Naomi up and I knew that she suspected something, but I didn't know what to tell her. So I told her that I have cancer and go into the city for treatment. Sometimes she would ask me to stay for tea at her house, and we would talk. But she kept prying, like she knew something else was wrong with me. She would ask me who my doctors are and say things like she knows good doctors right here in New Jersey. She said to me that I could trust her if something was wrong. One afternoon, I guess I needed to talk to somebody and felt as though I could trust her, so I told her what happened to me—how I got AIDS when I delivered Christian. She promised not to say anything, but the next day when I went to pick Naomi up at school, the other parents acted different towards me."

"How so?"

"There are a few mothers I say hello to while we all wait for the children to get out from school. We would just talk by the cars. But now they avoid me. I know she told them. They went to the principal. They said if there was a playground accident, she might infect other children."

It has been a few years since parents protested and an arsonist burned down the house of the Ray family in Arcadia, Florida. I am surprised this kind of hysteria is present and alive right here in New Jersey.

"I just don't want them to take out what happened to me on Naomi."

"What did the school principal say?"

"I don't know. She is going to have a meeting with these parents tonight. I wanted to talk with you before I see her. Maybe you can write a letter for me."

"I'll write a letter or call her, but first let's see if the principal can diffuse it. If I get involved, it may escalate the tension. But Janet, if I have to, I will fight for you so try not to worry. They cannot do this."

Janet exhales and settles back. She tells me about going to a Super Bowl party at Kyle's uncle's house.

"I brought a bowl of potato salad that I made and put it on the table. But no one would touch it."

"They just don't know any better, Janet." I might have done the same thing, but now I see the pain it causes her.

"I know, but it hurts."

"I'm sorry."

"Another time we were at his uncle's house, and there was something on television about AIDS. Kyle's uncle said they should just put all those people away someplace."

"Wow, Kyle's uncle has a problem."

"That was before he knew what happened. He's all right now."

I shrug. "Maybe he just doesn't like potato salad."

Janet laughs. I notice how Janet never wears make-up on her face and is always hurried. Today, she seems to rest herself on the vinyl seat of the chrome-legged office chair. She sits upright, her hands folded together on her lap and her elbows on the worn, imitation wood armrest.

"I began looking for support groups. Kyle was against it, but I convinced him to give it a try. I thought we would meet a few people like us, going through what we are. So I called the church that sponsored a group. I spoke with the priest on the phone, and he said to come down. He sounded nice so we tried it. But mostly they were drug addicts. We sat in a circle, and this one woman talked about how she would wake up in the street with a needle in her arm and would do anything for drugs. I can understand gay men who get infected because they love each other, but I can never understand how a person could do what she did to herself.

"One night Kyle and I were going to the movies with some people from the group, and they started doing drugs in the car. That was it. It freaked Kyle out. He yelled at them to pull over. We never went back after that."

"I'm sorry that didn't work out, Janet. I guess you had to try to find people just to be able to share with."

"Naomi's no longer asked over for play dates and wonders why." She takes a sip of her lukewarm tea. "I never pictured my life would turn out this way. I always thought we would all be a happy family."

Janet's world is chaotically upside down. If she had not been infected with AIDS she would be doing all the things I see my friends doing with their spouses and families. Going out to movies, dinners, watching their kids play school sports, or even taking vacations. Janet enrolls Naomi and Christian in after school activities and tries to keep up with it like the other mothers, but doesn't have the physical stamina. She so badly wants a normal life for them. Now, her days are filled with experimental drug therapy, hospitalizations, and figuring out how to help Naomi understand what is happening.

"It was easier when Naomi was in Catholic school. The nuns knew I was sick, and when I couldn't pay the tuition, they let her stay in school anyway."

"Did you tell the nuns you are infected?"

"Yes. One night I went to back to school night. I was so weak that I couldn't even make it up the school stairs. Sister Superior was watching me. I think she could tell I wasn't well. I needed to talk to somebody. So one day I went to see her. I told her how I got infected and everything."

"How did she handle it?"

"She made me tea and we talked. She told me that she was going to speak with Father Bernie to waive Naomi's school tuition. I just broke down and cried."

"Wow. That was nice of them."

"Yeah. One day around Christmas, I was alone in the house. We had no money, and we couldn't get Christian and Naomi anything for Christmas. I was just so depressed. Then there is this knock at the door, and it is Sister Superior with a tree and gifts for us."

Janet's story brings back a memory I would not have thought about in a hundred years. My father served in the navy, so we lived in temporary housing the government built because of the post-war housing shortage for returning veterans. When I was a young child, most of this veteran housing had already been bulldozed and turned into strip malls. We lived in one of the last projects. Later, it was razed by the town, so we moved again. All the kids and teachers at school knew we used food stamps. When my father was out of work and my mother got by day-to-day, she used this old yellow pot to heat tomato soup and divvy it out into our bowls. Sometimes we had it with bread, other times we'd spice it up with the extra packets of pepper or oyster crackers we took from fast food restaurants. Occasionally we diluted it with extra water to expand the amount. Tomato soup was coming out of my ears; we ate it so often.

"One day, a priest from Mount Virgin Church in Garfield showed up with a basket of food. His name was Father Olsen." Janet gives a slight smile as though to go ahead. I think she sensed that I'm not one to share stories, yet something about her coolheaded manner disarmed me.

"I just remember how glad we were to see that basket of food he brought over for Christmas. It was a straw basket, stuffed with canned foods, with cellophane over it." Janet smiles a you-fail-at-storytelling-but-I'm-still-happy-you-shared kind of smile.

"Why did you take Naomi out of Catholic school?"

"We had to move again because of Kyle's job."

"That's too bad. It sounds like the nuns liked you."

"Yes, they made plenty of exceptions for us."

"Are you all right?"

"I feel better, thank you."

We stand because Janet has to go pick up Naomi and Christian from school. We didn't realize our conversation had lasted so long. She lingers a moment and I notice she is wearing a dark purple dress, rather than the usual jeans, for the after-school meeting. The office is quiet and the pigeons are cooing. She had put on make-up, but it does little to hide her pasty complexion. I take her beige-raincoat from the coat rack behind the door and help Janet put the coat on. Her arms slide in with no resistance; the sleeves are disconcertingly big.

CHAPTER FIFTEEN

Janet's case is assigned to Judge Miriam Span, in the old Union County Courthouse in Elizabeth. I had heard about Roger Solmosy, the attorney for the New York Blood Center, who has a reputation as a tough New York lawyer. As I drive under the blanket of jumbo-jets swooping across the turnpike near Newark Airport and pass the stacks of hundreds of shipping containers, I replay the dozens of hostile letters he and I have already exchanged over moving Janet's case through the system. By the time I pass the fields of oil storage tanks, train yards and reach the recycling plant at exit 13A for the Elizabeth Seaport, I figure he will try to delay the case again. I have not met Solmosy yet, but the war between us is already vicious. Each time he writes a letter to Judge Span, I write two in response.

I follow the dilapidated neighborhood along Bayway Avenue to the Elizabeth Superior Court on Broad Street. I park around the corner and dig out a couple quarters from the ashtray for the parking meter. I walk around to the back street level entrance, just past the cement handicapped ramp. Once through the security check, I take the elevator outside the basement cafeteria up to the sixth floor. I covered this courthouse for Buttafucco and know my way around its bleak, unexciting labyrinth.

The doors to Judge Span's courtroom are as aged as the infrastructure and rusted railroad overpasses along the turnpike. There are decades of peeling, buttercup yellow varnish surrounding the tall black doors.

When I enter the courtroom, there is a large, over-weight man with uncut hair at the defense table. His suit jacket is cut large and drapes over him like robes. His eyes size me up from head to toe as I walk down the isle to the plaintiff's table. Solmosy. Next to him is Neil Reiseman, a tall, lean man in a tailored suit. Reiseman is an ex-army officer and the senior partner of his defense firm. I have not met Reiseman before today either, but I figure he did not get to be the senior partner of his law firm by playing fair. The animosity is so thick between Solmosy and me that we do not even bother with the usual courtesies. Reiseman shoots a quick glance in my direction, which I return without speaking a word.

"All rise." The bailiff comes out from Judge Span's chambers followed by a young woman, mid-thirties, in a black judicial robe.

"Counsel on the case *M v. New York Blood Center*, enter your appearance for the record." She says from the bench. One-by-one, we each enter out appearances for our clients on the record.

"Counsel, where are we on the case?" Judge Span already has a sense of my frustration with the court's failure, from the letters I have been sending her.

"Your Honor, my client has been in and out of the hospital fighting pneumonia. I have written the court and asked that her case be placed on an expedited track." I know the defense lawyers are just waiting for Janet to die.

"Excuse me, your Honor. How do we know Mr. Baxter's client is ill? Solmosy says laconically. "He has not provided any medical reports to the court."

"Your Honor, Mr. Solmosy knows my client is ill since it was his client who gave her the contaminated blood," I quip.

"Judge, I need time to review the case, gather experts, take depositions to protect my client." Solmosy talks as though Judge Span is junior to him and with a disdain for me. He has several ethical violations filed against him, and he is sentenced to several months of house arrest with an electronic ankle bracelet. Eventually, Solmosy is disbarred from practicing law, which he reduces on appeal to a four-year suspension. But this is later, and I have to deal with him now.

"Your Honor, I have to join in Mr. Solmosy's request for time." Reiseman adds. They wrestle in a tag-team against my case.

"Your Honor, you have to enter doner discovery order with teeth, otherwise they will just ignore it."

"All right, counsel. What do you need, Mr. Reiseman?" Judge Span asking them what they need, rather than using her authority to get them to move fast, disturbs me. Reiseman and Solmosy painstakingly detail the delays they need—I suspect they collaborated on this before I arrived.

"All right, Counsel. I will enter an order that discovery be completed in the next ninety days. I will set this case down for another case management conference. We'll see where we are then and set a trial date."

"Thank you, your Honor." I feel as though I got the best deal possible for the moment, and pack my litigation bag with discreet fury. There is a thickness in the courtroom that is apparent even to the other lawyers waiting in the seats behind the bar rail.

I make a stop at John's coffee shop for takeout tea to bring back to the office and check my watch. It is 10:00 a.m. and Janet will be here any minute.

"George?" Janet calls me from the reception area.

"Come on in, Janet." I am always glad to see her. "How do you like the fish tank? It is the newest addition to the office."

Janet laughs, "I like it." It's a large fish tank I picked up at a weekend flea market. Bubbles erupt from the mask of the miniature diver at the bottom. Six goldfish swim around it as though taunting the little plastic thing. I put plants and an underwater garden in the tank for the fish to swim through and around, a visual interpretation of the Beatles' Octopus's Garden, if you will. Sometimes, when it is late and I am alone, I sit back and chew a handful of Tums while watching the fish swim. The King-size bottle of Tums sits right next to the fish food. Janet takes one and sits across from me at the desk.

"Here, I got you a tea." I take the paper cups from the wet and ripped bag. I never seem to make it from John's Coffee Shop across the street without spilling the tea.

"I will have to be more careful. Sorry, what a mess." I begin to dry off Janet's tea container with the wet paper napkins from inside the bag.

"It's no problem." She smiles at my clumsiness, gets dry napkins from behind the coffee maker and helps to dry up the spill.

Janet's physical condition is getting more precarious. She is losing weight and looks paler. It is always touch and go with her. She's in the hospital, then out again. We begin to work on answering interrogatories in her case against the New York Blood Center and the hematologist who transfused her with cryoprecipitate.

There is an art to drafting interrogatory answers because you have to picture the other lawyers holding them up, reading the answers back to her in court. We have to be thorough but also leave some wiggle room. We begin going over her medical history.

"Janet, you were referred to Dr. Joseph Feldman for a hematology consultation by the OB-GYN because you gave a history of von Willebrand's disease. Do you recall what you told Dr. Feldman?"

George T. Baxter, Esq.

"His nurse gave me this form to fill out while I was waiting in his office. It asked if I had any bleeding disorders. I checked that von Willebrand's was suspected when I was a child. My mother told me that she had a sister who had it and that I had it too, because I always bruised so easily."

"Were you treated for it when you were a child?"

"No. We had this family doctor, and I think he tested me for it."

"What about when you delivered Naomi? Did you have any bleeding problems?"

"No."

"What did your doctor in Scotland tell you?"

"I don't remember; he told my mother."

"But he never treated you for it?"

"No."

"What was his name? I want to get the medical records from him."

"Dr. Alexander MacLeod, but he is probably retired now. I can ask some of my family back in Scotland if they know where he is. He was a friend of the family. He knew my mom well."

"Was he you mom's physician too?"

"Yes, but they were also good friends and she would talk with him, especially after my father left. Everything changed then."

"What do you mean?"

"Well, on the outside, to everyone, it looked like we had this nice family. My father wore his RAF blazer everywhere."

"What's that?"

"He was in the Royal Air Force. Everyone thought he was this stand-up, great guy, but he owed everyone money, cheated his partners, and when he left, and my mother blamed me."

"Blamed you?"

"Yes, they used to fight all the time, and he would hit her. I used to tell him to leave her alone and get out. I told her that she should leave him, so when he left her, she blamed me." Janet's eyes slightly glass and she pauses for a second. "She really didn't like me."

"Janet, come on? Are you sure?" I want her to feel better, but I am not sure denying that her mother ever loved her is the right approach.

"Oh, believe me, she made it very clear that she did not like me."

"Janet, don't all mothers and daughters have difficult relationships sometimes?"

"No. It was made very clear to me." Her response is the slightest bit brash; in retrospect, she was hurt that I tried to belittle her feelings. There is no denial for Janet about her childhood. She is too strong for that. I probably had difficulty accepting the violence and lack of affection Janet describes because I was the one in denial. Janet gets too quiet, like she's said too much, so I try to open up to her.

"When I was a child, my father would hit my mother too. My older brother or sister would interfere, like you. That is when we would escape to the movies." I remember watching Yule Brenner on the big screen in *The Magnificent Seven*, and Peter O'Toole in *Lawrence of Arabia*. I was really young and those movies shaped my idea of the hero—not surprisingly, Gregory Peck in *To Kill A Mockingbird*." She smiles briefly.

"Janet, what happened to your father?

"He moved to the States and married this woman he met on some business trips. Then he had a new family, and we never heard from him again. I have a younger sister and brother, and we really struggled. We went on government assistance and lived in public housing. I used to take care of them all the time. My parents fought so much that when my father left, I thought, good riddance."

"I raised my brother and sister after Mom died. Mom had family, but nobody helped us. Then, I met Kyle."

"How did you meet him?"

"He was our milkman."

We burst into laughter. Janet never complains or feels sorry for herself. Like me, she likes to state her past with the dispassion of a law brief.

"You mean, you actually married the milkman?"

She laughs. "My aunts and uncle didn't like Kyle because he didn't have a good job. They looked down on him, acted like he came from the wrong side of the tracks. But he was kind to us and helped us out. When no one would come to our wedding, I could not believe it."

"Did you ever hear from your father again?"

"Mom died from cancer, and I took care of her for a long time. On the day of her funeral, we were all getting dressed, and the phone rings. When I picked it up, there was this voice on the other end: 'Janet?' I asked, 'Who is this?' He said, 'Janet?' Then I said, 'Look, this isn't a good time right now. Whoever this is, my mother just passed, and we're leaving for her funeral.' Then he finally said, 'Janet, it's your father.'"

"I did not want to speak to him. I put the phone down. But after a while, my brother wanted to see him. Then my father said, why don't Kyle and I move to the States. He said he would help us. Kyle wanted to, so we moved here and stayed with him and his wife for a while. He had all these photographs around of his new life after he'd left us. Pictures of his trips to Disney World. And all I could think about was how we struggled in Scotland. How we never had new clothes but always used clothes. I began to argue with his wife, to the point where I would just stay in my room like a bratty teen. So Jim has an uncle in New Jersey, and we decided to move here from Michigan. I was pregnant with Christian when we moved."

"Wow. So that is how you got here to New Jersey?"

"Yes."

"Janet, I need find Dr. MacLeod in Scotland and get your childhood medical records."

"I'll ask my aunt if she knows where he is."

"Good. That will be a help."

It is past noon and Janet looks faint. We walk across the street to a café for something to eat while we talk. It is a small health food café with wooden floors and natural foods. I spot a table by the window.

"Let's grab that table."

Janet looks sheepish. "My doctors told me to stay out of the sun. It's the meds." She is frail and her complexion is pastier now.

There are only a couple of tables, but another one opens up, and I grab it for us. I go up to the counter and order avocado and chicken sandwiches with seven-grain bread. As I return to the table, I notice a few customers' heads turn toward Janet. I can tell Janet wants to talk.

"This seven grain bread is great, and the avocado and chicken are good for you." I place the plate before her then grab plastic folks and napkin from the counter for us.

"Thanks." She almost smiles, but looks away.

"Janet, what's up?"

"The bank is taking the house." She folds her hands on her lap and exhales for a moment.

"Why?"

"Kyle and I cannot make the mortgage payments."

"Maybe I can help you. The bank does not want your house. I can talk with them, convince them to restructure your payments, give you more time." I learned this through my own financial problems with Spencer Bank.

"No, let them have it," she says with a deep sense of resignation. "It was supposed to be our dream house, where we would raise Christian and Naomi. It is a small cape we bought when I was working, before I knew I was infected. Now, it is just a burden. Let them take it."

"Janet, are you sure?"

"Yes, I am sure."

Janet did not need to say more, and I did not press the issue. Janet's life continues to slide and her dreams fade. Janet and Kyle get by on his salary as a printer apprentice. Her plan in Scotland was to work in the States as a nurse and have both incomes when they bought the cape. Now, with Janet so ill and no medical insurance, they often move apartment to apartment, financially struggling, until they end up in a damp basement apartment. The apartment is outside the school district and they have to transfer Naomi again. Mildew is discovered behind the wall of that basement apartment, which is an extra health hazard for Janet's compromised immune system, so her doctors insist she move to another place. Once again, she has to uproot Naomi from school.

CHAPTER SIXTEEN

Though all I want is a quick settlement for Janet, big defendants, like those of Janet's doctor and the New York Blood Center, want to take the case to trial. I need to find a blood bank expert and a hematologist to testify. What I am about to tell you is how I find Don Francis.

Don Francis was the only government official to openly criticize the blood bankers for not testing the blood. *The Philadelphia Inquirer* covered Atlanta with a full-page photograph of the meeting and Don Francis banging his fist on the table, warning the blood bankers they were about to kill thousands of people. Randy Shilts' book *And The Band Played On* follows Don Francis through his frustrations with the politics of the blood industry and public health service in not taking action to avoid the AIDS epidemic. Dr. Francis is even the central character in the HBO movie adaptation of the same name. Don Francis is either a public health hero or a hotheaded CDC official, depending on which side of the fence you sit on. All I know is that I need Don Francis to testify about what happened in Atlanta between the Centers for Disease Control and the blood bankers. Like I said earlier, a lawyer cannot use a book or movie to prove his case. I need the actual Don Francis to come to court.

The year before I filed Janet's case, Patti and I flew out to San Francisco to see Marc Conant about Bill's case. My mother-in-law had to prep Courtney for the Friday spelling quiz in my absence. The trip was planned as business and pleasure. Patti and I checked into the Sheraton at Fisherman's Wharf and walked out to the end of pier 39. I snapped a few photos of her with Alcatraz in the distance. A few hours later, we took a taxi to Marc Conant's office.

Marc Conant dropped me a lead: Don Francis had been reassigned by the Centers for Disease Control from Atlanta to the San Francisco Department of Health. I instantly track him down. "Good luck," Marc clucks, "he's been gagged." As a government employee, he is prohibited from testifying or talking with lawyers about Atlanta.

The pleasure part of our trip abruptly ended when I took Patti back to the Sheraton, switched into a blue and white cab and left for the San Francisco Department of Health building. She stayed in the room and watched *Oprah*. The plan was to walk in like I belonged there and find Don Francis. I expected to be thrown out, but instead everyone was too busy and hardly noticed me. I asked a staffer to point out Don Francis to me. He looked around the room for a moment, then pointed to a tall, lean guy in khaki pants and blue oxford shirt standing over a desk. I exhaled and walked over to him.

"Dr. Francis?" He looked youthful, with sand-colored hair. Matthew Modine was the perfect actor to play him in the HBO movie, I thought to myself as I held out a hand.

"Yes?" Don Francis tried to figure out if he knew me.

"I'm George Baxter, a lawyer." He rolled his eyes. I kept talking to avoid being thrown out.

"I am here about a transfusion-AIDS case and I am wondering if I may ask you a few questions?"

"I am sorry, the government does not allow us to talk about it." Marc was right. He'd been gagged.

"What if I subpoena you?" I smiled.

"It has been tried. The government will quash the subpoena." He was not intimidated by that.

"Just a couple questions about Atlanta?" I would not move from the spot.

"I cannot help you, sorry." Dr. Francis was not wavering. Why should he? He would be risking his pension and legal sanctions. But, he was the only outspoken government employee to blow the whistle and I needed him to testify no matter what, but we were at an impasse. It was no use pushing him. That was the first time I met Don Francis.

Patti seemed to roll with the punches about cutting the pleasure part of the trip short and waiting at the hotel. At least, she didn't say anything about it. On the flight back home, she wore the gray University of California sweatshirt that we bought on our first day there. I knew how much she was looking forward to the vacation. When we arrived home late Sunday night, Abby jumped all over me. Abby had grown into an eighty-pound golden retriever. We had late night tea with my mother-in-law. I put a buck on Courtney's dresser because she aced her spelling quiz.

Now, a year later, Marc tells me that Don Francis has retired from the government. I cajole Don's home phone number out of Marc. I call Don Francis and remind him who I am. He agrees to meet me in San Francisco. Once again, travel bag slung over my shoulder, I catch the Friday late afternoon United flight. I check back into the Sheraton at Fisherman's Wharf and put Patti's stick-um notes on the hotel mirror. Their adhesive is weakening with every trip, collecting little s-shaped pieces of dust. I use cello tape to keep them up. On Saturday morning, I head over to a local café filled with fishermen. It is off the beaten track of tourists and serves its coffee in those heavy mugs. I read the business section of a day-old *San Francisco Chronicle*, sipping coffee and watching the fishermen come and go. I am meeting Don Francis in the hotel lobby at 8:00 a.m, so leave the coffee shop promptly at 7:45.

I sit down on the sofa in front of the fireplace and watch the ebb and flow of people enter and exit, but there is no sign of Don. A half hour turns into an hour, and still no sign of Don. The sounds of luggage wheels scraping the floor starts to become deafening. I begin to panic a little at the though of making the trip and not meeting him. I walk over to the check-in counter for my messages, but he has not called. I take the elevator up to my room and search through everything for Don's phone number. I left it on my desk in Hackensack. I go back down stairs and wait. It is 9:30 a.m. and I figure our meeting is off. Then, Don walks briskly into the lobby, his face flushed and hair messed as though he just finished a windy hike. It turns out that I gave Don the wrong hotel and he has been walking through hotel lobbies along the wharf looking for me. It's still the telecommunications dark age, before cell phones could have saved us from all this lag. Don's extraordinary effort to keep our meeting is impressive. I thank him by dumping two large black binders in his lap. The binders are filled with the documents I intend to use at trial. They are so thorough, with medical records and anticipated trial exhibits, that all the witnesses now call them the Baxter Binders.

Don and I work right there in the lobby; the revolving lobby doors a few feet away provide us with a intermittent flow of cold air that kept us alert. Without ever moving, we review each document and determine its significance. I am insecure and frightened to death about blowing the case, which is why I have methodically organized every piece of paper into the Baxter Binders.

In the lobby, Don takes me through the CDC data, which shows that gay men account for 75 percent of reported AIDS cases while intravenous drug users account for 20 percent. Don explains that's why the CDC wanted the blood bankers to use the core test—it identifies 90-100 percent of the people who make up 95 percent of the high-risk groups. "In a nutshell, that is the epidemiology of the AIDS epidemic," Don explains.

The flow of people coming and going through the revolving lobby doors has slowed by the time we close the binders. "Oh, it's dark outside," Don says, bemused. The hours passed us as expressionlessly as the hotel guests.

A couple of months later, Janet's case is still stalled before Judge Span, so I reserve Don for a video deposition on Bill's case. I reserve the Sheraton's smaller Conference Room B to save a few bucks. It is strange to see my name in big white letters on the hotel's directory of events in the middle of the lobby. A video deposition is where the lawyer calling the witness does it on video to preserve for use at trial later on. For example, if the witness, like Don Francis, is difficult to schedule for a trial day, his testimony is videotaped. It is an official proceeding, conducted just like it is taking place in court. Ed Matthews and other lawyers are present to cross-examine Don, a court reporter is present to transcribe the testimony, and a certified videographer records the video to be shown at a future time.

Don's video deposition is my first and I am unsure about the rules. It is my first national case; and here is Don, a folk hero and public health celebrity, as my first witness. I hide my nervousness from the other lawyers or else they will have me for breakfast. The only way is to fake it. I drink down coffee all morning to get that caffeine-sharp edge. As the camera lights are being checked, I pull Don aside for a few last minute instructions.

"Don, I have never done a this before. I'm not exactly sure about how to formulate the questions to avoid objections."

"Now you tell me, George." Don's cool about it.

"It's okay, Don. This is how we will handle it. Just answer the question you think I am trying to ask you." I resort to my old turnpike lawyering tricks and I am not sure Don will play along. "Ignore the other lawyers' objections." Don looks at me as though saying, "You can take the lawyer out of Jersey, but you cannot take the Jersey out of the lawyer."

"No matter what I ask, Don, just take my question as your cue to open up and talk; ignore the slug-fest between me and the other lawyers." I can handle the fighting; it is formulating questions in a way to avoid objections that worries me.

I made blowups of the CDC data, with pie charts that are easy to follow on camera. The videographer sets up a blue sheet behind Don for background and places small microphones on the jacket lapels of all the lawyers. I stick a blowup of the CDC's December 1982 Morbidity and Mortality Weekly Report under Don's nose, almost dropping it on his lap. All that coffee makes my hands jitter.

"Dr. Francis, I direct your attention to this MMWR dated December 1982. What significance did it have to you as a public health officer?"

Don looks right into the camera. "In December 1982, we had confirmation that AIDS was being spread by transfusions. This infant received a blood transfusion at birth and developed AIDS. When we traced the donor, we discovered he was a gay man dying from AIDS. He didn't show signs when he donated the blood, which means that an infected donor with no signs of infection can transmit the virus through his blood donation."

"Dr. Francis, please explain to the jury that will be watching this video what the CDC did after publishing this MMWR?"

"It was our worst-case scenario that AIDS was contaminating the blood supply. We immediately convened an emergency meeting with the blood industry to get them to begin testing donors. We had the means to screen out ninety-five percent of the high-risk donors who were transmitting AIDS."

"Dr. Francis, will you explain the epidemiology of AIDS as it was know by the CDC, blood industry and public health services by January 1983?" The caffeine almost passes for confidence.

"Yes. On January 4, 1983, we called a meeting at CDC headquarters in Atlanta to show the blood industry surrogate tests that would prevent contamination of the blood supply. We showed the blood bankers that seventy-five percent of all AIDS cases were gay men and twenty percent were intravenous drug users. We also showed them that the hepatitis B core antibody test successfully identifies ninety percent of the high risk gay men and one hundred percent of intravenous drug users, because both these groups have been exposed to hepatitis as a result of their lifestyles."

Don's San Francisco video deposition that day goes as anticipated: I ask a question; the other lawyers vociferously object; and Don goes on, making his points, oblivious to any arguing. No one cares about the lawyers' objections; that is for another day. Despite being under hot, glaring lights and in a contentious setting, Don's charisma, calm, and conviction come through on the video.

Don testifies about the frustration the CDC AIDS Task Force members had in Atlanta with Dr. Bove of the American Association of Blood Banks and Dr. Aaron Kellner of the New York Blood Center, who refused testing donors. He recounts how Dr. Bove and Dr. Kellner vociferously argued against what seems so reasonable and necessary to save thousands of lives. Don characterizes the blood bankers' response as "remarkably obstructive." Don saw the blood bankers' response as "basically an attempt to deny that there was a threat."

"The reluctance and the inertia that we at the CDC faced with the blood banks in that meeting was so ridiculous and so alarming that it got to the point of me literally pounding on the table and shouting to these individuals, 'How many deaths is it going to take before you will act? Do you need ten? Do you need twenty? Do you need forty? When we get to that level, then are you going to act?' This was a very heated meeting because of this incredible balance of those of us investigating the epidemic and seeing the urgency of the situation versus the blood bankers, who were the only ones who could take action yet so cavalier about it. The imbalance of this urgency from us and the negative response from them was a most disturbing time, one of the most disturbing times in my twenty years in public health."

Don testifies that when it became evident that the blood industry, FDA, and Public Health Services were not going to act, he wrote his own memo a couple of days later arguing the CDC needed to act on its own to prevent thousands of deaths over the next two years.

What Don Francis and the other members of CDC AIDS Task Force could not have known until the documents were uncovered in Bill's case is that the American Red Cross and the American Association of Blood Banks did not just cavalierly ignore the urgency; they planned to conspire against them. Rather than implement testing to save lives like Bill's and Janet's, the blood bankers planned to stick together against the CDC even before the overwhelming evidence presented in the meeting.

That was the first time I videotaped Don's testimony in Bill's case, about a year before Janet's case goes to trial. At times I am burning the candle at both ends, running coast-to-coast for both cases. Most of the time I would go with less than fifty bucks in my pocket, praying the credit card still had room on it to check out from the hotels. I would catch those flights hoping that no emergencies come up back home, because there was nothing in the checking account.

A year later, and I return to San Francisco to video Don again for Janet's case, this time with Roger Solmosy and Neil Rieseman. The Sheraton catering staff puts out a fruit dish, coffee and a few pastries in Conference Room B. The idea of pretending to be civil toward each other, sharing coffee and apple danishes and pear turnovers, strikes me as odd.

Solmosy has become formidable opponent who crosses the line. When I make demands for the production of blood bank documents, he refuses to produce them. I have to file time-consuming motions to get him to cooperate with standard court rules. Solmosy has a cold, metallic voice and uses pomade on his hair. It is more than just about winning to Solmosy—there is a dark side to him that makes a sport out of lacking compassion. This trait makes him a popular lawyer amongst blood bankers.

"Don't overstate the facts," said Dr. Aaron Kellner, president of the New York Blood Center, at the Atlanta meeting. "There are at most three cases of AIDS from blood donation, and the evidence in two of these cases is very soft. And there are only a handful of cases among hemophiliacs."

Dr. Kellner was against the CDC's proposed testing because it would cost the New York Blood Center millions to implement, and he was not about to absorb the cost. "We must be careful not to overreact; the evidence is tenuous." The April 1984 AABB *NewsBrief* states, "Irwin to Institute Anti-Core Testing; New York Blood Center Rejects Concept." Dr. Kellner states that his facility is "not convinced that AIDS is transmitted by blood transfusion . . . The evidence is still very shaky."

Dr. Kellner and the New York Blood Center still refuse to publicly acknowledge transfusion AIDS. Since a large percentage of the New York Blood Center's donor base is gay men who would be excluded from donating by core testing, it is purely a matter of economics and business. A smaller donor base means fewer blood products and less money; product safety is completely out of the equation.

The blood supply becomes so dangerously contaminated that it leads to another public health crisis: subsequent transmission of AIDS between family members of anyone who had received a transfusion. This secondary transmission becomes such a public health crisis that the CDC issues a warning in its March 20, 1987 *Morbidity and Mortality Weekly Report* entitled "Human Immunodeficiency Virus Infection in Transfusion Recipients and Their Family Members." The CDC warns that patients transfused in hospitals are at risk for transmitting AIDS to spouses. This is exactly what happens to Janet and her husband.

Tom Asher tells me about Dr. Theodore Keorner, at the University of Iowa Hospital Blood Center. Dr. Keorner started core testing at the blood center shortly after Dr. Englemen announced Stanford was screening its donors. Ted Keorner also teaches transfusion medicine at the medical school. I take Janet's hospital delivery records and catch a flight to Iowa City.

Ted Keorner's scruffy, long bread makes him look more like a woodsman than a physician. Ted is so unpretentious and naive to the ways of litigation that I worry Solmosy and Reiseman will have him for breakfast. He methodically takes me through Janet's transfusion record and shows me where there was never a drop in her hematocrit or hemoglobin prior to the twenty-one transfusions. "She was always within normal ranges," He tells me.

My search for a hematologist what will serve as a witness continues. Back at the office, I check the lawyer's journal expert advertisements and circle names in the law classifieds. I find one hematologist, Dr. Stephen Davis, who agrees to meet with me, so long as I bring a retainer check.

Dr. Davis is giving a patient chemotherapy when I arrive for our meeting. I wait in the small reception area until he finishes. He invites me into his private office to discuss Janet's case. There are legal files everywhere, on and under the chairs, against the floor, even on the window ledges. My eyes look for a patient's file on his desk, but there are only more legal letters. Most files have typed medical reports with his letterhead on them. I open Janet's file to show him Janet's delivery transfusion record, but he stops me.

"Did you bring the retainer check?"

"Yes, it's right here." I reach into my coat pocket and give him this month's mortgage payment. Sorry, Patti.

"Dr. Davis, my client's hematologist transfused her with twenty-one units of cryoprecipitate when she never had bleeding. Will you testify that it was a departure from the accepted standard of care for him to transfuse her before there was any blood loss?"

"Yes, I think I can say that," he says as he sticks the check in his pocket.

I am nervous about him. "Look, don't worry. As you can see, I do a lot of this. Besides, there are varying degrees of von Willebrands. Maybe your client has only a mild form of it, so she never needed the transfusions."

I am stuck with Dr. Davis at a witness, but without him, Janet's case could be dismissed.

CHAPTER SEVENTEEN

A few weeks later, I depose Janet's OB-GYN and the consulting hematologist at Neil Reiseman's office. Janet's OB-GYN is a middle-aged, mild-mannered man who freely opens his file notes to me. As I begin to question him about meeting Janet, rather than being defensive and concealing, which is what I expected, he is a direct and remorseful. He explains how when Janet mentioned the childhood von Willebrands, he referred her to the hematology consultant. Often he would look away during the deposition. When we finish, he stands up from the conference table; I notice the ends of his shirt sleeves are puckered from wiping away tears. It was the only time I have ever seen a defendant in an AIDS case show remorse or compassion. We agree to dismiss him from the case and his name is purposefully left out of this book.

Janet's hematologist, on the other hand, fights to win. He is a young, cocky adjunct professor at Columbia Medical School. "Dr. Feldman, you understand that you are under oath, don't you?"

"Yes." He has been prepped by Reiseman to keep the answers short or else I may pick up on something.

"And that woman next to you is taking down everything you say and making it a part of the court record?"

"Yes."

"When I ask you a question, it will be assumed that you understand it and that your answer is complete and honest. Do you understand that?" I need to let him know he is in my sand box.

"Dr. Feldman, what was the basis for transfusing Janet with twenty-one units of cryoprecipitate?"

He has a copy of his evaluation record that Janet filled out with him. "She gave a history of easy bruising and childhood von Willebrands."

"But, she never had any actual abnormal bleeding during her son's delivery?" I need him to admit there never were reasons for the transfusions.

"You can't wait for that in patients with von Willebrands without endangering her life, and maybe the baby's too."

"You transfused Janet before, during and after the delivery, though. She didn't need all of them?"

"Cryoprecipitate is always given in multiple transfusions."

"But, aren't there degrees of von Willebrand's?"

"Yes. She never came back after our first consultation." Janet had no medical insurance and could not pay for more visits.

"So you did not determine the severity of her condition?"

"I made a clinical diagnosis based upon her childhood history. Once you have von Willebrand's, it does not go away."

"Even though her hematocrit never fell?" I argue back.

"That's right."

"So you're saying that you transfused her prophylactically?"

"Objection." Reiseman jumps in.

"What is the objection?" I ask.

"To the word, prophylactically." Reiseman answers. It is a term that means to take a precaution. I picked it up in the medical records and use it in the sense that Janet's doctor transfused her to protect her against something that has not happened. "Well, if it was not prophylactically, then what was it?" I demand.

"I already told you. I made a clinical diagnosis of a patient who presented herself to me with a history of easy bruising, childhood von Willebrand's, and a family history of the disease."

I take the medical records from Janet's delivery of Naomi out from the file. The court reporter places an exhibit label on them. I slide them across the table.

"Dr. Feldman, show me in those medical records before you where Janet had a bleeding problem when she delivered her first child?"

I already know the answer. Janet never bled during Naomi's delivery, or was given transfusions.

"Dr. Feldman, were you aware of the risks of AIDS associated with transfusions you ordered for Janet?"

"It was very low, maybe one in a million." Dr. Feldman is like most physicians given false information by the blood bankers about the safety of its blood products. The AABB, American Red Cross and New York Blood Center claim that the risk was one in a million was not based on any sound medical or statistical study, but rather on manipulated information. The blood bankers estimated the risk by taking CDC's first couple of confirmed cases and dividing it into the number of annual transfusions. As transfusion-AIDS cases continued to increase, they never revised this statement. The blood bankers continued assuring physicians blood was safe using outdated data, so physicians transfused patients without proper indications. Only a few physicians, like Marc Conant, were aware enough to challenge the industry's misinformation.

An internal AABB memo uncovered during the Bill's case shows that while the AABB was assuring physicians on the frontline that blood was safe, at the same time they were consulting with their lawyers about shielding themselves from liability for a patient's lawsuits. The blood Bankers and their lawyers concluded that it is the patient's physician who has the legal obligation to tell them about the risk of transfusions. The plan was to scapegoat the smaller guys.

Dr. Feldman may have been unaware that the New York Blood Center was infecting metropolitan-area patients, but transfusing Janet with twenty-one units of cryoprecipitate that she did not need cannot be excused. Blood transfusions cost money, and I have no doubt in my mind that was a stronger motive than concern for his patient. Now, Dr. Feldman's strategy, like the New York Blood Center's, is to win, rather than compromise. Neil Reiseman will no doubt get another prestigious expert witness from a big name medical school to testify that even with mild von Willebrand's, there is no departure from accepted standards of care.

Walking out of Reiseman's office, I notice someone put a dent on the driver's side of my car. I kneel down in the street to inspect the crease in the center of the door. The door is damaged. It has been knocked off its alignment and does not close properly. I check the windshield for a note, but there is none. On the way home, driving north on the Jersey turnpike, the door begins to vibrate and slightly comes ajar. I grab the inside door handle and pull it towards me to shut it tight, but it is no use. I drive with one arm on the steering wheel and the other on the door handle, holding it shut as I drive on the highway.

The summer before 8th grade, my mother decided to move again to another town. We were on our own. My father had moved out of state and my brother was in the army. I had convinced her to let me finish out middle school at St. Brendan's in Clifton, New Jersey. I was tired of changing schools, standing up to different playground bullies, convincing new teachers to leave me alone. At St. Brendan's, I got along with everyone and the nuns accepted that I could not do the work, but decided to pass me anyway. My mother agreed, but I had to walk. Every day was the same: I walked a mile and half on River Road, along the Passaic River, pass the Marcal paper factory and high smoke stacks, under the rusted train overpass to the interstate highway 80 and 20 jug-handle. There are no pedestrian walkways, so it is all fast moving trucks. I would hold my breath and sprint between the break in the traffic across the jug-handle to the Clifton side. Another mile along the Lakeview Avenue Cemetery and I am at school. The walk never varied, five miles round trip, from Elmwood Park to Clifton in the rain, snow and chill.

Everyday I walked past an old 1952 Ford that was sitting on a gas station parking lot. Weeks went by and the "For Sale" sign progressively stood out; the window's fog and collected snow only made the sign more vivid. I convinced the owner to sell it to me. I was already 6' 1" and negotiated the payment plan like someone few years older, so he never thought to ask me my age. I got a part-time job mopping floors and cleaning restrooms at Woolworth's. Each weekend I showed up to admire the car and make a payment until the car was paid.

I could not legally register the car, so I unscrewed the license plates from my brother's car and parked away from the school so the nuns would not catch me driving home after class. The old car gave me some illusion of control. Each morning, I drove along River Road, looking out at the frozen Passaic River and the smoke from the paper factory from within the warmth of my car. "I earned this," I congratulated myself while changing lanes. It was scary and thrilling to sit perched behind the steering wheel, wipe the fog off the windshield with a tissue, put the gas peddle to the floor and merge into the jug-handle traffic. After awhile I got the knack of driving. Nobody would have given me driving lessons anyway. It felt safer than walking. On weekends, I would go for leisurely drives around town and look through the scratched windshield at the very Jersey landscape.

All that changed one morning when I was cowboying around a curve and slid into the curb. The left front wheel bent inwards and the car was unmovable. Panicked thoughts raced through my mind: "Take the plates off and run." "What should I do?" "What will I tell the police if they show up?" I should have simply abandoned the car and ran away, but I couldn't. It meant too much to me. Inevitably, a police car pulled up. As the officer walked towards me, I was unable to move from my seat and sat there in shock. It was out of my control.

"May I see your license and registration?"

"I'm 14," I burst. The cop's eyes widened and then went back to normal, like an adjusted camera setting. I got into the back of the police car. My mother had to come to the police station to get me. My father had to come back to New Jersey to take me to juvenile court—this was the first time. I already knew by then that driving the 1952 car on the highway bordering the river would be the closest I would get to control. The time had come for me to join everybody else I knew in their vast powerlessness.

CHAPTER EIGHTEEN

Janet collapses at home while trying to do the laundry. She's admitted to St. Clare's Riverside Medical Center in Denville with anemia, hypertension, congestive heart failure, acute renal failure, and anxiety. Time is of the essence now to move her trial. When she is discharged, Janet continues to meet me daily to prep for her video deposition. She comes in after Kyle gets home to watch Christian and Naomi, and we work into the night. I order a couple of pastrami sandwiches and small bottles of apple juice from the diner. She is weaker, but trying to hold on. I always try to feed her when she visits me, but the sandwiches sit on my desk in the round carryout Styrofoam plates, untouched and cold.

"Janet, what is that scar on your chest?" I point to the hook-shaped mark on the right side of her collarbone that was not there before.

"Oh, that's the Port-A-Cath my doctors put in at the hospital."

"What is a Port-A-Cath?"

"Well, my veins have collapsed so there's no place to put the intravenous medications, so they implant this Port-A-Cath to put the needles into."

We had talked at the hospital and decided to video her testimony for trial, just in case she doesn't make it. We meet frequently to rehearse.

"Janet, I will sit near the video camera so you can look into the camera when you answer my questions." Janet will be nervous, but I figure if she focuses on me she will block everyone else out.

"All right."

"I want you to think of each question that I ask you as your cue to tell the jury your story. Just open up and tell them everything." It is the same trick I used with Don Francis in San Francisco. "I want you to tell them about Naomi, too."

"Okay. I will.

"Watch my hands, my face. Remember the signals we worked out." I've worked out subtle gestures with Janet, just like I used to with witnesses in my turnpike days. A hand on my chin means keep talking; nodding my head means don't go there. There is too much at stake to leave things to chance.

"Okay."

"Have some apple juice?" I am nervous and worried for her. The color has drained from her face. I twist the bottle cap off for her, then I try to toss it into the wastepaper basket by the door but miss it.

"I guess basketball is out." We both laugh.

"Yeah, you better stick to law."

I enjoy making Janet laugh because everything is so irreversibly hard.

"Do you want to call it a night?" I see she is tired.

"I'm all right."

After a couple of more hours, Janet tires. We sit back and talk. Janet has graciously come to terms with her all that has happened to her. She never complains, and just wants her family taken care of. Her love for Naomi, Christian and Kyle is almost palpable.

"Janet, when you had an appendectomy in 1967, and a tonsillectomy and adenoidectomy in 1965. Do you know if there was a bleeding problem?" I leave no stone unturned when looking for excessive bleeding in Janet's history.

"No, I was just a child and don't remember." Janet would have been just six years old then so I did not expect her to.

"Why was the adenoidectomy done?"

"I remember I had unexplained bruising and they went inside to see if they could find anything wrong."

"Same family doctor?"

"Yes, Dr. MacLeod." She has not been able to reach him. "He's probably long retired by now."

We pick a little at the cold sandwiches. Janet sips juice through the straw in her bottle. She pushes the bottle away.

"What's wrong?"

"I don't know how to explain what has happened to Naomi. I've tried bringing her to the public library to get children's books about losing a parent, but she won't read them. I've tried reading them with her and leaving them lying around so that she'll pick one up when she's ready, but nothing works."

"It's tough to deal with for anyone, and must be impossible for a young child."

"A couple of nights ago, she locked herself in the bathroom."

"Why?"

"She wanted to be alone. She sat on the toilet lid and refused to come out. I had such a migraine and was so exhausted. I sat on the floor outside the bathroom door and just said, 'Naomi, please. Mommy has a migraine. Please come out so I can tuck you into bed.'"

"She must be afraid of losing you, Janet."

"After a while, the door opened and she came out. She wanted me to lie with her for a while before turning the lights out. She rubbed my head and started to ask me questions about who will take care of her when I am gone."

"Have you thought about a guardian?"

"Yes, Kyle's aunt. But Naomi wants to know if she and Christopher can stay together. She really loves her brother. Naomi asked me who will love her if something happens to me. I told her not to worry; someone will always be around to love her. She has a lot of questions, and she is so precocious for her age. She sees things on television and asks me about them."

"Yeah, I try to check what Courtney watches too." The few times I do see her, at least.

"Finally, I told Naomi it is time to go to sleep because she has school in the morning. I lean over, kiss her good night, and turn off the bedroom light. I was so upset that I put on a pot of water for tea. I get out a cup and saucer from the cabinet and look around the kitchen at Naomi's drawings and cards that hang on the refrigerator door. I begin to relax, until I see the Polaroid that Jim took of me holding Christian in the hospital after he was just born. And then I realize that is when they infected me with AIDS.

I jumped up, grabbed a large kitchen knife from the sink, raised it up, and lost it. I slashed away at the photo. I mean I really lost it and was slashing at it until it was shredded into pieces."

I feel sorry for Janet and wish there was something more I could do. "If there was one thing you could do with Naomi now, what would it be?"

"I would probably like to take her and Christian to see Disney World." We laugh, but in my head, I know—even if she doesn't—that the hurt from her father's vacations to Orlando while she took care of her entire family in Edinburgh is cleverly disguised as humor. I search for a way to help make it happen. I just do not have a nickel to spare. Every last penny is used on her's and Bill's case, with nothing left over. Patti borrows money from her parents for groceries. It is the end of a long night, so I walk Janet to the car.

When I get home, Patti and Courtney are sleeping. As usual on the late nights, Patti leaves a plate in the refrigerator with a stick-um note. I microwave the dinner and sit alone at the kitchen table, thinking about Janet's life, how similar our childhoods were. But now, in her final days, she hangs on for her family.

It is Thanksgiving weekend, November 1992. I trace my five fingers on a piece of paper to resemble a turkey and write Patti and Courtney a Thanksgiving card. "Happy Thanksgiving. Without you, life would be very boring. I am sure there are times that you do not realize it, but I know how lucky I am to have you as a family."

I had been trivializing Patti's needs, seeing only the immediacy of the fight for Janet and Bill.

"What are you complaining about?" I would argue when Patti called me at work to tell me a check bounced or another late notice came in the mail. "Janet is in the fight of her life, has lost everything meaningful, and I have to do this for her now."

Once, I was struggling to find some money to pay bills on Bill's case when Patti called, frantic about a shut-off notice.

"You cannot go through life with blinders on," Patti warns me. "It is as through you have tunnel vision," she yelled over and over again. I know she is right, but I cannot hear reason above her shrieking. Patti and I dated for four years through college, got married in law school, and we had never taken a break even once.

"There is no second chance to win these cases," I argue back. Patti is no longer as graceful at rolling with the punches. But when I get home late, there is always a plate of leftover dinner with a note on the refrigerator door, treating me with the patience I can no longer see in Patti's face.

CHAPTER NINETEEN

It has been two and a half years since I started Janet's case and it is one trial delay after another. The court's inability to fast-track Janet's case frustrates me with the whole civil court system. I write Judge Span another letter for an expedited trial date. I detail the urgency of fixing a firm date because Janet is slipping away. Judge Span has us come in for another case management conference.

It is a typical January afternoon in Elizabeth. The sun has not been seen in days, the cold goes through my coat, and the trees have long been dead. I use the court's rear entrance and walk up the long cement handicapped ramp, step-by-step, so I can picture Janet using it for trial. The place is depressing.

There are a few other lawyers in Judge Span's courtroom waiting for conferences too. I check in with the court's sheriff deputy and I don't exchange pleasantries when I enter Judge Span's courtroom. We know why we are here. They want more delays, and I want a trial. Judge Span comes out from her chambers and takes the bench.

"Good afternoon, Counsel. Mr. Baxter, why don't you begin?"

"Your Honor, the last time we were here, you gave us a firm trial date. Now, Mr. Solmosy and Mr. Reiseman want another adjournment."

Solmosy argues that he wants more time to serve expert reports. Rieseman joins in the request for more time.

"How much time do you need, counsel?" I already sense Judge Span is reneging on the firm trial date she set, so I interject.

"Judge, you said we had a firm trial date. My client is sick and time is of the essence. There is no reason to continue these unnecessary delays."

"How do we know Mr. Baxter's client is sick, your Honor? Did you bring a doctor's note, Mr. Baxter?" It has been two and a half years of Solmosy obstructing Janet's case. He rarely produced the donor records, used by the New York Blood Center, for the contaminated cryoprecipitate, stonewalling all my discovery requests.

"You don't need to see a doctor's note, Mr. Solmosy. You have her hospital records." I always update them with Janet's latest medical records.

"Your Honor, the bar convention is coming up in December and I have already booked my trip," Reiseman says.

"Well, you should not have booked a trip when there is a firm trial date set in the case." It is as though my pleas for an urgent trial date are meaningless. This is exactly what the blood bankers had in mind when they expected most transfusion AIDS patients to die quietly before costing them any money. They relied on the gamesmanship of their lawyers, like Solmosy, who use the dysfunctional court system to their advantage.

"When is the bar convention, Mr. Reiseman?" Judge Span asks, leaning toward the adjournment. I am shocked that she cannot see the urgency.

"Wait a minute, Judge. You gave us a firm trial date and that has to mean something." I took Judge Span's trial date as a promise.

"When can everyone agree to be ready?" Judge Span asking defense lawyers this is like giving them carte blanche with the trial calendar.

"I am ready now." The medical system let Janet down and, now, the court is about to let her down too. I begin to boil over with frustration at the ease with which they delay Janet's case again.

At that moment, the court becomes silent and all heads turn toward the back door. An EMS worker wheels Janet into the courtroom in a wheelchair. Janet is so weak that her head bobs from side to side as the ambulance attendant pushes the wheelchair over the small bumps on the floor.

The ambulance driver approaches the bailiff, but I quickly gesture to him to bring Janet down the aisle alongside me at the counsel table. Janet's head is buried in her chest. She just can't lift it up, and she has a gray hospital blanket around her. Judge Span pauses and looks at me.

"Your Honor, this is my client, Janet M." Everyone is caught off guard by Janet's ghastly appearance.

I had called Janet's doctor and explained how important it is that Janet be allowed to leave the hospital and be in court. I promised to hire a private ambulance to pick up Janet from her hospital bed, bring her to court, wait, and bring her back to her bed at the hospital. He reluctantly agreed: "At least it will be on your bill." A desperate move, but we are desperate.

Janet sits beside me in her wheelchair, her straw-like hair obscuring her face and neck so that all you can see is her hair and her blanket.

"Your Honor, I object to Mrs. M being here." It does not take Solmosy but a minute to get over Janet's appearance.

"She has a right to be here. She is the plaintiff." I argue back.

"Your Honor, I do not know if it is safe to have Mr. Baxter's client in here. She may be contagious. She should have a mask on." The inhumane maneuvering in Solmosy's jockeying infuriates me. Judge Span looks at me as though Solmosy raised a credible argument for removing Janet from the courtroom.

"She doesn't need a mask, Mr. Solmosy." Solmosy goes on about not wanting to catch anything just because he is in court for his client.

"Your Honor, look for yourself." Janet sits beside me, still unable to lift her head from the blanket. "My client is ill and time is of the essence. She has a right to a timely trial, and time is of the essence."

Reiseman reminds Judge Span he already booked his tickets for the Bar convention. "It is in Disney World," he shrugs.

"Is that a fucking joke?" I argue back. We move closer and closer. Fingers are pointed and a scuffle erupts.

I push Reiseman out of my space and Judge Span hits the panic button. Sheriffs' deputies rush in like a SWAT team and restrain me. The deputies wait for Judge Span's order to escort me off to the county jail. I am concerned about Janet, sitting there, sensing a violent skirmish but unable to raise her head to see. After a moment, calmness settles back into the court, and Judge Span dismisses the sheriffs' deputies. The entire courtroom is in shock. Judge Span could have jailed me for contempt, but lets it slide.

We all just stand there for a moment, shocked by what happened. Other lawyers and spectators watch quietly. Once the deputies release me, I stand firm next to Janet, pretending it is all business as usual. I put my hand on Janet's shoulder, over the gray hospital blanket, to let her know it's all right. Her lawyer is not going to jail.

Judge Span stands up from the bench, collects her notes, turns to leave, then looks back at us. "February 8, counsel. Be ready." Judge Span goes into her chambers.

The ambulance driver and I push Janet's wheelchair up the aisle. I am thankful that I get to go home, but Janet has to go back to the hospital. The adrenaline pumps through my veins and I do not know what came over me. Nothing matters now except getting Janet through this. Professional protocols and rules of court are out the window. As I push Janet's wheelchair to the elevator, heads turn toward us.

"Janet, how are you doing?" I am still a little shaken by the courtroom fight. She has a migraine. She tries to look at me, but cannot open her eyes. The ambulance driver and I wheel Janet down that cement handicap ramp and we load her into the waiting ambulance. All she has to do now is hang on for ten more weeks.

CHAPTER TWENTY

A Winter snowstorm hits on the week of Janet's trial and the Jersey turnpike is even more hazardous than usual. Snow has blown through the large holes of the ramshackle water repellant plant, where windows used to be. The building is desolate and surrounded by snow covered trailer cars and trains. My still-unfixed car door pops open, and there is a blast of cold air from the fast-moving, treacherous roadway beneath me. With one hand on the steering wheel, I reach over with my other hand and slam it shut. The front end rattles on the packed snow bump along the way. I filter out the noise and concentrate on Janet's trial ahead.

"When the doctor first told me that I had the virus, I thought I was going to die straightaway." The courtroom lights are dimmed, shades are drawn over the windows, and the jury watches Janet's video deposition on the court video monitor. "I don't know where I'm going to end up, but wherever it is, I know that I'll be all right. It's Naomi, Christian and Kyle I worry about. They won't know what to do without me."

It is February 8, 1993. Janet's trial begins three years after I file her case. Janet's hematologist has made a settlement offer for $750,000 on the eve of trial. They figure it is more money than I have ever seen before and that I will take it. The New York Blood Center refuses to settle and threatens to delay Janet's case even more with lengthy appeals even if we win a jury verdict. There is pressure to tread carefully now because there's money on the table, and trying to win more from the jury is counterproductive if it means Janet will not survive for it.

Judge Span is on the bench and the court's video monitor sits on top of a gray metal media cart in front of the courtroom, angled toward the jurors. Janet's image is on the monitor screen with my office conference room in the background. She looks just as I saw her through the lens of the video camera on that day, months earlier, in my office.

"Janet, describe for the jury that will be watching this video how your life has changed." My voice is heard asking the question on the video, but the camera always stays on Janet.

When the day of Janet's video deposition came, the videographer covered my conference room windows with a blue paper curtain to block out the daylight. He set his camera and lights on Janet, who sat at the other end of the conference table. He pinned a microphone on the lapel of each lawyer, did a sound check, and we began.

The night before, I asked Janet to wear something smart-looking for the jury. She thought for a minute, and then said, "I know what I'll wear." She came for her video deposition wearing a navy blue dress with a white-lace collar. The dress sags over her frail body and her complexion's pallid, but she exudes elegance.

"Janet, what went through your mind when your doctor told you that you are infected with AIDS?" I sat next to the cameraman so that Janet would look at the camera when answering the questions.

"All I knew about AIDS were those pictures of sick and emaciated people I saw on television. I worried if Christian was all right, so I had him tested three times, and he's negative. I worry about Kyle because he'll never be able to handle it when I'm gone. I worry about Naomi. I watched my mother die from a long illness with cancer, and it was hard on us. I don't want Naomi to see me go through anything like that. Sometimes I was purposefully mean to Naomi so she won't miss me so much when I'm gone." Janet tries to fight it back, but a tear rolls down her cheek.

"But Naomi doesn't understand what's happened, and she just keeps loving me."

"Janet, are you all right?" I offer her a break.

"Yes." Janet's focused and keeps talking. "I worry about who'll love her. No one will ever love Naomi the way I love her."

The blood bankers objected to the way Janet just kept talking even though there was no question pending.

"So what's the objection? I asked her a question, and she's still answering it." I argued back. "You're interrupting my deposition. I'm going to continue." I reminded Janet to disregard the objections and just continue telling her story. The night before, we talked about how they will use court rules to try and prevent her from telling her story. My instructions to Janet were, "Forget court rules, just talk to the jury." I know ignoring court rules is offensive to our sense of justice, but I've seen them distorted enough for the wrong reasons.

Janet did exactly as planned, telling her story to the camera. I didn't even use the gestures I had planned to use.

I walked over to the videographer's camera and checked Janet's image in the monitor that day. I wanted to make sure the camera was capturing her just right. I watched Janet testify through the camera for a minute to make sure the jury would see the same image I was seeing in front of me.

"Janet, what happened when you came home from the hospital with Christian?"

"I didn't know that I was infected from the blood that they gave me, and I infected Kyle. I knew something wasn't right with me, but my doctors kept saying it was just anxiety, nerves, and I should sleep with the window open. I felt tired all the time. I would give Christian a bath before bed, and the steam of the water would put me to sleep. I'd have to put my head down on the edge of the bathtub."

Janet tells her story and focuses on me as though no one else is in the room. Our long sessions together made her comfortable opening up, and so that's how Janet's video deposition looks to the jury.

Just when I had imagined that nothing else would go wrong, Janet was readmitted to the hospital with pneumonia. This time her T cells were below two hundred and twenty, and it looked bad. Janet was unable to make the trial so I show the jury the video.

"I used to like to do things with Naomi, Christian and Kyle. I played soccer back at home and now I'm tired all the time. The medications I take make me sick and nauseous. I worked as a nurse in Scotland, but now I'm too sick to work. Every time I go into the hospital, Naomi's frightened that I'm not coming back. Last time, she asked me, 'Mommy are you going to die?' And I don't know what to tell her."

"Janet, just a couple more questions?" There's a pause on the video, then my voice is heard asking the next question.

"Have you ever used intravenous drugs?" Since Solmosy stonewalled my donor discovery efforts, I go through the known risk factors to establish that the transfusions were the cause of Janet's infection.

"No." She answers succinctly.

"Janet, I have to ask you these questions for the record."

"All right."

"Have you ever had sexual intercourse with another man besides your husband since you were married?"

"No."

"Have you ever had any other blood transfusions besides the twenty-one units of cryoprecipitate?"

"No."

"Thank you, Janet."

The monitor screen goes fuzzy and the video has ended.

The senior claims executive from the hematologist's malpractice insurance company has come to court. He is a tall, congenial man in his fifties with gray hair. He sits behind the counsel railing, but stands and leans over to drop a folded piece of paper on the counsel table. I unfold it and the offer is raised to a million dollars. I turn around and hold up my thumb, indicating a higher demand.

"Please turn the lights on," Judge Span directs the court bailiff. He opens the window shades and turns on the overhead lights. The blast of light makes everyone squint. Janet is conspicuously absent from the courtroom. The jurors look drained from watching the ninety-minute video in the dark.

"Ladies and gentlemen, I'm going to give you a twenty minute break to stretch. Please be back on time." Judge Span looks tired too. Dr. Davis, the hematologist I found an ad for in the legal Yellow Pages, is in the courtroom and we go out into the hallway for last minute prepping. We sit on the bench across from the courtroom checking my notes again and again. The jurors re-enter the courtroom and I know we have to go inside too. Since the courtroom fracas, Reiseman brings a huge, six foot four, 250-pound lawyer who looks like a Giants' lineman with him to court, who stays at his side. It's more for show than for safety.

The jurors straggle back into the courtroom after the recess and I begin checking over my notes at the counsel table. There's a tap on my shoulder and I turn around. The insurance adjustor raises the offer to 1.5 million. He tells me that is all the money he can get from the company, but I know they are holding back. Solmosy reminds me that he will tie Janet's case up with appeals if I win. "She won't live to see a settlement," he snarls. They are working together to wear me down. I have to find a way to pin Reiseman and Solmosy against one another. Divide and conquer—that's my strategy. Once again, I raise my thumb to indicate a higher amount.

When all the jurors are back into the jury box, we resume the trial.

"Mr. Baxter, call your next witness." Judge Span is ready.

"Yes, your Honor. Plaintiff calls Dr. Stephen Davis to the witness stand." Dr. Davis has a scrimpy file with a few notes. I thought he would bring more of Janet's file with him.

"Dr. Davis, you are a hematologist licensed in the State of New Jersey?"

"Yes."

"And you reviewed the plaintiff's records to give an opinion to the court about her transfusions?" Just as I finish the question, Dr. Davis begins twitching his nose.

"Yes," He answers, twitching and slightly tilting his head in the air.

"Dr. Davis, are you all right?" I'm bewildered by what's happening to him on the witness stand.

"Yes, I'm all right." Dr. Davis' nose begins to bleed, on the witness stand. He tilts his head further back for a moment.

"Dr. Davis, would you like a break?"

"No, no. I'll be fine."

"Dr. Davis, are you sure you don't need a recess?" I am trying to yank him off the witness stand but he is not getting it.

"No, no." He insists. He reaches for the tissue box at the edge of Judge Span's bench, rolls up a piece of tissue, and puts it into his nose to stop the bleeding.

"Dr. Davis, let's take a recess?" The jurors have disapproving expressions on their faces at this behavior. He refuses to step down to use the men's room to clear his bleeding nose. With 1.5

million on the table, there sits my key witness, with tissue paper stuffed up his nostril. Everything is unraveling before my eyes.

"Dr. Davis, do you have an opinion that Janet's hematologist departed from the accepted standard of care by transfusing her with twenty-one units of cryoprecipitate?"

"Yes. He should have waited."

I can't believe that he answers the most crucial question before the jury with tissue hanging out of his nose. Judge Span looks at me with a raised eyebrow. Janet's hematologist insists it was not a deviation from the accepted standard of care to make a clinical diagnosis with her history. It will come down to who the jury likes, and this is a disaster. When it is over, Dr. Davis steps down from the witness stand, completely unaware of his awkwardness—confidently, even.

"The jury didn't like your witness, Mr. Baxter." Judge Span politely says from the bench. Like I needed her to say that. I could see it on their faces.

Two weeks into the trial, Janet miraculously bounces back, as she has again and again. She comes to court and I want the jury to hear her from the witness stand. Solmosy and Reiseman object, since the jury has already seen the video. Judge Span allows Janet limited testimony that is not duplicative of the video. That is all I need.

"Your Honor, I call my client, Janet M to the witness stand." The day has finally come when I say these words. She made it.

"Good morning, Janet." I stand near the jury railing, so she and the jury are facing each other.

"Good morning." She calmly says, facing me.

"Janet, you were discharged from St. Clare's Riverside Medical Center yesterday?"

"Yes. I was there for two weeks for pneumocystis pneumonia." Janet has a migraine.

"How do you feel now?"

"I feel fatigued and feverish. I can't really do much."

"Janet, did you ever tell Dr. Feldman that you had Von Willebrand's disease?"

"No. I said that I was suspected of having it when I was a child."

"Objection." Reiseman looks at Judge Span. She looks at me. We know that I have crossed the line of her prior ruling about no duplicative questions from what was covered on the video. It was worth the try.

"Thank you, Janet. That's all I have." It is best to end now.

Another evidentiary problem with proving the connection between the New York Blood Center's cryoprecipitate and Janet's infection is the chronology of the lateral transmission between her and Kyle. Kyle steps on to the witness stand.

"Kyle, I have to ask you a few questions for the record?" Kyle is taciturn and reserved, with dark eyebrows and an aquiline nose; his disposition is not affable, like Janet's. He was always working and we did not get the chance to practice his testimony.

"All right."

"Kyle, have you ever had sex with another man?" I have to go through the same high-risk questions with Kyle to rule other sources for the infections.

"No."

"Have you ever used intravenous drugs?"

"No."

"Have you had sexual intercourse with another woman other than your wife since getting married?"

"No."

"Kyle, have you donated blood?"

"Yes, the New York Blood Center used to have blood drives at work and I donated." I ask Kyle to hold up the donor card. It is proof that all the while he donated blood for the New York

Blood Center, he was negative for AIDS. The blood bank started testing donors for AIDS during the time Kyle donated blood. The card existed to show Kyle's donation history and that he was a healthy donor.

Janet's medical records, on the other hand, show that during the same time, she was already infected by the transfusions she got earlier. It is the proof of their chronology of infections, showing that first, Janet was infected, and then she had to have infected Kyle. The donor card excludes Kyle as a possible source of infection for Janet, and vice versa.

"Kyle, tell the jury how your life has changed?"

"I worry about the time."

"What do you worry about Kyle?"

"Everything."

"Kyle, what do you mean everything?" I have to get it out from him for the jury.

"I worry every time Janet goes into the hospital that she's not coming back." Kyle's voice begins to crack.

"Kyle, what else?" It's hard putting Kyle through these questions but the jury has to hear his answers.

"I worry that since I have the virus too, what'll happen to Naomi and Christian once all this starts happening to me." Kyle cannot continue.

"Thank you, Kyle. That's all I have." I hand him the tissue box from Judge Span's bench. Beneath his detached and tough exterior is a devastated husband and father.

The insurance adjustor taps me on the shoulder again. This time he whispers to me that the trial is not going well for me. I know they are distracting me with offers during the trial on purpose, so I have an idea about how to fight back and handle them. I asked around and found a brand new lawyer, Gregg Paster, to come to court. Gregg's fresh out of law school and just passed the bar exam. I introduce him to the adjustor.

"This is Gregg Paster. I want you to communicate all the offers to him."

Then I hold three fingers up to Gregg, in front of the adjustor: "And Gregg, do not disturb me with their offers until it is reasonable." They are gambling that I will fold, putting pressure on me by whispering and sliding offers under my nose when I am cross-examining a witness. I am perspiring under my jacket, fatigued and coming off the caffeine, but play it close to my chest. I keep thinking, "Divide and conquer." I have to pin Janet's hematologist and The New York Blood Center against each other. The stakes are higher than ever.

CHAPTER TWENTY-ONE

I get up at sunrise for the ride down the Jersey turnpike to the Elizabeth courthouse. Abby brings back Mrs. Nelson's newspaper again while I sip a coffee. I toss it on her steps before I drive away. The packed snow on the roadway pops the driver's side door open again. I get to court early and pace the hallway outside the courtroom. As the jurors straggle in, I notice one juror, a middle-aged woman, teaching the Macarena to a couple of others in the jury room. The laughter from the jury room is disconcerting. You can never tell what seven random people, from all walks of life, chosen for jury duty, are thinking.

Inside the courtroom, I stand at the counsel table as the last juror files into the jury box.

"Mr. Baxter, are you ready to proceed?" Judge Span asks from the bench.

"Yes, your Honor. I call Dr. Alexander MacLeod to the witness stand." Janet and Kyle are in court and sit behind me. Janet's fighting a migraine but tries to hide it from the jurors. Janet's childhood doctor from Scotland walks down the courtroom center isle to the witness stand. The bailiff holds out the bible and swears him in.

A few days earlier, after Dr. Davis testified, I went back to the office in the evening. As usual, I kicked the mail piled against the door. I noticed the red light on the answering machine blinking. There was a message from a man with a thick Scottish accent. I called him back, and the phone had one of those antediluvian rings to it.

"Hello, is this Dr. Alexander MacLeod?"

"Yes, it is." I could not believe I found him. These were the days before Google and internet searches. I pictured Dr. MacLeod as a country doctor in a small Scottish village, reading by candlelight and describing things as "bonnie."

"Dr. MacLeod, I'm George Baxter, a lawyer in the States. I am calling you about an old patient, Janet M."

"Yes, I remember her. I knew her mom quite well. How is Janet?"

"Well, I am sorry to tell you this, but she has AIDS."

"Holy Mother of Jesus!"

"She got it from a blood transfusion here in the States, when she delivered her son, Christian."

"How is Janet doing?"

"Not so well, I am afraid. Janet didn't know she was infected right away, and she infected her husband, Kyle."

"Holy Mother of God!"

"I need you to come and testify for Janet. Will you come? I will pay your travel expenses."

"Yes, I will come." He thought for a second. "May I bring my wife?"

This doubled the cost of flying Dr. MacLeod over, and my credit card was already run up to its limit. But what choice did I have? I needed him to testify.

Dr. MacLeod and I talked into the evening about what happened to Janet, the transfusions, the trial and her condition. I got home late again. Patti left a plate out on the stove with a Valentine's Day card. I missed Valentine's day. A week earlier, we had an awful argument. I had been intercepting the mail to pull out the delinquent notices from just about everyone. But with the trial, I stopped.

"You lied to me. You're a liar."

"What are you so upset about?"

"The loan officer from Spencer Savings called, George." She found out that I was using mortgage money for the case. More than once, her credit card was declined or a bill collector called. But this time, Spencer Savings Bank called because I had not made a mortgage payment in months. Too often it comes down either to the case, money for food, or the mortgage payment. That "diamond in the rough" thing has worn thin.

"Look, I'll take care it." That's what I always say. I mean it when I say so, but then I never quite can.

"Why didn't you tell me things are so bad?"

"Because I knew you would act like this."

Everything else is secondary to Janet's case. I expect Patti to accept that, but our differences make it almost impossible. I grew up in a family that occasionally needed public assistance when my father was between jobs. Patti, on the other hand, grew up in a middle-class, affluent family where people like my family were considered a drain on society. Her father has never been late with a bill. While all of Patti's friends have husbands with salaried jobs that can afford to host barbecues, she wonders if there is any light is at the end of this tunnel. Patti took something for her migraine and goes to bed without another word. I threw a blanket on the couch and slept on it. I pray that Courtney does not wake up in the middle of the night and notice.

"Dr. MacLeod, thank you for coming here today. The jury is not used to your accent, so may I ask that you answer my questions slowly?" The jurors lean forward and struggle to understand him through the thick Scottish accent.

"Yes, I will try." Dr. MacLeod is a small, polite and unassuming man who I worry cannot stand up against cross-examination.

"Dr. MacLeod, you are a licensed medical doctor in Scotland?"

"Yes, I am. I was Janet's family's physician in Edinburgh. I was her doctor until she was twelve. Then her family moved away." Dr. MacLeod talks fast and it is still difficult to understand his Scottish accent. Earlier in the morning, I picked him up at the hotel. I tried to prep him on the ride but he was too overwhelmed with New York skyline to the east and Newark skyline to our west, as well as the dense industry, commerce and flights heading in and out of Newark Airport to hear a word I said. The heavy concentration railcars, power plants and smokestacks threw him into sensory shock. He just stared out the window, fascinated. You'd think he'd just seen Mount Rushmore.

"Dr. MacLeod, please remember to talk slowly. Did there come a time when you tested Janet for von Willebrand's disease?"

"Yes. She doesn't have it." There is a slight buzz from the jury.

"So it is your testimony that as Janet's childhood physician, you tested her for von Willebrand's disease and ruled it out?"

"Yes, that's right. Janet does not have von Willebrand's." Judge Span leans forward from the bench and takes notes.

The night before trial, Dr. MacLeod and his wife came over for dinner. Patti bounced back from our argument and made that special chicken dish with grapes and mushrooms; her mother's recipe. Patti is a gracious host with a genuine penchant for making people feel comfortable. She served coffee and dessert in the living room while I asked Dr. MacLeod about Janet's case.

"Dr. MacLeod, if Janet's von Willebrand's condition was mild, then they could have waited before giving her all twenty-one units of cryoprecipitate?"

George T. Baxter, Esq.

Dr. MacLeod stopped sipping the coffee and slowly put his cup back down on the table. He was having difficulty getting something out.

"I knew Janet's family well. After her father left them, Janet's family moved into public housing. Janet's mother started drinking and became very unstable. I am afraid that she took all her anger out on Janet. When Janet was brought into the hospital with bruises, her mother told everyone that the child bruised easily because she had von Willebrand's. I was asked to test Janet when she was a child, and she did not have it."

"You mean that Janet's mother made the story up to deceive the hospital when Janet was brought in with bruises?"

"She was a very unstable woman."

"Janet's physicians gave her twenty-one transfusions that infected her with AIDS for a bleeding disorder she never had?"

"I am afraid so." We all just looked at each other. If Janet's mother had not made up this story to protect herself, life may have treated Janet with a little more kindness.

"Dr. MacLeod, just so that the jury is clear, does Janet have von Willebrand's disease?"

"No, she does not have von Willebrand's."

"Thank you, Dr. MacLeod."

"Mr. Reiseman, cross-examination?" Judge Span asks.

"Dr. MacLeod, you say that you tested Janet for von Willebrand's when she was a child, and she doesn't have it?" Reiseman fishes for something, anything to rebut the testimony.

"Yes, that's right." Dr. MacLeod politely replies in that Scottish country doctor way.

"Do you have proof of that?"

Dr. MacLeod takes out a faded old notebook with a red rubber band around it. It's one of those black and white marbled notebooks school kids use. He holds it up for Reiseman to see.

"May I see that?" Reiseman opens it and anxiously searches through it for a moment. "Dr. MacLeod, it says here that Janet bruises easily and von Willebrand's is suspected?"

"Janet had fallen in the playground at school the day before. She had a bruise. But I tested her at the Royal Infirmary and I can assure you that she does not have it." Dr. MacLeod is firm. I learn later that he often testifies for the police in Scotland.

I turn around at the counsel table to check on Janet. Her eyes are closed because she is fighting a migraine. The night of Dr. MacLeod's arrival we had all met at the hotel for dinner. It was a reunion for Janet and Dr. MacLeod. His wife went back to the room early, but we stayed in the restaurant at the Sheraton for hours talking, eating hamburgers and sipping beer. I had never seen Janet so comfortable and happy. There was even a slight spring in her step when she volunteered to go up to the counter for the beers.

Reisman backs off. It is no use to keeping Dr. MacLeod on the witness stand. He has no choice. His client blew it and gave Janet contaminated cryoprecipitate for a bleeding disorder she never had.

There is a tap on my shoulder. It's Gregg. Dr. Feldman's adjustor is ready to settle the case, but the New York Blood Center will not. Judge Span excuses the jury so that we can go into her chambers for a serious settlement discussion. We use the empty courtroom to negotiate Janet's settlement.

Judge Span tries to broker a settlement. First she privately talks with me in her chambers while Reiseman and Solmosy wait in the courtroom. She wants my bottom number to tell them. Then she has Reiseman and Solmosy back into chambers to get their numbers. Like I said, negotiating a settlement is no different from haggling in the street or bluffing at a card game. The settlement talk goes on for hours while the jury waits.

Adrenaline and caffeine have kept me going for three weeks now, and I add another hundred thousand dollars to my demand. I cannot trust this Macarena jury with the fate of Janet's settlement. Reiseman folds and I get a good, confidential settlement from the hematologist. Reisman will now sue Solmosy and the New York Blood Center, in order to get back what they lost to Janet. I give him access to my expert witnesses as a part of our deal. Divide and conquer. It is a clean deal, with no appeals. She was paid a confidential, settlement within thirty days.

I walk over to Janet and Kyle, who wait in the empty courtroom.

"Janet, it's over."

She exhales.

"We are settling with Reiseman, and he is continuing the case against the New York Blood Center."

Trial exhibits are everywhere, jurors are waiting to continue the trial, and trial adrenaline still pumps through my veins, but we are going home in the middle of the winter afternoon.

Don Francis and Marc Conant testify against the New York Blood Center to help Reiseman recover the money paid to Janet. Weeks later, when the dust settled, Reiseman calls me and offers to buy lunch. We shake hands and he tells me, over spaghetti and meatballs, that the New York Blood Center has filed an appeal in the case. When the waiter clears our plates, there are tomato sauce stains splattered all over the table. I cannot believe this is the same person I got into a brawl with months earlier.

In 1993, after Janet's trial, the Federal Food and Drug Administration goes public with its blood industry concerns and obtains a consent decree that requires the American Red Cross to clean up its act. The media, however, barely notices the story. The Federal Food and Drug Administration has to sue the American Red Cross in Federal Court and get an injunction to compel the blood bankers to comply with the agreed upon safety regulations.

Janet and I continue our friendship. I help her set up trust funds to care for Naomi and Christian after she is gone. We go to Prudential Securities where she sets up her first money market account.

We sit at a table in a small conference room when they bring in a one hundred thousand dollar check, which she withdrew from the settlement funds. Janet folds the check along the perforated line so that it stands on the table and she stares at the number. She is lost in thought for a moment.

"Janet, what are you doing?" I smile.

She calmly looks at the check. "I just want to look at it for a minute."

"Okay." I laugh.

Janet told me during one of our evening sessions that she didn't know where she would end up, but wherever it is, she knows that she would be all right. It is leaving Kyle, Naomi, and Christian behind that she worries about. It wasn't just the money, but what it will do for them. Janet bought another house where she planned her family will live after she is gone. It is a split-level with maple tree outside the large picture window in the living room that faces a quiet street. The brick house is about twenty years old with white clapboard siding, a small cement patio and swimming pool in the back yard. Janet takes me down the basement stairs and shows me the storage and laundry area. There is also a new van parked in the driveway that is more dependable than her old one. Janet's life seems back on track, as it might have been had none of this happened to her—at least from outward appearances.

Months later, I drop by to see Janet again. This time, she is confined to the couch, covered under a quilt she made for Naomi. I am taken aback by her shaved head with nylon stitches on the side. Although frail, Janet had insisted on doing the laundry and fell, hurting her head, while carrying the basket down the basement stairs. Like that day in court, Janet does not have the strength to lift her head or talk, but her eyes are open and fixed on me.

"Janet, I'll talk, and don't try to say anything." I talk with her and Kyle but do not want to overstay. I say a few words just to connect with her.

"I like what you did with the house. I bet Naomi and Christian like it. That's a nice hairstyle you have there." Janet moves her hand toward me.

"Janet, I'm going to leave now so that you can rest. I will come back to see you next week."

Janet gestures for me to move closer. I don't know what she wants at first, but I can tell she isn't ready for me to leave. I kneel beside the couch and lean toward her. She tries to lift her head, but has difficulty. I notice a thin, delicate branch on the maple tree tapping against the outside of the living room window. It is cold and gray outside and the lone branch sways in the wind. Its leaves are long gone and it just silently hits the window, again and again. Janet finds enough strength to raise her arms a few inches—just enough so that I realize she wants to hug me. I move closer; she puts her arms around me. She holds me tight and will not let go. She just holds on to me as I kneel.

The next evening, as I sit down for dinner with Patti and Courtney, the phone rings. Patti answers it, as usual. Patti says into the phone, "Just a minute, he is right here."

Jim gives me the funeral details. I was beginning to think that Janet had cheated death. I fooled myself into thinking there was more time, that she would bounce back, as usual. But Janet knew it that was the last time she would see me, and that hug was her goodbye.

The day of Janet's funeral, I procrastinate all morning, unable to dress. Eventually, I put on a fresh white shirt and dark suit. I stand in front of the bathroom mirror, trying to make a

Windsor knot, but my hands fumble. I don't know why; I have made this knot a thousand times. Sweat splotches my shirt, rendering its starched, upright shape limp. Finally, I make any knot and head for the car.

I put the key in the ignition and start the engine but cannot put the car into gear. I feel anxious, sick to my stomach and weak, but I have to get to Janet's funeral. I put it into gear and drive forty feet to the end of the street, but stop. I cannot go. I feel like I am being choked, and sit in my parked car with my left hand holding the driver's side door as though it hadn't been fixed. Winter scrapes against the windows and cars honk at me to move, but I cannot go.

I was sad, but I was angry and wanted justice. Maybe revenge. I knew that if I did not find a way to hold those responsible for the national blood policy accountable, then Janet's death, all the misery she and her family suffered, would be meaningless. Janet's determination won compensations for her family, and I can make my mortgage payments now, but nothing can bring her back. I decide right then, in the car, to go all the way against the American Association of Blood Banks in Bill's case and expose the blood bankers' conspiracy, with no intention to settle. I drive in the opposite direction of the funeral home, to the office.

PART III

CHAPTER TWENTY-TWO

It has been over a year since Judge Scuito sent that certified letter to the last known address of the donor in Bill's case. The letter came back with no forwarding address. Bill's blood donor has disappeared from the face of earth. I fear the donor's trail has either gone cold or he had died. It's a moot issue now and the court drops it. Even though I fought the blood bankers for a couple of years over donor discovery, the delay served in their interest because the donor is gone, and Bill's health is waning.

A box with a Lawyer's Service delivery labels on it blocks my office door at work one morning. I check them over and the box is from Matthews. Tom Asher suggested that I subpoena the internal records of the American Association of Blood Banks for the period between mid-1982 through mid-1985. These are the years from when the AIDS epidemic appeared in the blood until the blood bankers began screening donors. It is in this window of time that Janet, Bill and thousands of other people were given contaminated blood by the industry. After protracted delays and stonewalling, the blood bankers finally produce the documents. The cardboard box feels like Christmas. I use the sharp edge of a scissor to open the box, sit on the floor, and wade through them for a week. It's an old lawyers' trick to bury incriminating documents among thousands of useless documents, so I search for that one smoking gun. On the fourth day of combing through the lackluster, I find a confidential memo, dated January 24, 1983 Report to the Board, Committee on Transfusion Transmitted Diseases, by Joseph Bove, its chairman. In a chronological sequence, this internal document came right after the American Association of Blood Banks and the American Red Cross got together and put out the January 16, 1983 industry joint statement against the CDC's Atlanta recommendations to test donors. Publicly, the joint industry statement denies the risk of transfusion AIDS, but in this internal memo, they admit more cases are on the horizon after the another infant is infected with AIDS from a blood transfusion in a Texas hospital.

Dr. Bove writes, "This increases the probability that AIDS may be spread by blood. There is little doubt in my mind that additional transfusion related cases and additional cases in patients with hemophilia will surface, and that the CDC continues to actively pursue more transfusion-related cases."

This document is important because the blood bankers continued to argue that the CDC's evidence, presented in Atlanta, was not conclusive, though they themselves believed it was true. I lean back against the wall and read the part about the blood bankers purposeful plan to delay action for as long as possible. Dr. Bove writes, "The most we can do in this situation is <u>buy time</u>. By that I mean it will be necessary for us to take some active steps to screen out donor populations who are at high risk of AIDS. For practical purposes, this means gay males." But then, Dr. Bove warns against any such action, writing, "We are reluctant to do this since we do not want anything that we do now to be interpreted by society (or by legal authorities) as agreeing with the concept—as yet unproven—that AIDS can be spread by blood." The final sentence that catches my eye is this: "I hope that we are equipped psychologically to continue to <u>act</u>

together. I have been in contact with the American Red Cross (Dr. Katz) and the Council of Community Blood Centers (Dr. Menitove) and believe that the three of us can, together, work out whatever new problems arise."

I cross-reference Dr. Bove's memo with Dr. Cumming's February 5, 1983 Red Cross memo stating, "To the extent the industry, American Red Cross, Council of Community Blood Centers and American Association of Blood Banks, sticks together against the CDC, it will appear to some segments of the public at least that we have a self interest which is in conflict with the public interest, unless we can clearly demonstrate the CDC is wrong." It is clear to me that while the blood bankers continued to refute the CDC's evidence of transfusion AIDS, they knew the blood supply is being contaminated.

The first time I met Dr. Bove was two years earlier. I drove up to the Yale University Blood Bank, New Haven, to depose him. It's a two-hour drive from Hackensack. I prayed all the way there for my car to make it. It had over two hundred thousand miles from the turnpike lawyering days. The steering wheel rattled with every pothole on I-95, but it got me there on time.

I checked the address of this old cottage converted into an administrative office building just off the Yale campus. I went inside and saw a fireplace in the reception area. The place had a smell that was both floral and soupy. It was luxurious in that New England way: quaint, but a lot of resources went into making it seem quaint. Dr. Bove's assistant shows me to what was probably a bedroom, now used as his conference room.

Dr. Bove walked in. "Good morning." No handshake extended or other pleasantries. He was all business. "Good morning, Dr. Bove." I wondered why he had agreed to appear without a subpoena. I handed the Atlanta meeting minutes to the court stenographer to mark as plaintiff's exhibit. She placed a sticker on it and I slid it across the conference table. "Dr. Bove, I am handing you the minutes for the CDC's meeting on January 4, 1983. Were you present at the meeting?"

"Yes." His name is listed right at the top of the official attendee's list.

"Did the Centers for Disease Control recommend that blood banks test donors with the hepatitis B Core antibody test?"

"No." His denial of something that is stated right in the minutes caught me off-guard.

"No?"

"No." Dr. Bove's single word answers indicated that he has been through this before. I fumble through the Atlanta minutes while Dr. Bove continued testifying.

"The group never reached a consensus that AIDS was transmitted by blood."

I found the page I was looking for in the minutes and showed it to him. "It says right here that 90 percent of people with AIDS also have the hepatitis b core antibody?"

Dr. Bove took aim at the CDC's study population as having been too small to be meaningful and attacked the reliability of the core test. He argued core testing was unreliable because it had too many false positives, which meant that good blood would have been discarded, causing severe blood shortages. Dr. Bove is the kind of guy that has an answer for everything, and I better hone my cross-examination skills.

He leaned forward from across the conference table. "I'll tell you what we could have done. We could have closed all the blood banks, and then you would have had a different crisis," he reprimanded.

To that day, almost eight years after Atlanta, Dr. Bove insisted the AABB and Red Cross made the right decision.

Dr. Bove did not want a subpoena to appear because he intended to have me for lunch. I was no match for this professor of transfusion medicine at Yale.

Driving back to Hackensack on I-95 South, it occurred to me that Dr. Bove, in his dual capacity as both a member of the FDA Blood Products Advisory Committee and chairman of the AABB Transfusion Committee, had more influence over the regulatory process of the blood supply than the CDC, which is charged with preventing epidemics. Truly the fox guarding the hen house.

Back at the office, Roslyn calls me from Florida. It's unusual for her to call me because she just leaves everything about Bill's case up to me.

"Roslyn, how are you?"

"Bill's sick. He is at Halifax hospital with pneumonia."

We talk about making Bill's case move through the legal system faster. It has already been three years, with the appeals and all.

"I will do all I can, Roslyn." The battle between the blood bankers and me is personal—they are pulling strings to delay the case, tapping a foot as they wait for Bill to die. I am discouraged by the court's inability to move Bill's case faster, and even more discouraged at the disappearance of the donor. The only way I get to sleep is with the help of Patty's Valium. I never asked for my own prescription because that would be admitting that I needed the crutch. If Patti was out of Valium, then NyQuil.

I decide to take matters into my own hands rather than wait for the court and ask Judge Scuito for a conference. Judge Scuito has the lawyers come into court to hear me out. I want to hire a private investigator to either find the donor or bring back his death certificate. The blood bankers argue that since the private investigator is an extension of my office, I would be privy to confidential donor information. I convince Judge Scuito that by appointing a private investigator as an officer of the court, the donor would answer only to him. Judge Scuito agrees, so long as I pick up the tab.

I ask around the courthouse for a private detective recommendation and the name Al McClutchy comes up. McClutchy is a tough, retired police detective who spent time in narcotics enforcement. "He's the kind of guy who gets the job done," lawyers in the coffee shop would say.

McClutchy agrees to meet with me at my office. Al is 52, slightly balding with broad shoulders. His waist-high baseball jacket is unzipped and I notice a small revolver peep out from his belt. We talk for a while and he tells me about his task force drug raids. Al mentions how he has contacts in the department of motor vehicles and police force that may be useful in tracking down the donor. Judge Scuito appoints McClutchy as an officer of the court and off he goes to find the donor.

A week later McClutchy calls me at home. "George, I want to give you a heads up."

"What do you mean?" I worry it is bad news, that the donor is dead.

"I found your man."

"Al, where are you?"

"Key West, Florida."

I instantly know the donor is a gay male. Key West is a gay hot spot like San Francisco. This is consistent with the CDC's epidemiological profile of high-risk blood donors.

"Did you talk with him?"

"Yes."

"Will he agree to answer a few questions?"

"I convinced him it's the right thing to do."

Judge Sciuto calls us all back into court to discuss questioning the donor. After wrangling over limiting my intrusion into the donor's privacy, as the blood bankers argue, Judge Sciuto decides on written interrogatories. These are written questions that are answered under oath. First, however, I have to submit my proposed interrogatories to the court so the blood bankers can object to them. This simple process moves at a snail's pace. Over the next month, we appear in court again to argue over the content and structure of my questions, as though we are in a creative writing workshop. Once Judge Sciuto has ruled on the form of the written interrogatories, Al McClutchy returns to Key West to have the donor answer them.

I had taken depositions from every employee involved in the blood drives at Bergen Community Blood Center. It turns out that donor 29F0784 was recruited during an off-site bloodmobile drive. I even depose the driver of the bloodmobile that day and learn that the "self-deferral" and "high-risk" materials were simply placed on a table, but no one could say if the donors actually read them.

I consult with Marc Conant about preparing the donor interrogatories. Marc tells me a problem with blood bank "self-deferral" pamphlets is that donors don't always understand them or do not admit to being gay, since being gay at that time elicited terrible vitriol. The gay community in the mid-Eighties had no support, no presidents or celebrities making videos about how "it gets better." Back then, it only got worse. In some cases, gay men have not even admitted it to themselves. A man who has a single homosexual experience may not consider himself gay. I decide not to ask the donor if he is gay, but rather ask him this question: "If the blood bank had told you not to give blood if you ever had sex with a man, would you have donated blood?" I figure this question gives me "causation" and give 29F0784 the opportunity to sidestep the word "gay."

Al returns with the donor's answers, and Judge Sciuto calls us all back into court to hear them. Donor 29F0784 is a thirty-year-old man who lived in Bergen County, New Jersey but relocated to the Florida Keys. His answer to my question is, "I would not have donated blood if I had been informed by the

Bergen Community Blood Center not to donate blood if I ever had sex with another man."

I prevail over the blood bankers' objection, that Donor 29F0784's answer is to be read to the jury at trial and can be used as evidence against them. Rather than being forced to go to trial with only circumstantial evidence and inferences linking the blood bank's negligence to Bill's infection, now there's direct evidence. In Legalese, it's simple proximate cause that "but for" Bergen Community Blood Bank's failure to ask the donor this question, the donor would not have donated the blood that infected Bill with AIDS. It is also an example of how donor self-exclusion, which was proclaimed to be working by the blood bankers and FDA, was a disaster.

Bergen Community Blood Center is against the ropes because they did not follow the minimum screening protocols to protect Bill. Anthony Passaro is the director of the blood center. He is a businessman with no medical background. The deposition is short because I want just one question answered by him. So with a court stenographer at the conference table making a record, I ask him, "Mr. Passaro, if the American Association of Blood Banks had recommended that you—not you personally—that the Bergen Community Blood Center do a certain laboratory test for screening donors, would it have been done at the blood center?"

"Yes."

It is a powerful one-word answer that establishes, on the record, that had the AABB recommended core testing, Bergen Community Blood Center would have done the testing. I look at Roger Ellis across the table and nod. We have a settlement. Anthony Passaro subsequently resigned as director of the Bergen Community Blood Center. His next business venture was a "nostalgic" ice cream parlor in Ramsey.

This leaves just me and Matthews, Bill and the AABB.

CHAPTER TWENTY-THREE

The AABB wants to compel the donor to submit to an AIDS and hepatitis B core test, after arguing for years, even in front of the New Jersey Supreme Court, that such an intrusion will collapse the volunteer blood system. When AABB asks Judge Sciuto to enter an order to compel donor 29F0847 to submit to an AIDS and core test, my suspicion that the blood bankers were using the donor's "right of privacy" argument all this time as a delay tactic is affirmed.

It's a crafty legal maneuver. Their plan throws my strategy out the window and costs me nerve-wracking weeks ahead. The AABB figures that if Bill's donor is core negative, then the case is over—no matter how deceptive they claimed the test was. On the other hand, if the donor is core positive, it's still not evidence he was core positive at the time he donated the blood that infected Bill. It could end their case, or be no risk to them.

I am so anxious about the outcome that I call Don Francis and ask him what he thinks, but I am not comforted by what he says. His exact words to me are, "George, there's over a 90 percent chance the donor is core antibody positive." As always when given such a percentage, the smaller 10% is more shrill, more troubling than the more fertile 90%. I never predicted Matthews would go back on the donor's "right to privacy," but he did—nothing is predictable. It is a chess game in which rooks are allowed to move diagonally one second and back to its normal straight line the next, with nobody acknowledging the aberration. If the AABB wins because of their sly tactics, it will be over and no will know what they did.

A few weeks later, Judge Sciuto calls us back into his chambers with the result of the donor's test. Sure enough, donor 29F0784 is core positive and AIDS positive. "Judge, they just proved me right. They proved the CDC AIDS Task Force recommendation would have saved my client's life." I blurt out in court.

As expected, the blood bankers argue that the donor's recent positive test results cannot be admitted into evidence because they do not establish the he was positive when Bill was transfused. The hypocrisy of standing on the donor's right to privacy as the pillar of the volunteer blood supply, but then forcing him to submit to testing, is outdone by further manipulation: they pull strings to keep the test results hidden from the jury.

I arrive back in San Francisco for Marc Conant's deposition. I check back into the Sheraton and stick Patti's post-it notes on the mirror, as usual. She wrote me new ones, since we've finally been able to afford new, not generic yellow Post-It's. I go for a long walk along the marina toward the Golden Gate Bridge. As a ritual, I have walked along the water to calm my nerves since my first trip here in 1989, four years ago. I thought about how, within that time, I met Janet, fought her case, and did not attend her funeral. I had seen her die gradually, her immune system lapsing into further disrepair with every conversation, yet I could only recall her laugh, her reluctant sarcasm, the robust love she had for her family. This is the forth year I see Christmas lights illuminate the boats in the marina, more familiar to me than my own house's Christmas lights.

I jump into a cab and head to Marc's Divisadero Street office. Everyone is ready to begin. Marc's conference room has a large glass window with a two-way view of the reception area. Patients are coming and going as we begin the deposition. The court stenographer is set up at the end of the table, next to Marc. Matthews and I sit opposite each other. I always doodle on my legal pad during these depositions. It's a nervous habit.

"Dr. Conant, you cannot testify to a reasonable degree of probability that this donor was core positive when he donated blood based upon his subsequent test result, can you?" Matthews fires away.

"Yes, Mr. Matthews. I—"

"Just because the blood donor tests positive for AIDS and hepatitis B this year, in 1991, that it does not mean he was positive in August 1984, when he donated blood." It is Matthews' personal mission to discredit Marc Conant for the blood bankers. They despise Marc so much that privately they call him a "whore," which is how lawyers describe an expert who will say anything for a price.

"Mr. Matthews, I can tell you that based upon the donor's age—" Matthews cut him off.

"Dr. Conant, isn't it possible that the donor was not AIDS positive in 1984?"

I interrupt before Marc answers. "Objection to the form of the question." I'm worried Matthews may wear down Marc. There's no way I can let Matthews get away with this old lawyer's trick of getting Marc to agree that anything is possible rather than sticking to his medical opinion.

"Dr. Conant?" Matthews practically spits his name. "Isn't it possible that the donor in this case, 29F0784, was not hepatitis B positive when he donated blood?"

"Objection." I hit the conference table. It makes a load smacking sound that startles everyone in the office. I am still angry about the blood bankers' hypocrisy in compelling the donor be tested and now trying to bury the results.

"Let the record reflect that Mr. Baxter just hit the conference table," Matthews leans back. He delivers smug half-smile.

"I object to your characterization of my hitting the table." I know the transcript cannot reflect this level of aggression.

"Mr. Baxter, you're obstructing the deposition." Matthews adjusts his jacket lapels. "Ask Dr. Conant questions later if you don't like his answers." "I'm not obstructing anything and object to your characterization. I'm protecting the record." I have to protect the record: you cannot put toothpaste back in a tube once it is out. "Why don't you ask your next question?" Matthews and I bicker like schoolchildren.

Matthews will not let it go, and pretends like his accusations are questions. "Dr. Conant, you cannot say, with any degree of medical certainty, whether this donor was AIDS positive or not when he donated blood in 1984?"

"Objection." I slam the conference table again. This time the whole table shakes and even patients on the other side of the glass window in the reception area turn their heads. "That question has been asked and answered. I am not going to allow you to badger Dr. Conant with the same question again and again just because *you* don't like his answer."

"Gentlemen, please." Dr. Conant interrupts. "You are upsetting the staff and patients." I look out the window at the San Francisco rooftops and pretend to relax, but it is just not possible.

"Dr. Conant, isn't it possible—"

"Objection, Mr. Matthews—"

"Mr. Baxter, you are purposely obstructing this deposition and I am going to report this to the court—"

"Mr. Matthews, you may report me to the court, the postmaster, or anyone you want, but you are not getting away with asking an improper question today." I will not risk Matthews rattling my witness.

"Counsel, please." The court stenographer pleads. "I can't take you down with you talking over each other."

"Dr. Conant, don't answer that last question." I quickly say.

"Mr. Baxter, you can't instruct the witness not to answer my question."

Matthews is right. The court rules don't permit me to tell Dr. Conant not to answer the question. But who's playing by the rules? Tempers flare. The patients in the reception area are stunned.

"Dr. Conant is here to testify about his medical opinion that he holds to a medical probability, not to speculate about possibilities." Staff and patients no longer pretend to casually ignore the commotion and fighting, and watch intently.

"Gentlemen, please. You are scaring my staff. They have to take care of patients."

"Dr. Conant, do you understand the difference between the question about 'possibilities' rather than your opinion that is based on a medical 'probability'?" There is too much on the line to allow the case go down the tubes based upon this trick.

Marc looks me in the eye. "Yes," he assures.

"Then go ahead and answer the question." I calmly say, praying that he got it.

"Mr. Matthews, I can tell you that to a reasonable degree of medical certainty this donor 29F0784 was core positive when he gave the blood that infected Mr. Snyder." Marc testified how based upon a well-known study, "Hepatitis B in Homosexual Men: Prevalence of Infection and Factors Related to Transmission," *146 Journal of Infectious Disease* (8 July 1982), and the donor's age and gender, it is highly predicable when he became sexually active and exposed to hepatitis. And, based upon the age of donor 29F0847 when he donated the blood that infected Bill, the donor had already been sexually active for several years and exposed to hepatitis. The AABB's plan backfired. I underestimated Marc's ability to not be bullied by Matthews.

It is dark outside by the time Marc's deposition winds down. The pace of the office has slowed to a few patients in a mostly empty reception area. Two men sit in the chairs near the water cooler; one of them has his head buried into the other's shoulder, and they are holding hands. As time goes, caterers bring trays of food into the office. A new rush of friends and patients gather for the holiday party.

"Gentlemen, as you can see, we are preparing to have our office holiday party soon. You are welcome to stay if you like." That's Marc, always gracious. Matthews packs up, mumbling something about catching a flight.

Marc's office is decorated with Christmas trays and poinsettias. The conference room where we spent the afternoon in battle is darkened and quiet. Some men brought their partners, and I recognize some as patients from the reception area. Marc introduces me to party guests as his "lawyer friend from New Jersey." I shake hands and mingle with Marc's patients and friends. It is my first gay party.

It seems like a lifetime ago that I stood in this very reception area for the first time, afraid to sit among the patients or to pick up a magazine. As the night goes on, I ask Marc, "How do you do it?" Looking around the room. "How do you deal with helping keep so many patients when you know you can't save them?"

Marc pauses, looks around the room, and says, "My friend, almost half of them will not be here next year. But they need help now, and you do what you can for them. Like how you helped that woman." Marc is, of course, referring to Janet. I hear the pop of champagne drowned out by laughter and clinks of glasses. Marc's words have stayed with me since that evening.

CHAPTER TWENTY-FOUR

"Ladies and gentlemen, the evidence in this case will show that 'but for' the negligence of the defendant, the American Association of Blood Banks, the infected donor, known as donor 29F0847, would have been tested, prevented from donating blood, and my client, Bill Snyder, would not sit here before you now, infected with AIDS." Bill's trial begins on May 6, 1994. My mouth is dry; I'm so nervous. I take another sip of water from the paper cup on the counsel table. I catch a glimpse of Roslyn and Patti sitting together in the first row.

"You will hear testimony about a Centers for Disease Control meeting that took place on January 6, 1983, in Atlanta, eighteen months before Bill was transfused, where the blood bankers were warned to test blood donors at risk for transmitting AIDS with a test called the hepatitis B core antibody test." Keep it simple, keep it simple, I think to myself. "That is the last time we will hear that long name. From now on I will call it the core test. It's not difficult, and if I can get it, so can you." I did not realize my comment was self-deprecating. I use the moment to swallow another sip of water. "Gay men made up seventy-five percent of all the known AIDS cases, and intravenous drug users made up another twenty percent. And, the core test detected over ninety percent of gay men and one hundred percent of the intravenous drug users, all at risk for transmitting AIDS."

Nervous energy and caffeine runs through me. I loaded up with coffee in the courthouse café less than an hour ago. I reach for the 18x36 blowup of Dr. Bove's internal memo to the American Association of Blood Banks board of directors I left on the floor, leaning against the counsel table. Slowly, I place it on the court easel, waiting for an objection.

"Objection. Mr. Baxter can't show the jury documents not yet in evidence." Matthews says in a commanding way.

"Your Honor, I intend to offer Dr. Bove's memo into evidence during the trial."

Judge Van Tassel cautions the jury. "Ladies and gentlemen, remember I instructed you earlier that what the lawyers say in their opening statements is not evidence." Judge Edward Van Tassel, 71, has a remarkable likeness to Richard Nixon. They called him back from retirement because the trial is supposed to continue for a couple of months. He is slow moving, partially the reason it took weeks to select a jury. The other reason it took so long is because prospective jurors heard it would be a two-month trial and ran for the hills. "The objection is overruled."

I place Dr. Bove's memo on the easel facing the jurors. "After the Atlanta meeting, the defendants, American Association of Blood Banks and the American Red Cross, immediately put out a joint industry statement on January 16, 1983 against the CDC's recommendations to test donors. Publicly they said there was not evidence that AIDS is transmitted by blood. However, privately they said something else." I highlight Dr. Bove's words with a yellow marker and read them to the jurors. "AIDS could cause a major problem in the blood collecting sector. My current best guess is that we are dealing with an infectious agent able to be spread by blood and blood products and that individuals who receive large quantities of factor concentrate are at risk."

I pour another cup of water from the court pitcher on the counsel table. The courtroom is filled. I sip the water and put the cup down to give the jury a moment to see the document on the easel. "Remember, while publicly denying the risk of transfusion AIDS and refusing to test donors, Dr. Bove tells the defendant's board, 'There is little doubt in my mind that additional cases in patients with hemophilia will surface. The most we can do is buy time. We do not want anything we do now to be interpreted by society or legal authorities as agreeing with the concept, as yet unproven, that AIDS can be spread by blood.'" I check over my notes on the legal pad at counsel table. I never got over losing my first case before Judge Hamer, so I write out all my questions on a legal pad to get them just right. I look back at the jurors, trying gauge whether they are with me. Their poker faces make me uneasy. Juror number one, the foreman, is an older man—a little too conservative looking for my taste, with a tweed jacket and *The Wall Street Journal* peeping out of his briefcase. He seems like the type to be a leader with the other jurors. The younger woman next to him in the front row always seems to look to him for approval.

"Ladies and gentlemen, the evidence will also show that donor 29F0847, whose platelet was transfused into Bill on August 23, 1984, tested both AIDS and core positive. The defendant, American Association of Blood Banks, was negligent because they failed to act in a reasonable and prudent manner by refusing to implement core testing that would have identified donor 29F0847, and prevented Bill from being infected with AIDS-contaminated blood. I ask that you return a verdict for Bill and Roslyn Snyder."

I practiced and tested this opening statement on taxi drivers, friends and airline passengers trapped in the seat next to me. Last night, Patti and Courtney sat in kitchen chairs and timed the opening, exactly forty minutes. Patti walks up from behind and squeezes my shoulder for reassurance.

"Ladies and gentlemen, Mr. Baxter has finished his opening statement. Now we are going to hear from Edwin Matthews, counsel for the defendant." Judge Van Tassel turns to Matthews. "Mr. Matthews?"

"Thank you, Your Honor." Matthews confidently rises from the counsel table, notes in hand. He moves closer to the jury railing with his shoulders square on the jurors and looks right into their eyes. He could sell them Furbies if he wanted to.

"Good afternoon, Ladies and Gentlemen, and your Honor." Did I forget to acknowledge Judge Van Tassel when I started my opening? I can't remember. "I am Edwin Matthews, with the law firm of Cuyler, Burk and Matthews. I am proud to stand here before you to represent my client, the American Association of Blood Banks. Let me tell you a little bit about the AABB. It is responsible for over ten million transfusions a year that save lives." Matthews steps away from the counsel table and walks to the center of he courtroom. He lowers his voice to a level of deep sadness. "I know this is an emotional case. Nobody feels as badly about what happened to the plaintiff as I do. If you are human, you cannot help but feel sorry for Mr. Snyder." He pauses a moment. Then he perks right up. "But, it is not our fault. We did not put AIDS into the blood he received. It is no one's fault." It worries me that Matthews is more convincing at feigning sympathy for the blood bankers than Charlton Heston was in portraying Moses.

"You each took an oath to decide this case on the evidence you hear in this case and not on emotions. And the evidence will come from that witness chair." Matthews points at the empty witness chair. On the eve of trial, Matthews hit me with eleven expert witnesses straight from the Who's Who list of prominent blood bankers, government people and scientists. They did so last minute because they wanted to send me off on a wild goose chase around the country to depose witnesses when I needed to be in the office preparing for trial. It was their strategy all along to buy time, figuring my client would die in the meantime.

"The evidence in this case will show that my client, the American Association of Blood Banks, did everything possible short of closing down the blood banks." Matthews is old school, slow and methodical. He talks for a couple of hours about how the core test is not even an AIDS test and that had they used it as such, there would have been blood shortages from discarding so much good blood. I cringe at the counsel table over the subtle difference between a surrogate test that could have detected AIDS in more than ninety percent of the donors at risk and an actual test for the viral agent. I pray the jury understands the difference.

"You will hear testimony from Dr. Luc Montagnier, from the Pasteur Institute, in Paris, France, that until he isolated the viral agent in the Spring of 1985, there was no test to detect the viral agent of AIDS." He goes through his prominent witnesses one-by-one. He tells them that even Dr. Dennis Donoghue, the former Chairman of the Federal Food and Drug Administration's Blood Products Advisory Committee, which considered core testing and rejected it, will testify. Matthews tells the jurors that they must decide the case based upon the knowledge at the time of Bill's transfusion.

"Look at what the industry practice was when the plaintiff was transfused." Matthews is in full stride now and very compelling. He passionately argues how the blood bankers claim they did not put AIDS into the blood, they were consistent with the industry practice, compliant with the FDA which regulates blood as a biologic, and did nothing wrong. "We don't even know the plaintiff." Or the other 29,000 people they infected.

Matthews stands squarely before the jurors and warns: "If you decide the case for the plaintiff, it will open the floodgates for other lawsuits."

George T. Baxter, Esq.

Behind me, Bill can barely keep his neck straight. He is exhausted from being in court all day. It's too much for him. Patti's seat is empty; she left to get Courtney out of school. I can feel the ebb of caffeine from my limbs. Matthews' confidence is pristine; not a single strand of his silver hair sticks out of place. He annunciates his t's and could probably play a king in a Shakespeare play. He walks back to the counsel table, to gestures of admiration by his people.

CHAPTER TWENTY-FIVE

It's late Thursday afternoon when we finish showing the jury the San Francisco video testimony of Don Francis I did the year earlier. Matthews tells Judge Van Tassel that he needs to video a witness, Dr. George Grady.

"Your Honor, I object." Judge Van Tassel excuses the jury and asks us to come into his chambers to discuss it. As usual, Judge Van Tassel relaxes with a buttered roll and coffee sent up from the café, which he enjoys while Matthews argues that Grady is now unavailable to come to Hackensack for trial.

"Judge, I am in the middle of presenting my case. I can't go to Boston now, without notice, for a video of Dr. Grady." Matthews knows it is a major disruption.

"Dr. Grady is unable to make the trial and he is a crucial part of the AABB's case."

"When do you want to do this, Ed?" Judge Van Tassel is actually considering it.

"This weekend, Judge." Matthews is getting his way.

"Judge, I can't go to Boston this weekend, I have to get ready for my next witness."

"Oh, I think you can handle it, George."

"But, Judge. I have exhibits and a witness to prep for Monday." I was looking forward to crashing on the couch over the weekend too.

"Go ahead and do it, George. Go to Boston tomorrow. I will excuse the jury for the day. I have a doctor's appointment Friday anyway."

On Friday morning, I catch a shuttle flight out of Newark into Logan Airport. I rent a car, get a map, and make my way over to the Massachusetts Department of Health. The streets are old with high curbstone and brick. The tires of my car make a guttural noise over the stone streets. The buildings are old and drab. It reminds me of when I lived with my grandmother in Malden, not too far from here. That year, I was thirteen and had lived in three different states with four different relatives and attended four different schools. I went there for about three months before I took off one evening. I said I was going to the corner store, but grabbed a bus at the Malden bus station and headed back to Jersey.

The conference room is ready, with the court reporter at the end of the conference table and videographer making last minute lights and camera adjustments. "Where's the coffee?" I ask, before I even say hi. Dr. Grady is in another office somewhere, getting last-minute pointers for the deposition. The court stenographer asks me, in her Massachusetts' accent, for the case caption for her transcript. She is a young woman, with dark brown hair and a flouncy white blouse. I notice her slightly naive manner in the way she asks me for the case caption. She is probably covering the deposition per diem, not attached to an agency. I take it as a cue to try the conspiracy and negligence theories with her while we are waiting. I want to soften the room up to my cause before the bad guys come out. I sum up Bill's case to her about how the core test detected over ninety percent of people at risk for transmitting AIDS but the blood bankers refused to use it. The cameraman listens too. "So, what do you think? Should they have used the test to save lives?" She doesn't answer, and stays impartial. I turn to the cameraman for his reaction, but he too tries to stay impartial. I had to try.

Matthews and Dr. Grady, in his fifties, come into the conference room. He is wearing a yellow short-sleeved button-down shirt with a pencil pouch in his shirt pocket and looks nervous. Dr. Grady looks even more uncomfortable when the cameraman adjusts the lights and does a microphone check. Under the lights, I see his hair is thinning on the top; I can almost see it happen as Matthews begins his first question.

"Dr. Grady, for the record, you are the Director of Communicable Diseases at the Massachusetts Department of Health?"

"Yes."

"And, you were also a member of the American Association of Blood Banks, Committee on Transfusion Diseases?"

"Yes."

"Did the Committee on Transfusion Diseases consider using the hepatitis B core antibody test as a surrogate test for AIDS?"

Dr. Grady goes on about how the core test was thought to have too many false positives to be a reliable AIDS test. In other words, since 5-7 percent of core positive donors do not actually have AIDS, the test was not efficient enough to use. He said it would have resulted in throwing a way good blood. Matthews asks him for a final expert opinion about whether the AABB was negligent for not recommending it to screen donors by the time Bill was transfused. Dr. Grady agrees it was not. "Thank you, Dr. Grady." Matthews is satisfied.

It is my turn to cross-examine Dr. Grady. "Dr. Grady, good afternoon." Since he is uncomfortable, I remind him that he is under oath. "Dr. Grady, I am going to ask you questions, and this court reporter is making a record of your answers." Dr. Grady's conference table is actually in an outer office to his office. It is the workspace he uses to meet people without bringing them into his private office but there is clutter everywhere, files and projects under his supervision piled on the credenza against the wall. The edges of the files protrude out in awkward triangles because he didn't bother to pile them neatly, probably expecting a secretary to do it for him. "So if you don't understand a question, you have to tell me. If you answer my question, it will be presumed that you understood the question and gave a complete and honest answer. Do you understand this before we begin?"

"Yes."

I slowly pull a document from my file and hand it to the court reporter to mark as an exhibit. She places a yellow exhibit sticker on the first page. I show it to Dr. Grady, he looks at Matthews.

"You can't use this memo, Mr. Baxter. It post dates your client's transfusion and is prohibited by rule 407."

All hell breaks loose. I slam the conference table. The Massachusetts court reporter and cameraman are uneasy with how fiercely Matthews and I go at each other, but this is worth fighting over. It is Dr. Grady's internal AABB memo privately admitting the benefit of core testing. He states it will reduce the transfusion incidence of hepatitis, while "as a bonus," catch donors at risk for transmitting AIDS. The memo directly refutes the AABB's legal strategy of claiming false positives and blood shortages. This is the first insider memo that admits core testing is a good idea because it will reduce both transfusion AIDS and hepatitis.

Matthews fights desperately to keep Dr. Grady's memo off the camera and out of the record. New Jersey Evidence Rule 407 prohibits using a subsequent corrective action taken by a defendant as evidence of prior negligence. The social policy behind this rule is that if litigants can use a defendant's subsequent remedial action as proof of prior negligence, then no one will take corrective actions, instead choosing to hide or deny their culpability. The downside to this policy is that it often keeps the truth from coming out. Dr. Grady's memo is dated January 1985, after Bill's transfusion. Matthews argues strenuously that I am not permitted to show the document. I argue that even though the memo is dated after Bill's transfusion, it refers back to blood bankers' knowledge at the time of Bill's transfusion. I ignore Matthews and show the memo on camera, then hand it to Dr. Grady. Dr. Grady jerks his head backwards. "Mr. Matthews, don't interrupt me. I am going to ask this witness about his memo."

"Gentlemen, please calm down. I'm not used to this kind of confrontation." He begins sweating through his yellow shirt.

"Dr. Grady, you state in this memo, and I quote, 'bonus.' You use the word 'bonus.' You say, 'The use of hepatitis B core antibody as a surrogate test will not only reduce the incidence of hepatitis but also, as a bonus, AIDS too." Bill's donor 29F0847 is both hepatitis B and AIDS positive, just as the memo predicts. I push the memo across the table toward him. The court reporter does a double take. Even she realizes its significance.

"That memo is prohibited—"

"No, Mr. Matthews. That is for Judge Van Tassel to decide."

"Please. I am not comfortable with this kind of confrontation." Dr. Grady practically squeals.

Matthews opens his mouth to object. I strike the table again hard enough that the memo falls to the floor.

"Mr. Matthews, stop interrupting my cross-examination." The court reporter puts the document back on the table. "Dr. Grady, you wrote in this memo that core testing would reduce the incidence of transfusion hepatitis—"

"Objection—"

"And as a bonus, AIDS—"

"Objection—"

"Dr. Grady, answer the question."

"May we go off the record?" Dr. Grady asks timidly. The cameraman and court reporter look to me for consent. I nod reluctantly. The camera is shut off and the court reporter stops typing.

Dr. Grady shakes. He echoes again that he is not used to this kind of confrontation. "I was trying to change things from the inside. Some people do it from the outside, but I wanted to do it from the inside." It sounds like a confession.

His attempt to compare himself to Don Francis is embarrassing. Dr. Grady went along with the blood bankers, fully aware that thousands of people were getting contaminated blood products. It should have been shouted from the rooftops, but instead it was an insider club secret. Core testing was finally adopted in 1986, a year after this memo, to reduce the transfusion incidence of hepatitis and AIDS as predicted by the CDC. The move was three years and thousands of lives too late.

On Monday, Matthews and I fight it out before Judge Van Tassel over allowing the jury to see it. Matthews wants to exclude Dr. Grady's memo under Evidence Rule 407 that precludes it as a subsequent remedial action. Even though core testing is eventually used to screen for both AIDS and hepatitis, the blood bankers want to keep it from the jury. The AABB tells the jury that core testing is unreliable to screen donors for AIDS and would have caused blood shortages. But this is obviously not true, because they use it now.

Judge Van Tassel finishes his mid-morning buttered roll and coffee from the court café, after ordering the jury to give us time to argue in his chambers. There is something humorous, in the mist of all this fighting, about waiting and watching the crumbs from his hard roll flake all over his morning newspaper. I've never seen a jaw move so elastically from somebody's face.

"Your Honor, Dr. Grady's February 1985 memo is written after the plaintiff's transfusion." Matthews insists I cannot use this memo or even refer to the fact that core testing is used now.

"I am not using Dr. Grady's memo to establish the blood bankers' negligence, but rather to impeach them." A document may be admitted into evidence to attack credibility. I want to admit the memo into evidence because it refutes the blood bankers' claim that core testing is ineffective and would have caused blood shortages. The jury has to know the truth. The decision is left to the discretion of Judge Van Tassel.

Matthews bites back. "The rules of evidence specifically exclude acts of subsequent or corrective action, like Dr. Grady's memo, from being admitted into evidence." I relished in the fact they tried to sabotage my case by sending me to Boston, but their plan backfired. I couldn't have Judge Van Tassel puncture this glee.

"No judge, the fact that they finally did use anti-core testing in 1986 goes to the credibility of their argument that it was ineffective and would have caused blood shortages." Judge Van Tassel sits back and takes notes, wiping crumbs off his chin.

"It is prejudicial to admit the document." Matthews fights hard.

"All right, counsel." Judge Van Tassel looks up from his notes as though he has made up his mind. "I am granting Mr. Matthews' motion to preclude Dr. Grady's memo from evidence. Dr. Grady's memo goes to a subsequent remedial action that is precluded from evidence."

Judge Van Tassel's ruling becomes a major trial victory for the blood bankers. We all know the truth but have to continue the trial like some kind of foxtrot.

"Your Honor, why not allow the jury to see the evidence and let the chips fall where they may?"

"I have already ruled, Mr. Baxter."

George T. Baxter, Esq.

I was forced to go to Massachusetts during trial for something Mr. Matthews should have done months ago, and now the evidence that could win my case is completely useless. There is no use in arguing with Judge Von Tassel. He is resolute in his decision.

By not being allowed to introduce any evidence about subsequent use of core testing, Judge Van Tassel just punched the blood bankers' ticket and gave them a free ride. Almost all of my planned cross-examinations are now precluded.

CHAPTER TWENTY-SIX

It is early morning, and only Abby and I are awake. Three yellow legal pads filled with notes and questions form a tower on the kitchen counter. I open the back door and Abby runs outside. I try to eat a bowl of corn flakes for energized thinking, but most of it stays in the bowl. Abby scratches at the door with my neighbor's newspaper in her mouth again. She wags her tail and leaves the newspaper on her bed. "Abby, what are you doing? You are going to get me into trouble with old Mrs. Nelson." On my way out, I drop the newspaper back on her steps.

It is surreal as I top the Essex Street hill and take in the sunrise over the Hackensack courthouse dome. Behind it, across the Hudson River, the buildings of New York seem to reach for the cloudless sky. It is a peaceful moment, but my nerves are on edge over how today goes at trial.

It is too early to go inside the courtroom, so I sit in my car in the empty court parking lot and pop a meditation tape into the cassette player. I lean my head on the car seat, which resembles a pebble from overuse, and exhale a deep breath. I could have gotten away with being an ambulance chaser for the rest of my life. I was happy to have just finished law school. Bill's case makes me challenge myself day after day. The sunrise fades and more cars fill the parking lot.

George T. Baxter, Esq.

I step out from the third floor elevator with the legal pads tucked under my arm and look around the hallway for the only blood bank expert I have in the case. Dr. Edgar Engleman, the only blood banker in the country who defied his industry, was sitting on that hard oak bench outside the courtroom checking over his notes.

"Dr. Engleman, thank you for coming." I extend a handshake. It took two years and more than half a dozen trips to Stanford before Dr. Engleman agreed put his reputation on the line and gamble on me to set the record straight with Bill's case.

Dr. Engleman began screening donors while the industry was still denying transfusion-AIDS and the FDA blindly listened to them. He appeared before the FDA's Blood Products Advisory Committee on December 16, 1983, to urge them about the need to do something, but the other blood bankers ridiculed his efforts. With a tweed jacket and thinning brown hair, he sits on the bench calm and composed, in such jarring contrast to my nervous energy.

The courtroom is filled with spectators and the defense table has extra legal talent siting at it today. Everyone stands as the bailiff leads the jurors into the jury box. When the last juror sits down, so does everyone else.

"Mr. Baxter, are you ready to call a witness?" Judge Van Tassel asks from the bench.

"Yes, your Honor. Plaintiff calls Dr. Edgar Engleman." He walks from the back of the courtroom down the aisle to the witness stand. The lawyers and industry people stare at Dr. Englemen like piranhas ready to eat his flesh. The bailiff holds the court's Bible out. Dr. Englemen puts his right hand on the Bible and raises his left hand. "Do you swear to tell the truth, the whole truth, and nothing but the truth, so help you God?"

"I do." Dr. Englemen sits down in the witness stand.

"Proceed, Mr. Baxter." Judge Van Tassel is all business in the packed courtroom.

"Thank you, your Honor." I keep my legal pads close at my side. They are tattered and torn from looking at them over and over again.

Bill's entire case rests on Dr. Engleman's shoulders, because he is the only blood banker who will testify. I am not the most polished lawyer, so I push ahead reading each question from my legal pad.

"Dr. Englemen, you are the director of the Stanford University Hospital Blood Bank in Palo Alto, California?" It's the first question on pad number one.

"Yes, I am."

"How long have you held this position?"

"Fifteen years."

"Dr. Englemen, did there come a time when you decided to use a surrogate test to screen blood donors at Stanford who were at risk for transmitting AIDS?"

"Yes. After the Centers for Disease Control published its MMWRs, it became evident that testing was imperative to protect the patients at Stanford."

"Dr. Englemen, will you explain to the jury what significance the MMWRs have to you as a blood banker?" I am following the questions on my pad like a script.

"It is the Morbidity and Mortality Weekly Report, the CDC's way of communicating urgent information about an epidemic or public health emergency to the medical and blood-banking community."

"Did you routinely rely on the information in these MMWRs to make critical public health decisions?"

"Yes, as do my colleagues."

I show Dr. Englemen a blowup of the CDC's July 16, 1982 MMWR. "Dr. Engleman, is this July 16, 1982 Centers for Disease Control's Morbidity and Mortality Weekly Report the kind of information that was relevant to you as a blood banker?"

"Yes, it is."

I turn to Judge Van Tassel. "Your Honor, may I put this blowup on the easel and have Dr. Englemen step down to explain it to the jury?"

"Yes, go ahead, Mr. Baxter."

Dr. Englemen steps down and walks to the court easel that I placed very close to the jurors. I want the jury to bond with Dr. Englemen. I also move right up to the jury railing so it's the jurors, Dr. Englemen, and me.

"Dr. Englemen, will you read and point to the jury that part that is relevant to you?" I hand him a yellow highlighter too.

"Three hemophiliacs who are infected with AIDS have no other risk factors other than the blood products they used." Dr. Englemen highlights the text as he reads it to the jurors. "A twenty-month-old infant with no other risk factors for contracting AIDS except a transfusion, was infected with AIDS. When the CDC tracked down the donor, they learned he was dying from AIDS."

"What did that mean to you as a blood banker?" I always ask him his opinion as a blood banker to establish the T.J. Hooper *reasonable person* standard. I asked similar questions of Dr. Francis, but he testified as a public health expert.

"It meant that our worse-case scenario had been realized, that AIDS would get into the blood supply and infect people if something was not done to prevent it." Dr. Englemen looks professorial at the easel before the jurors. He is not charismatic like Don Francis or Marc Conant, but he is convincing. "The baby contracted AIDS from a donor who appeared healthy when he donated, ending any legitimate dispute over whether AIDS was transmitted by blood."

To compensate for Dr. Englemen's conservative style, I repeat his answers to the jury. Like, "Dr. Englemen, are you saying that as a blood banker, this was conclusive evidence of the link between AIDS and blood transfusions?" The jurors look at him for the answer.

"Yes." Dr. Englemen answers.

I do it again. "So are you testifying to this jury that by December 1982, the Center for Disease Control had established conclusive evidence that AIDS was transmitted by blood?"

"Objection, your Honor. Mr. Baxter is repeating Dr. Englemen's answers, or making a statement and then asking him to agree with him. It's improper."

"Mr. Baxter, rephrase the question." Judge Van Tassel politely suggests.

"Yes, Judge. Dr. Englemen, was there any doubt in your mind by December 1982 that AIDS was transmitted by blood?"

"None."

I move from the counsel table closer to the jury and look at them as I make my statement in the form of a question. "Did I hear you correctly, because if I heard you correctly, that means the American Association of Blood Banks ignored the evidence?"

"Objection. Mr. Baxter isn't only testifying now, but he is asking compound questions. First he asked the witness something about evidence, and then he babbled something else." The jury burst out in laughter at Matthews attack on me.

"I object to that objection, judge." I look at the clock on the wall. "It's only 11:20, and everyone knows that I don't begin babbling until after lunch."

There is uproarious laughter from the jury that is louder than before. It catches Matthews off guard.

Professor Latin, my first year torts professor at Rutgers Law, used to say, "If I call on you and you don't know the answer, you better be funny." Needless to say, I was funny more than I was right.

I never stop when Matthews makes an objection; otherwise he may control the flow of my questioning. I simply ignore him, which irritates him more.

"Dr. Englemen, when did you begin testing donors at risk for transmitting AIDS at Stanford?"

"The evidence was pretty compelling that something had to be done and I started routine testing of all Stanford's donors by June 1983. I allowed no blood to come into Stanford's hospital community that was not tested."

I had leaned all the blow-ups against the front of the counsel table. I grab Dr. Bove's December 1983 memo to the AABB board and put it up on the easel.

"Dr. Englemen have you had an opportunity to review Dr. Bove's Report to the Board in preparing to testify today?"

"Yes, I did."

"Dr. Englemen, will you read and highlight the parts that are relevant to the opinions you have in this case."

Dr. Engleman goes to the easel and stands between it and the jury, yellow marker in his right hand. "This is an internal memo from Dr. Bove to the AABB board in December 1982, which says AIDS is a 'major problem in the blood collecting sector.' He continues, 'My current best guess is that we are dealing with an infectious agent able to be spread by blood and blood products and individuals who receive large quantities of factor concentrate are at increased risk.'"

"Dr. Englemen, what significance does that internal memo have on your opinions in this case?"

"It shows that they privately acknowledged the evidence linking AIDS to the use of blood products."

Next I put Dr. Bove's January 28, 1983 Internal Report to the Board on the easel. The easel is little wobbly so I adjust it. "Dr. Englemen, did you rely upon Dr. Bove's January 28, 1983 memo in preparing to testify today?" He doesn't wait for the next question about what relevance it has to his opinions. He just leaps into his answer.

"This is an internal memo to the AABB board just weeks after the CDC published its MMWR about the twenty-month-old infant being infected with AIDS from a blood transfusion that we discussed earlier. Dr. Bove writes to the board, 'This increases the probability that AIDS is spread by blood.'"

"Dr. Englemen, please read and highlight the next line for the jury?"

"Dr. Bove writes, 'There is little doubt in my mind that additional transfusion-related cases and additional cases in patients with hemophilia will surface.'"

"Please read the next line to the jury?"

"The most we can do in this situation is buy time. By that I mean it will be essential for us to take some active steps to screen out donor populations who are at risk of AIDS. Additionally, Dr. Bove says, 'We do not want anything that we do now to be interpreted by society or legal authorities, as agreeing with the concept, as yet unproven, that AIDS can be spread by blood.'"

"Dr. Englemen, what relevance does that have to your opinions in this case?"

"It clearly demonstrates that privately they admit there is a link between AIDS and blood products but want to 'buy time,' as they put it."

I zero in on the final questions of Dr. Englemen's direct examination. All the other questions were to lay the foundation for him to give his expert opinion as a blood banker against the AABB. I pick up the third legal pad from the counsel table to read the questions exactly as I wrote them out the night before. I pause for a minute to look over the next question and at Dr. Englemen in the witness stand. I am still in a state of disbelief that he is here.

In the weekend last year which Patti and I had planned as business and pleasure, we were catching the flight home on Sunday evening. I suggested we check out Chinatown for the rest of the afternoon—our first non-business excursion of the weekend.

"What about Ed Englemen?" Patti wanted to know.

"It's no use, Patti. He has not returned a single call."

"Look, we are out here, you might as well call him." As we were putting on our coats, I picked up the room phone and dial Stanford. I look at Patti, who was waiting to get this over with. She checked the bathroom and closets to see if we had left anything, though she had already done so twice already. Dr. Englemen's assistant answers the phone. I recognized her voice by then, and she knew mine. She was always gracious with the way she let me down.

"Hello, it's George Baxter. I am in San Francisco and I thought as long as I am here maybe I can meet with Dr. Englemen." As I talked, I signaled Patti to grab a bottle of water for our walk.

I almost dropped the phone when Dr. Englemen's assistant told me to come down to Stanford by 6:00 p.m. I checked the time on the digital clock radio next to the bed. It was already 3:00 p.m. We rushed out the door and rented a car at nearest the Budget counter.

The tall palm trees that perfectly lined each side of Palm Drive, Palo Alto, Stanford's main entrance, all the way down to Stanford tower, were picturesque. Spanish tile roofs and stained-glass windows bespoke of affluence. Everything was so symmetrical. It sure isn't the state college where Patti and I met in our junior year. I drove around the campus looking for the Stanford Blood Center on Welsh Drive.

There was just one chair in his office. He was not expecting me to show up with Patti. Instinctively, I grabbed a chair from the reception area, lifted it through his doorway and over his desk so that Patti could join us. He went along with the temporary disruption to his office so Patti could join us. She kept apologizing and staring concentratedly at his stapler.

The clock on his wall said 5:15 p.m., so there is a rushed feeling. He was polite and asked about our trip, but I went straight for the questions.

"Dr. Englemen, I read that you started screening donors for AIDS here at Stanford in June 1983?"

"Yes, that's true." He cleared his sinus and breathed inward. "All the blood donors who came to Stanford had to be tested for abnormal T cells on the day of donation. If the donor had abnormally low T cells, then we rejected their blood."

"Did the testing work?"

"Let me put it this way," Dr. Englemen proudly proclaimed, even through his wheezy head cold. "We rejected one donor who was allowed to give blood at several Bay Area blood banks. He had AIDS, and we prevented his blood from entering the Stanford hospital community."

"Dr. Englemen, my client's transfusion was on August 23, 1984, more than fourteen months after you began testing here at Stanford. Would you agree that it was negligent for a blood center not to test donors by then?"

"Yes, I agree with that." He did not even hesitate to answer.

"Will you testify in my case?" This time he paused reluctantly, as though he did not want to embarrass me with Patti there.

"George, how many lawyers are in your firm?" He already knows that I am a sole practitioner from my letterhead and endless faxes to him. "I will only back a winner, George."

There was another deadening pause, and the clock struck 6:00 p.m. Dr. Englemen tried to convince his industry and its regulators to do something about unsafe blood, but was brutally criticized for it. The blood industry accused him of using nothing more than a marketing gimmick to attract patients to Stanford hospital, and his staff was ostracized at trade meetings.

"Dr. Englemen, if I have questions, may I call you?" That was the first time I met Dr. Englemen. I flew out to his office three times after that, uninvited, even after he continued ignoring my calls.

"Dr. Englemen, I hope you are not going to make me fly out here each time I have a question?" I asked him, on my third trip to Stanford.

"I just wanted to make sure you are not a quitter, George." He smiled.

The courtroom is quiet as the jurors watch me read my next question to Dr. Englemen. It looks amateurish, but I have to protect the record and get it just right.

"Dr. Englemen, based upon your education, training, and experience in blood banking, do you have an opinion as to whether the American Association of Blood Banks was negligent in not recommending surrogate testing to screen donors before Mr. Snyder was transfused on August 23, 1984?"

"Yes, I do. It was negligent."

I flip the page on my legal pad to read the next question. "Dr. Englemen, do you have an opinion that the American Association of Blood Banks failed to act in a reasonable and prudent manner by not recommending hepatitis B core antibody testing as a surrogate test for AIDS by August 23, 1984, when Bill Snyder was transfused?"

"Yes. The evidence showed a clear link between AIDS and blood products by then. The American Association of Blood Banks failed to act in a reasonable and prudent manner by not testing donors."

I breathe a sigh of relief. No matter what happens now, I got in the prima fascia case. That means the basic criteria of the case, a negligent act by the defendant that causes an injury to the plaintiff. I sit down at the counsel table, turn around and acknowledge Patti, Roslyn, and Bill, who sinks into his wheelchair.

"Mr. Matthews, cross-examination?" I was hoping for a short recess so Patti could make a café run and bring back some apple juice for my much needed energy surge. I also wanted the jury to have time to absorb Dr. Englemen's testimony.

"Yes, your Honor." Matthews checks the alignment of his jacket and tie, stands from the counsel table and walks over to Dr. Englemen. His expensive tie is in a neat, diamond-shaped knot near his collar and looks like the head of a cobra. "Dr. Englemen, how much are you charging to testify here today?"

"I charge $350 per hour, Mr. Matthews." There is an instant buzz from the jury that makes me uncomfortable. Matthews knew he would get a reaction from the jurors over that question. Most jurors have jobs in which their two-month long absence will create a hardship. Dr. Engleman's hourly fee is more than what most of them make in a week. It was particularly caustic because Matthews knew I sought out blue-collar, *The Daily News*-reading versus *The Wall Street Journal*-reading jurors for my case, and was now using my asset against me.

"And how many hours have you billed Mr. Baxter, so far in this case?" I quietly cringe in my seat. Mr. Englemen's bill, with all the meetings, depositions, travel to Hackensack, is over twenty thousand dollars.

"I would have to check, I don't know for sure." That is because I have not paid him, and he has been sympathetic enough not to ask.

Matthews begins to throw hypothetical numbers at Dr. Englemen, asking him to take a guess at the time he spent on the case. "Sixty? Eighty? Maybe a hundred?"

"I have to go back and check." Dr. Englemen really does not know.

"You're being paid a lot of money to be here today."

"It is the same rate I charge if I am back at Stanford seeing patients."

"Do you claim the income you make from testifying in your taxes, Dr. Englemen?"

"Objection, your Honor. Dr. Englemen's already testified that he does not know." Matthews agrees to move on to his next question rather than have my objection sustained before the jury. He has got his mileage out of these ad hominem questions by distracting the jurors from the facts of Bill's case, antagonizing Dr. Englemen for his income and lifestyle. It is the kind of cheap but crafty cross-examination trick lawyers use to get jurors to reject a strong testimony.

"Dr. Englemen, you did not use core testing at Stanford, did you?"

"No, we used the T cell test."

"And, that is because you were already studying T cells at Stanford?" The blood bankers have prepped Matthews well. He tells the jury about a grant Stanford received for a sophisticated state-of-art device to study immune T cells. "Since you did not use core testing, then you have no first hand knowledge about it?"

"I relied upon the data coming out from the Centers for Disease Control published in their MMWRs."

"Was it not the industry standard to not test donors with core testing in 1984, prior to the plaintiff's transfusion?"

"The evidence was good that—"

"Answer my question."

"Mr. Matthews, a reasonable blood banker—"

"Dr. Englemen, answer my question."

I cannot let Matthews box Englemen into a yes or no answer to his narrowly constructed question.

"Objection, your Honor. Mr. Matthews is not allowing Dr. Englemen to answer the question."

"Mr. Matthews, let Dr. Englemen finish his answer." Judge Van Tassel hardly looks up from taking notes.

"Go ahead and finish your answer, Dr. Englemen." I say, as I sit back down at counsel table.

"The evidence was good that something had to be done. A reasonable blood banker would have implemented one of the surrogate tests recommended by the CDC. I used the T cell test because we were already studying it. However, other blood banks could have used core antibody to screen donors at risk for transmitting AIDS."

Matthews boldly takes my own blow-up of the December 10, 1982 MMWR and puts it on the easel. "Dr. Englemen, read the title of this exhibit for the jury?"

"Possible Transfusion-Associated Immune Deficiency."

"Possible, right?" Matthews demands. "Doesn't the word possible convey it was still unproven? There was no consensus in the blood banking and public health community."

"The evidence was good—"

"It was only a working hypothesis. Nothing could be done until Dr. Luc Montagnier isolated the viral agent."

"It was not necessary to wait until the viral agent was isolated," Dr. Englemen retorts forcefully. It was a crisis and a working hypothesis should have been enough. They only waited for the viral agent to be isolated because it affected a part of the population nobody liked: drug addicts and homosexuals.

"Isn't it possible, Dr. Englemen, that dedicated public health experts can disagree?"

"Objection to what is *possible*, judge?" I hate that word, "possible."

"He can answer the question. Overruled." I cringe and my quashed attempt.

"Mr. Matthews, any legitimate doubt about how AIDS was transmitted and how to prevent it from contaminating blood ended by mid-1983." Englemen sticks to his guns and does not cave in to Matthews' bullying. This frustrates Matthews so much that his tie is noticeably askew, so he tries a softer approach.

"Tell me, Dr. Englemen, do you believe there was an industry conspiracy?"

I bite the paper cup I am sipping my water from as I cringe for the second time. I did not see that question coming. I had briefed Marc Conant and Don Francis on the conspiracy theory, but never shared it with Dr. Englemen. We never discussed it because, frankly, he is far too intellectually conservative to abide by such sensational terminology.

"Dr. Englemen, do you believe there was a conspiracy in this case?" Matthews repeats. I stop my nervous doodling and put down the pencil.

"Yes, I do." Dr. Engleman says. "There was a conspiracy to just do nothing."

I slowly lift my head and look at Dr. Englemen in surprise. He did not hold back.

Matthews is a smart and seasoned trial lawyer, but his disdain for Dr. Englemen got the better of him and he broke the golden rule: never ask a question unless you already know the answer.

CHAPTER TWENTY-SEVEN

Bill and Roslyn visit my office so we can rehearse their testimonies. Bill is a reticent man whose stoicism prevents him from airing complaints. Although it is a quality in people of his generation, I know it will hurt him in court. He needs to open up to the jury, make them feel like it could have been any of them in his chair. Roslyn marches through the door first, like she did three years ago. I can recognize the rhythms of their footsteps by now: Bill's is slow and steady, Roslyn's is brisk but backtracks frequently in order to help Bill walk. Today, the footsteps are doubled.

"Hi George. These are our boys, Alfred and Steven." It is the first time I am meeting Bill and Roslyn's boys. They are barely fifteen but 6 feet tall and 180 pounds. Their arms and legs are muscular, sinewy like tree trunks. Alfred is slightly larger than Steven. They are restless, catapulting themselves from their chairs every few seconds to examine something different: the copier, the San Francisco poster, the fish tank. Steven begins to prod the fish tank, as though trying to catch the plastic diver's attention. The whole tank begins to shake and I can hear the water slosh around.

"Steven, sit down!" Roslyn shrieks.

Though I am just as tall as the twins, I am not sure I would be able to handle them if they became agitated. Roslyn, barely

5'2, grabs Steven by the elbow tries to seat him back down next to Alfred, but he won't budge.

"Stephen, please sit next to your brother," she tries again. Roslyn is one of those people whose tenderness comes through the cracks of a stern, inflexible disposition. I used to dismiss her as abrasive, but I see now that it is how she has to be.

She walks over to Alfred. His eyes, almost completely shut, resemble tadpoles. He utters something throaty but inaudible. Roslyn takes out a handkerchief and wipes the saliva collecting on the side of his mouth. The brain damage is more severe than I thought.

"Steven, sit over here." Bill's firm voice surprises Steven, and he sits down without a complaint.

"I usually leave them with my sister when we come up from Florida to see you, but she wasn't home yet," Roslyn explains. I admire her for not being apologetic.

"That's okay." I try to relax Roslyn. They are cold so she gives them their coats and seats them in the other room. She calmly tells them over and over again to wait for her.

"Bill, I want to go through you testimony for tomorrow with you."

"Sure, all right." He says, watching the boys through the open door.

"Did you look over the questions?" I have two legal pads filled with questions I intend to ask Bill. I copied them and sent them down to Florida weeks ago for him to look over. Bill stares at me blankly.

"Bill, it is important that you open up to the jury. I know this is hard for you, but you get only this one chance to testify, and then it is forever over."

"Sure." The twins cannot settle down.

"Alfred, stop it." Roslyn barks. Alfred gargles indiscernible speech.

"I am dropping them off at my sister's and I will be back." Roslyn tells me.

"All right. I will begin with Bill and be ready for you by the time you get back."

"Alfred, put your coat on." Roslyn begins to reach for his coat from the back of the chair. It is a wool, maroon baseball jacket with leather arms. It looks heavy, but Roslyn instinctually helps Alfred put his arms through the sleeves. Alfred's hands are huge, the size of baseball gloves. He stands still and patiently waits as Roslyn does the same with Steven. She zippers them up and leads them out hand-in-hand. Bill sits across from my desk and looks lost without Roslyn beside him.

I go through the pages of questions with Bill, but he cannot get beyond one-word answers. "Bill, this is your chance to tell the jury about what they did to you. Do you understand?"

"Yeah, I understand." Bill's face has turned ashen and drawn. He fades after barely twenty minutes.

"Just try to relax on the witness stand. The jurors want to help you, but you have to tell them your story."

Bill nods that he understands. Roslyn drops the boys off in Fairlawn, about fifteen minutes from my office. When she returns, Bill is too exhausted. Roslyn and I spend an hour going through her testimony while Bill lays supine on the lined-up chairs in the reception area.

By the time I get home, Courtney is asleep. Patti stayed up and waited with a plate of dinner leftovers. That is the way trial is, in court all day, nights prepping the next witness, running on caffeine and adrenaline. Patti and I sit at the kitchen table and Abby nestles her neck on my knee. I pet her head and realized how happy I was to have Patti's company while eating dinner after 11PM.

"Courtney's teacher sent home a note today for talking during class." Patti gives me a snapshot of my other life. "I am going to see him after class tomorrow, but I will be in court in the morning to sit with Roslyn."

Patti moves my plate aside once I'm done and squeezes my hand. "Don't worry. You're doing great."

"All rise." The courtroom stands in unison. The jurors come out from the jury room door and fill the jury box. Judge Van Tassel takes his seat. I keep checking over my questions for Bill, sipping water.

"Mr. Baxter, are you ready to proceed?"

"Yes, your Honor." I turn to push Bill's wheelchair to the witness stand, but he stops me. Bill is too proud for that, but he cannot make it on his own. He finally gives up and looks up at me. I lean over and lend him my right arm. He takes it to lift himself up from the wheelchair. I feel his weight on my arm as we carefully take slow, methodic steps to the witness stand. My stomach churns when I realize how light he feels: barely more than a heavy grocery bag. I cannot believe there was a point in time where I avoided shaking this same man's hand.

Bill is nervous, so as I ease him into the witness stand, I whisper, "Bill, they want to help you, so relax." I walk back to the counsel table and begin to question him as planned.

"Good morning, Bill." I want him to have a moment before we begin.

"Good morning." He mumbles.

"Bill, how are you feeling today?"

"I'm weak. I'm always tired." He is not looking at the jury like we discussed. I begin with the first question on my legal pad.

"Bill, tell the jury how you felt when you first got the news that you received a transfusion from a man who has AIDS?"

"I got scared."

"What do you mean, scared?"

"I had only seen those people on television with AIDS and it frightened me."

"What did you do after you received the letter from the blood bank?"

"I got tested at Halifax and I got AIDS."

"Bill, tell the jury how your life has changed because of your infection with AIDS?"

"This disease, it has taken over my life. The medications they give me make me sick."

"How do they make you feel, Bill?"

"Nauseous, like I need to throw up. I am tired all the time." Bill is freezing up. He is too shy and afraid to look at the jury. I have to do something. I pour a cup of water and bring it to him. As I hand it to him, I whisper again, "Bill, try to relax. They want to hear what happened to you." Then rather than go back to the counsel table, I remain close to him at the witness stand.

"Bill, please tell the jury what you mean by weak?"

"This disease is all through me. I am always too sick to help my wife with the boys."

"Did you used to help Roslyn more with the boys?"

"Yeah, she needs my help with them."

"Why Bill? Tell the jury why Roslyn needs your help?" Bill explains about the boys, as he fades before my eyes. I have to make it quick for him, but the jury has to hear a little more.

"Bill, are you all right to continue a little longer?"

"Yeah."

"Tell the jury how your life has changed since you were diagnosed with AIDS?"

"I stopped kissing my wife. I used to like to kiss her, but now I don't because I don't know how this disease spreads. Maybe if I kiss her she could get it."

"What else, Bill? What is different for you?"

"I keep my toothbrush away from Roslyn's toothbrush. I make sure mine doesn't touch hers or the boys' toothbrush." Bill is drained. So I ask a final question.

"Bill, what disturbs you the most with your illness?"

"I don't know how Roslyn will take care of the boys without me. I don't want them put into some mental hospital or something. I heard stories about those places. I don't want that for them." Our practice session lasted forty minutes, but on the witness stand, Bill has clammed up after five. I need to go through his hospitalizations for the jury, but it is cruel to let him continue. After Bill's final answer, I sit down at the counsel table.

"Mr. Matthews, cross-examination?" Judge Van Tassel asks.

"No, your Honor." Matthews is a smart trial lawyer who knows better than to cross-examine a witness like Bill. There is nothing to be gained by it for him. I am relieved that Bill's testimony is over, but I am more worried than ever that Bill cannot make it through the trial.

"All right, ladies and gentlemen, I am excusing you early today. The lawyers and I have housekeeping that we have to do, so you get to leave early this Friday." The jurors seem to like Judge Van Tassel and smile at him. "Remember my instructions to you not to discuss the case." Different jurors reciprocate and wish the judge a good weekend as they file out.

"Mr. Baxter, who is your next witness for Monday?" Judge Van Tassel waits until the last juror is out.

"Dr. Conant, your Honor."

"All right, counsel. Have a good weekend." Judge Van Tassel says, leaving the bench.

Roslyn parked her rented car in the handicapped space outside the courthouse's side entrance. Patti, Roslyn, Bill and I get into an empty elevator down.

"Thanks, George." Roslyn unexpectedly says to me.

Patti joins in and lightens the moment. "Yeah, nice job honey."

We reach the street level handicapped ramp and I wheel Bill out from the court building. Together, we lift Bill from his wheelchair and help him into the car.

That evening, Courtney and I break out the frozen pizza dough. Once again, we throw flour all over the pizza pan and use a rolling pin to flatten the dough. Patti picked up a new metal rolling pin that I know will give the end product its crispness. I twirl the dough over my head, singing a made-up Italian song. We were excited to see how Cracker Barrel and gourmet pizza sauce would enliven the satisfying but bland fare we were used to back when I couldn't pay my mortgage. I take it out from the oven and cut it up with the new pizza cutter Patti also picked up. It has a small sharp wheel at the end, and glides over the pizza.

After dinner, I lay down on the coach and don't wake up until early Saturday evening. Patti is cooking and Abby is laying on the floor at her feet. Abby is always nearby, and we have to be careful not to trip over her.

"What are you making?"

"These are for next week's dinner. There is no time to cook during the week with court." Patti fills a half dozen freezer bags with a beef stew and puts them into the freezer.

"Will you help set the table?" Patti asks. "It is almost dinner." I begin getting the plates from the cabinet. "Also, tell Courtney to start getting ready for dinner?" The kitchen phone rings.

"Hello?" Patti answers. By the way she is talking, I can tell it is someone who has never called us before. I flail my arms and raise my head, asking her to tell me who it is. Patti holds up her finger and impatiently gestures for me to wait. Then she says to the person on the other end of the phone, "He is right here."

Before she lets go of the phone, she says, "Honey, it's Judge Ciolino. He has something to tell you and doesn't want you to get upset."

I look at Patti with apprehension. Why would the Judge Peter Ciolino, the boss of all the judges, the man on the forth floor of the courthouse, be calling me at home on the weekend?

Patti reluctantly hands the telephone to me and I receive the news: Judge Van Tassel has suddenly died from a heart attack. I cannot believe it. I was just in court with him the day before, and now he is gone. My stomach feels twisted and I lean over a table chair.

"They want a mistrial," Judge Ciolino says. I already knew that the instant he gave me the news. There is no way Bill will survive or I can afford to start over again. It is an absolute disaster.

On June 4, 1994, *The Record* carries the article on Judge Van Tassel's untimely death in the middle of trial. I stop at the Van Emburge Funeral Home on Ridgewood Avenue and give my condolences to Judge Van Tassel's family. I meet Judge Van Tassel's wife and two daughters. We exchange a couple of stories about the judge. They tell me how he enjoyed being called back from retirement to try the case. As I stand in the reception area, large groups of people wearing black contrast with the pristine white arrangements of orchids, chrysanthemums and lilies in the parlor. The impersonality of it was something I would never have seen in Janet's funeral, or rather, something I never did see. I remember it rained that day, and I try to imagine the rest. The only attendees are Kyle, Naomi and Christian. Scottish bagpipers play dirges as the children watch, because they cannot bear to look at the polished wood coffin in the dirt. The casket emits a hollow percussion from being pelted by rain.

CHAPTER TWENTY-EIGHT

On Monday, I head over to the courtroom, partly because I do not know what else to do with myself. It is like having a phantom limb. I have put years into Bill's case and now, weeks into the trial, and it screeches to an abrupt and unfair end. I pack up my files and exhibits, which are still splayed out on the table from Friday like the set of a play. I place the MMWR blowups back into the brown paper they were wrapped in the day I got them from the printer. Dr. Bove's blowup is still leaning against the counsel table where I left it, practically sneering. The quiet and emptiness of the courtroom is so vast I can sink into it. "What the hell am I supposed to do now?" I ask myself. I have no other cases, and put all my energy into winning this one.

Marc Conant walks into the courtroom after arriving from San Francisco. He walks down the court isle toward me and it only takes a second for him to realize that nobody else is coming.

"What is going on, George?" He asks, puzzled.

"Let's go have lunch." We walk down to Miyoshi's Japanese restaurant on Mercer Street. Marc puts his duffel bag on the floor. He came straight from the airport.

"Sorry I didn't tell you earlier." I pick the small grains of rice on my sushi off the seaweed one by one, unable to eat.

"So, what does this mean?" Marc asks.

"It is an automatic mistrial. After five weeks, a mistrial."

"I am sorry to hear this, George. Is there anything I can do?"

"No, it is the way it goes sometimes, I guess." I am trying to appear professional; it's not working.

"You came a long way, George."

"Well, I started in 1989."

Marc ignored my self-effacing joke. "Closer than any other lawyer I know." He tries to remind me how after three years of gathering evidence, tracking down witnesses and winning the appellate court decisions, we got all the way to the courthouse door with Bill's case. Marc's attempts to console me are useless.

"Coming close only counts in a game of horseshoes," I retort. "This was supposed to be big." This was supposed to be case where the people who gave 29,000 people AIDS were hauled into court.

"I know," Marc sighs. We barely talk for the rest of lunch. I call Roslyn; she takes Bill home to Florida where he can rest. I call Don Francis; he is apologetic but irate. I do not have the courage to call Ed Engleman.

I want to be alone so I walk to the office. I throw the mail aside and sit on my chair, unable to move. The office is so quiet I can hear the buzzing sound of the ceiling light. Even the pigeons are quiet.

Judge Ciolino invites Matthews and me to come into his chambers. It is a view looking out over Hackensack from the top of the rotunda. I grew up seeing this dome only from the outside, and didn't even think there would be an office it, let alone that I'd be sitting there one day. What an anticlimactic place to get such dreary news, I think to myself. Judge Ciolino does not take the time to ask for our thoughts or arguments. It is apparent that he has already made up his mind, and we are there as a matter of protocol. I sit in the chair across from him, looking over his shoulder at the window.

"George, Ed, how are you gentlemen?"

Matthews puts his hand on his chest. "My deepest condolences over Judge Van Tassel, Your Honor."

"We're all taken aback by Judge Van Tassel's passing, Your Honor," I mumble, still slouching.

Matthews wastes no time: "Under the circumstances, Your Honor, we move for a mistrial."

"There is not going to be a mistrial." Judge Ciolino snaps. "I asked you to come in so I could tell you what *I* have decided to do." I cannot believe what I am hearing. "I have ordered the daily trial transcripts, and I am giving the case to Judge Stark to continue."

Matthews immediately objects. "Judge, we are halfway through the trial. It is prejudicial to my client."

"Judge Stark will read the transcripts at night while she continues the trial."

Who is this Judge Stark? I ask myself. Is she some kind of super-judge who can read weeks of testimony by night and fill in the rest by day?

Judge Ciolino continues, "There is not going to be a mistrial, Counsel. I already explained what happened to the jury and they understand. They will be in Judge Stark's courtroom to resume the case on Wednesday. That is what I have decided. Thank you for coming in."

I hold on to my professional composure long enough to make it out of Judge Ciolino's chambers and to a bench in the hallway. I collapse on the edge of the bench, repeating something along the lines of "Holy Shit," over and over again.

On Wednesday, I head to over to our new courtroom to resume Bill's trial. I run into juror number five on the elevator. Jurors and lawyers do not usually talk with each other during a sitting trial, but being trapped in the small elevator and after all the agony transparent in the courtroom, we exchange a "good morning." The jurors must have expressed their willingness to sit in on the trial longer than anyone expected. I am sure their commitment factored into Judge Ciolino's decision. Juror five is a slender, middle-aged woman married to a prominent lawyer in town. She seems like the type to own a vacation home in Vermont. She always pays attention and looks alert during trial, but her face never reveals any emotions that I can read. When I get into the courtroom, other jurors are still arriving and waiting in the jury box. Juror one has stopped wearing a necktie now, which tells me he is settled into trial. This is no Macarena jury. It is clear they feel like they are doing something that is important to see to the end.

As Judge Stark picks up her notes, I notice Matthews looks more agitated than his usual composed demeanor allows. Bill stayed in New Jersey after hearing the news of the continued trial. Marc Conant, who got the news just when he reached the airport at San Francisco, bought a ticket back to New Jersey and is now on the witness stand.

"Dr. Conant, did you review the Halifax medical records of Bill Snyder in preparing to testify today?" I plan on using Marc to go through Bill's hospitalizations, which Bill was unable to do.

"Yes, Mr. Baxter. I have reviewed all of Mr. Snyder's medical records, including the look-back notification of donor 29F0847."

"Dr. Conant, based upon your review of the medical records, are you prepared to offer your expert opinion, based up a reasonable degree of medical probability, whether Bill Snyder was infected with AIDS from the transfusion he received on August 26, 1984?" I read it straight from my note pad.

"Yes, Mr. Baxter, I am." Marc turns toward the jury and flips through Bill's chart for a minute. "Bill Snyder was transfused on August 26, 1984 with a unit of platelets that came from a male donor, identified as 29F0784. Later, in a subsequent blood drive, the blood center discovered that this donor has AIDS. A letter was sent to Mr. Snyder advising he be tested. Mr. Snyder tested positive for AIDS at the Halifax Medical Center. Mr. Snyder has no other risk factors. He is not homosexual and does not use intravenous drugs. Therefore, it is my opinion, based upon a reasonable degree of medical probability, that Bill Snyder was infected with AIDS by the transfusion he received on August 26, 1984."

"Your Honor, I am going to ask Dr. Conant to explain Bill Snyder's prognosis to the jury. It is very sensitive, so with your permission, I would like to wheel Mr. Snyder out from the courtroom during this part of the testimony."

"Go ahead, Mr. Baxter." Judge Isabel Stark is young and sharp-tongued, which cuts lawyers right down to size. She wears a feminine, white-laced collar on her judicial robe.

All heads turn to watch Roslyn and the bailiff wheel Bill from behind the counsel table, up the courtroom isle, and out the door into the hallway. The sound of the wheels scraping against the floor as they leave echoes and remains in the room even after they are gone. I am hoping these dramatics will convey the tragedy of Bill's story, which Bill was unable to do in his short testimony.

"Dr. Conant, will you please explain Bill's prognosis to the jury?"

"Based upon Mr. Snyder's T cell count and viral load, I would say that he may live another twelve months."

"Can you explain to the jury T cells and viral loads?"

"Certainly. May I use the easel?" There is large white paper on the easel to draw on.

"Use anything you feel you need to help the jury understand you answer."

Dr. Conant picks up a black crayon and draws the outline of a locomotive train heading toward another line. The thick black crayon has a very dramatic affect. Dr. Conant takes a step back to observe. "I am obviously not an artist." A few jurors laugh. "Bill is this train heading toward this line, the cliff. When he reaches the cliff, he will drop. The viral load, that is, the speed at which viral replication is occurring, is the speed of this train heading to the cliff." The jury's mood abruptly shifts back to solemnness.

"Dr. Conant, where on the tracks of your drawing is Bill Snyder today?"

"Bill Snyder is right here." Marc draws an "X" down the tracks close to the steep cliff lines. "Bill's T cells are his immune system. The lower his T cell count, the less immunity he has to opportunistic diseases. Bill's T cell count is below 230. That means he has no immune system." Marc highlights the "X" he drew on the tracks. "Bill is about right here. When he reaches this point, his lungs will fill up with fluid. He will be unable to breathe and will suffocate from pneumonia. Bill has fought off pneumonia three times at Halifax, but the next time it is not likely he will survive." There is a long silence after Marc Conant's gripping testimony.

"Your Honor, may I bring Mr. Snyder back into the courtroom?"

"Yes, Mr. Baxter." Judge Stark's piecing eyes tell me she understood my theatrical strategy. Roslyn and the bailiff wheel Bill back into the courtroom, down the aisle and maneuver his wheelchair behind me at the counsel table as the jurors watch.

"Proceed, Mr. Baxter." Judge Stark says as soon as Bill is settled again.

"Yes, your Honor." I look over the Cumming Red Cross memo about the industry "sticking together" against the CDC, in the stack of blow-ups leaning against the counsel table while Dr. Conant, the jury and Judge Stark patiently await my next question. The American Red Cross document is crucial to proving the blood bankers' conspiracy and, thereby, shattering the industry standard. I decide to go for it, slowly lifting it from the stack.

"Objection, your Honor." Matthews jumps to his feet. "Mr. Baxter can't show that document."

"All right, counsel, hold it. Let's excuse the jury." Judge Stark has the bailiff lead the jury back to the jury room. They're used to clearing out while Matthews and I fight out legal objections by now.

Judge Stark jumps in with her own questions. "Dr. Conant, are you familiar with this memo?"

"Yes, your Honor."

"How familiar?"

"It has been produced in a number of Red Cross transfusion cases that I have testified in, your Honor."

"All right, Mr. Baxter, continue with the proffer."

"Dr. Conant, read the parts of this memo that you intend to rely on?"

Dr. Conant points to the memo and reads it for Judge Stark. "This part here: 'Of those actions which have been suggested, the only two things we are not doing are asking direct questions of gays and testing blood samples. As time goes on we are liable to get more and more pressure to utilize these means also. If AIDS continues to double every six months, the concentration in gay males continues, and absent evidence to the contrary, the pressure is likely to be overwhelming in 6 to 12 months. Even if the evolving evidence of an epidemic wanes the CDC is likely to continue to play up AIDS—it has long been noted that CDC increasingly needs a major epidemic to justify its existence.

Then, Dr. Cumming continues, 'To the extent the industry, the American Red Cross, the Council of Community Blood Centers and the American Association of Blood Banks, sticks together against the CDC, it will appear to some segments of the public at least that we have a self interest which is in conflict with the public interest, unless we can clearly demonstrate that the CDC is wrong.'"

"Dr. Conant, explain how the memo you just read for judge Stark is relevant to your opinions in the case?"

"The American Red Cross memo, is dated February 5, 1983, and spells out how the industry, the American Red Cross, the American Association of Blood Banks, and Council of Community Blood Centers, have to stick together against the CDC. Similarly, Dr. Bove's memo, just a couple weeks earlier, also states how they are sticking together. It shows the industry leaders have decided to stick together against the CDC's recommendations to test blood for AIDS." A conspiracy, plain and simple.

"Thank you, Dr. Conant." I sit down at the counsel table. My proffer of the Red Cross memo is complete.

"Your Honor, this document has already been excluded by Judge Van Tassel." Matthews fights that she cannot now change a ruling in the middle of trial.

"I am going to permit Mr. Baxter to question Dr. Conant about it in the presence of the jury."

"It is hearsay. It is not even our document," Matthews fires back.

"I am going to permit Mr. Baxter to use it."

"You are handing me reversible error." Matthews argues to Judge Stark, pointing his finger.

"Your objection is overruled, Mr. Matthews." The wrath emanating from Judge Stark's bench is intimidating.

"It is reversible error." Matthews is relentless.

"Take it up with the appellate court, if you don't like it," Judge Stark snaps. The jury re-enters the courtroom. I am now permitted to ask Dr. Conant my questions in front of the jury. I go through the documents with Marc, emphasizing that the AABB and the Red Cross "stuck together" in order to delay testing blood. A few hours and a few legal pads later, we conclude.

"Dr. Conant, do you have an opinion whether the American Association of Blood Banks' refusal to recommend core testing to screen blood donors caused Bill Snyder to be infected with AIDS?"

"Yes, clearly it did. The donor in this case is both core and hepatitis B-core positive and would have been detected had they been testing the blood." I flip the pages, but cannot find a question I have not asked.

"Your Honor, the plaintiff rests its case."

CHAPTER TWENTY-NINE

They come, and they go, for weeks. Blood bankers from all around the country. Dr. Paul Holland of the Sacramento, California, Blood Center; Dr. Donald Louria of the New Jersey School of Medicine; Dr. George Grady, director of the Massachusetts Department of Health; Dr. Harold Oberman of the University of Michigan Hospital Blood Center; and Dr. Ernest Simon, ex-deputy director of the Federal Food and Drug Administration's blood division. Some in person, others by video. They pass by me unscathed, since Judge Van Tassel's ruling tied my hands from mentioning that the blood bankers eventually, in 1986, used core testing for hepatitis B, and, "as a bonus," AIDS.

I don't know who actually pulls the strings for the blood bankers' case, but whoever it is has enough influence to reach across the pond for a scientific giant, the most famous retrovirologist—if not the only famous retrovirologist—in the world, Dr. Luc Montagnier from the Pasteur Institute in France— the man who discovered HIV. He is to catch the Concorde from Paris to New York's John F. Kennedy Airport, where he will be then shuttled by helicopter to the nearby Teterboro Airport and brought to court. Dr. Montagnier ultimately wins a Nobel Prize. Over the past few years, his face has been all over magazines, scientific and health journals, and the lecturer's circuit. And now, he will arrive at our dingy Hackensack courtroom to testify against me. He is the blood bankers' celebrity witness. I fear the jury has forgotten the testimony of my witnesses by now, and a star like Dr. Montagnier will clench the case.

The morning of Dr. Montagnier's testimony, I drive to court absurdly early because I could not sleep. I drive through the parking lot of Sears, then the parking lot of Costco, then Dunkin' Donuts, and finally the court, aimless and unsure of what else to do. I sit in my car and watch the sun rise over the Hackensack River as my mind drifts back to the morning I sat on the floor outside Professor Slocum's door, desperate to get back into law school. I spent three days waiting outside his office to see him. It was my first year at Rutgers Law. Courtney was a baby; I was hauling ass working full time at a law firm. I needed extra money so I worked days, nights and weekends, researching law and writing briefs. I used to say that I am learning law on the job, but that did not help me pass my law school exams. I failed a couple of courses, including torts, and they were kicking me out. I was so devastated that when I got home, I could not tell Patti what had happened. I just ate dinner pretending that I would someday become a lawyer; I made knock-knock jokes and cleared the dishes and tickled Courtney's feet. After brushing my teeth, I lingered in the bathroom for more than an hour.

The next morning, I didn't know what to do, so I left for school as I had every other morning. I sat in a Newark coffee shop watching students go to class. I just sat there morning after morning for two weeks, in complete disbelief that I would never go to class like that again. I just could not accept it. There had to be a way out of this trouble. Finally, I got an idea and I went to see Alfred Slocum, a sixties-radical-type black professor with a long goatee and shiny bald head, the dean of minority admissions.

I never acknowledged being admitted under the minority admissions program. Rutgers's minority admission program was color-blind, based more on educational and economic disadvantage rather than race. They admitted me because I never finished high school and served in the Marines. I kept this hidden because I wanted to be on track for the good ole boys club.

Professor Slocum always stretched my name out when we spoke: "M-i-s-t-e-r Baxter." I tell him that I've calculated my grade point average and, even with the failure, my overall GPA is a B, higher than what is required to stay in school. He is angry about the double standard that the scholastic standing committee used to kick me out: if I were black, they would have let it slide. He says it pisses him off because it means they have different expectations for white students and black students, and this offends him. He agrees to help me with an appeal. A couple of weeks later, we argue my case before an ad hoc committee of faculty and students.

I pace the hallway while the committee decides my fate. When Professor Slocum comes out from the deliberations, I can't read his face. Then, he cracks a smile: "M-i-s-t-e-r Baxter, you're back in." We agree that I will take the rest of that semester off and come back in the spring. As I step into the elevator, he asks, "Mr. Baxter, you are coming back, aren't you?"

It never would have occurred to me to quit.

The hallway is filled with blood bankers and people who want a glimpse of Dr. Montagnier. Marc Conant told me that the blood bankers circulated a press release saying that Dr. Montagnier was coming to testify, so local reporters scramble for an update on the trial before Judge Stark takes the bench. Curious courthouse workers and litigants gather in the hallway to see what is going on. It is probably a good thing Bill isn't here; he wouldn't be able to deal with the noise and spectacle. I am relieved when Judge Stark sits down and the court hushes to a quiet, with only the occasional click of a camera. But then I remember who I am supposed to cross-examine, and I am not so relieved anymore.

I doodle on a legal pad at the counsel table as Dr. Montagnier is called to the witness stand. I draw Fred Flintstone and put a polka dot necktie on him. I also doodle the Mayflower on the high seas with its sails full of wind, always sailing away. These are the same images I have been drawing on note pads since the sixth grade.

"Your Honor, Dr. Montagnier has to catch the Concord back to Paris this afternoon, so I request that his testimony be completed without a recess." Matthews makes clear that this geek-jetsetter needs to get back to his glamorous life in Europe. You can almost hear his car and helicopter on standby in the parking lot.

"That's all right, Mr. Matthews." Judge Stark is congenial about the request, in a way that seems to apologize for her sharpness during Marc Conant's testimony. "Mr. Baxter?"

"Yes, your Honor. I will try." Frankly, I have no cross-examination planned for him. I want him off the witness stand as fast as possible.

Spectators greet Dr. Montagnier as he confidently walks down the aisle, stopping to shake a hand or two. His head is remarkably square, with a jaw that seems to dip down from its otherwise precise geometry. Wave-like strands of hair fall to the left side of his face. He takes the witness stand.

"Please state your name for the record?" The bailiff asks him.

"Dr. Luc Montagnier."

"Please place your right hand on the bible?" The bailiff holds the bible to give him the oath before testifying. There is a surprising awkwardness about Dr. Montagnier when he raises the wrong hand and thrusts it out, as though saluting Adolf Hitler. A couple of jurors exchange glances. He quickly raises his other hand, but is uncertain whether to place his hand on the Bible or in the air. Perhaps he is not accustomed to American courtrooms. Jurors and court personnel continue to exchange glances over his clumsiness.

"Please place your *right* hand *on* the Bible." The bailiff directs. "Do you swear to tell the truth, the whole truth, and nothing but the truth, so help you God?"

"Yes." It sounded more like "oui."

Matthews begins going through Dr. Montagnier's qualifications. I interrupt Matthews by standing up and agreeing to stipulate Dr. Montagnier as an expert, to avoid the jury hearing his impressive credentials. But Matthews is too experienced to fall for this and insists on going through them for the jury anyway. So for the next twenty minutes, Matthews proudly gloats through the resume and accolades of Dr. Montagnier before the jury, like a proud father showing off to his country club friends.

"Dr. Montagnier, you are from the Pasteur Institute in Paris, France?"

"Yes."

"And, in the spring of 1984, you isolated HIV, the causative agent of the AIDS virus?"

"Yes." Dr. Montagnier speaks with a heavy French accent.

"Dr. Montagnier, before that great discovery, was it possible to have a test that could test donors for AIDS?"

"No no, no."

"Dr. Montagnier, there has been testimony in this case that the hepatitis B core antibody test would have worked as a surrogate test for donors at risk for transmitting AIDS. Do you agree with that?"

"No, no. It would have caused too many false positives."

The moment I hear Dr. Montagnier spout the usual blood bankers' defense jargon—"false positives"—the mystique of this giant fades. I figure the blood bankers bought him. Dr. Montagnier tells the jury there are parts of southern Italy, for example, where many people have been exposed to hepatitis but are otherwise healthy. They would all be rejected as blood donors because they have antibodies for hepatitis, even though they don't have AIDS.

Matthews boldly grabs my own blowup exhibit off the table to show Dr. Montagnier. It's the CDC date from the Atlanta meeting. He plans to have his celebrity witness discredit the testimony of my celebrity witness, Don Francis.

"Dr. Montagnier, I want to ask you about this study that the plaintiff's experts have relied on?"

"Objection." Everyone looks at me. "Judge, that's an epidemiology study and Dr. Montagnier has been offered as a virologist." I am not sure where there this objection comes from, but I cannot back down now. The blood bankers stare agape at my audacity to challenge to this visionary's scientific credibility.

"Your Honor, I was never informed that Dr. Montagnier was going to testify about this CDC study." I am grasping for anything that might work.

"Judge, it is for impeachment. Mr. Baxter's experts used this study when they testified." Matthews is surprised Judge Stark is listening to my objections.

"But, your Honor, not only is Dr. Montagnier not an epidemiologist, but also there's been no foundation laid that he is even familiar with this study."

"Mr. Matthews, ask Dr. Montagnier whether he has seen this study before today," Judge Stark orders.

"Dr. Montagnier, have you seen this CDC study before today?" Matthews complies.

"No, I have not." Dr. Montagnier flips the pages of the CDC study, slightly bewildered about what is happening.

Judge Stark takes over and voir dires Dr. Montagnier. That is when a judge examines the witness herself to determine if the witness has the credentials or knowledge to testify about evidence. "Dr. Montagnier, when was the first time you saw this study?"

"Just now when the lawyer handed it to me." Dr. Montagnier still does not get it.

"So the first time you saw this study is this morning when Mr. Matthews gave it to you?" She asks again.

"Yes." Dr. Montagnier confirms.

"The objection is sustained." Judge Stark surprises everyone, and most of all, me.

"Your Honor. Mr. Baxter's experts used this study when they testified. Are you telling me I cannot examine Dr. Montagnier about Mr. Baxter's evidence?"

"Dr. Montagnier just said he has never seen this document before today when you handed it to him. I am not allowing you to examine with it," Judge Stark lashes back.

"Judge, you are precluding me from questioning Dr. Montagnier about the study plaintiff's experts relied on?" Matthews dares to ask again.

"Mr. Matthews, I am not permitting you to question this witness who is not an epidemiologist about an epidemiological study he admits he never saw before."

Mathews asserts that Judge Stark just handed him another reversible error. "I want it clear for the record." Matthews is threatening an appeal over the ruling. After all, the blood bankers flew Dr. Montagnier all the way in from France and his testimony was just cut short.

Matthews sits down at the counsel table still muttering something about reversible error. This surprise ruling limiting Dr. Montagnier's testimony pulls the rug out from under him. Now it's my turn.

"Dr. Montagnier, I have just a few questions, if you don't mind?" I want to keep it simple.

"Yes." He replies.

"Dr. Montagnier, southern Italy was not a Centers for Disease Control AIDS 'hot spot' like New York, Los Angeles or San Francisco, was it?"

"No."

"So the need to take precautions in these 'hot spots' was greater than in southern Italy?" It's basic epidemiology.

"Yes."

"Dr. Montagnier, are you aware that Dr. Englemen used the T cell test to screen donors at Stanford?"

"Yes."

"Well, would you agree that before you isolated the viral agent, that Dr. Engleman's T cell test was a good surrogate test to screen donors at risk for transmitting AIDS?"

"Yes."

The blood bankers were not prepared for him to agree. Neither was I.

"Objection."

"Judge, he just answered the question." I quickly argue back.

"Overruled." Judge Stark allows the answer to stand. I just turned Dr. Montagnier into my own witness.

"Thank you, Dr. Montagnier." I know when to quit.

Judge Stark excuses the jury. Matthews and his associates collect their notes from the counsel table. They look absolutely frustrated.

"Mr. Matthews, thank you for bringing Dr. Montagnier in to court for me." I could not resist the jab. Matthews mutters something about reversible error.

CHAPTER THIRTY

The courthouse café on the third floor has the worst coffee ever. The amount of coffee lawyers and court personnel drink warrants the stainless steel vac on the counter to be refilled every half hour, but the demand does not make it taste any fresher—instead, it tastes watery and the grounds get stuck between your teeth. Its only distinctive flavor is aluminum, and its only redeeming quality is convenience. Let's just say it does the job. Day after day of the trial, it sharpens my fuzzy confidence just enough for me to look the defendants in the eye. I cannot not fool myself into believing that Dr. Montagnier was brought down by my skill or trial acumen; it was all luck and I know it.

Dr. Kleinman, the next witness, is not one of the industry players present at the Atlanta meeting. He looks young enough to be a college athlete, but is the director of the American Red Cross's Lost Angeles Regional Blood Center. This is the first time I see him, and his square jaw and upward-tilting grin makes me uncomfortable. His youthfulness paired with his power over one of the largest regional blood centers are enough to make him a sure hit with any jury, and I worry his country club charisma eclipses his insolent, irritating pomposity.

"You're trying to mislead the jury," he announces. "Liar," he mouths to me silently. "He is being dishonest," he says out loud, directly after. Even Matthews has to quiet him down in order to take us through his direct examination. He questions Dr. Kleinman about all the CDC MMWRs in that painstaking way that is meant to tire and bore us. One by one, he refutes each one of the conclusions drawn up by my witnesses a week earlier. He debunks each testimony with an air of victory, as though reciting an acceptance speech for prom king. What troubles me is that he sounds intelligent.

"The infected baby was one case out of a millions of transfusions that year—it was no reason to create hysteria." He makes eye contact with the jury. "People would have postponed surgeries if they thought they were at risk of AIDS from blood." Shouldn't the patient have the right to decide that for themselves? I wanted to bark back at him but I had to control my temper. I did want my irritation to make his clean-cut, professional demeanor to look like a positive quality by contrast.

"So there was no consensus in the public health community that AIDS was transmitted through blood products?" Matthews insists.

"No, there was no consensus." Dr. Kleinman begins slandering Dr. Engleman. "His grand gesture of testing blood was just a marketing gimmick."

"Objection, you Honor—"

"It had no provable impact on safety," he talks over my objection.

"Excuse me, I have an objection." His tactic is to make the jury reconsider my credibility and I cannot let him do it.

"We all know what you are trying to do," he hisses.

"Your Honor, will you instruct Dr. Kleinman not to address me when I make an objection?"

"Dr. Kleinman, please allow Mr. Baxter to make his objections. Your counsel, Mr. Matthews will respond." Judge Stark calmly instructs Kleinman.

"He is trying to mislead the jury, your Honor." Dr. Kleinman is like a pit-bull.

"Judge, objection." I move close to Dr. Kleiman but out of hearing for the judge and jury. "Don't worry Dr. Kleinman, you will get yours in about five minutes." It is a playground fight now.

"Judge, objection." Matthews caught it.

Before sitting back down at the counsel table, I wait to catch Dr. Kleinman's eye hold five fingers at my chest. Matthews takes Dr. Kleiman through the industry standard of care argument. "It was not required by the FDA to test blood for AIDS when Bill Snyder was transfused." I catch Matthews and Kleinman exchange a smug smile.

"Dr. Kleinman, I have only a couple questions. You are the director of the Los Angeles Red Cross Blood Center? I try to lure Dr. Kleinman into a sense of his own aggrandizement.

"That's right." Dr. Kleinman's confidence is made of iron.

"And, Mr. Matthews asked you to testify today as an expert witness for the American Association of Blood Banks?"

"Yes." His quick answer reveals that he is annoyed, but he masks over it with a fake-cute sheepish smile.

"And as a blood bank expert, you want this jury to believe you? To accept your testimony as true?"

"Yes." He says, feigning patience.

"You want this jury to trust and rely on your testimony as an expert in blood-banking safety?"

"Yes." Dr. Kleinman reassures the jury by looking at them.

"You have not withheld anything from them, have you?"

"No." Dr. Kleinman does not take his eyes off the jury.

"Then how is it, Dr. Kleinman, that you did not mention the FDA blood recall that the FDA recently charged you with?"

"Objection." Matthews says immediately, before he has really process it. I do not think the blood bankers told Matthews about this recall.

Pandemonium breaks out at the counsel table as I ignore the objection and place the FDA Inspection Report under Kleinman's nose. I obtained it through a Freedom of Information Act Request.

"Judge, Mr. Baxter never gave me notice of this document." It is against court rules to surprise opponents with documents, but there are always loopholes if you look hard enough.

"It's cross-examination, your Honor. I didn't know if I would need it."

Dr. Kleinman looks at Matthews for help. Matthews keeps fighting for him. "Judge, I was not placed on notice about this document. Mr. Baxter cannot use it."

"I am using it to impeach Dr. Kleinman's credibility as an expert witness."

"I asked Mr. Baxter to produce a list of all the documents to be use at trial and this was not included." The lawyer in me feels a little bad for Matthews, because I know he is too smart to have used Dr. Kleinman as a witness. The blood bankers had definitely not informed him.

"It is a cross-examination, your Honor." I insist.

"The objection is overruled, Mr. Matthews." Judge Stark puts an end to the fighting.

I stand face to face with Dr. Kleinman at the witness stand, holding the FDA blood recall notice. "Dr. Kleinman, do you recognize this recall notice? Your name is on it, right here?" I point to his name in the lower corner of the document as responsible head. "It says here that the Food and Drug Administration forced a massive recall at your blood facility. Fourteen hundred units of blood that were unsafely tested for AIDS? Right?"

"Objection. Mr. Baxter is not allowing my client to answer the question."

"Let Dr. Kleinman answer the question, Mr. Baxter," Judge Stark states.

"It was the difference of interpretation over an FDA regulation. That's all." Dr. Kleinman widens his eyes begins to turn his head towards the jury to deploy his usual connect-with-the-jury-with-your-wide-incredulous-eyes trick, but I cut him off.

"Look at this document." I point to the FDA Inspection Report. "It says here, when the first test proved those units positive for HIV, you reran the test. The second test came out negative, so you labeled it *completely* nonreactive to HIV and sold it to hospitals all over Los Angeles?"

"It is a matter of interpretation." Dr. Kleinman says flippantly. It is as though putting profit before patient safety is what all the cool kids are doing.

I obnoxiously wave the FDA recall in front of his face.

"When you recall fourteen hundred units of unsafe blood, it not like a car recall. The blood has already been used. It has already been put into someone's arm." It has already given someone AIDS.

"You never actually got those units back, right?" I cannot help my voice from being raised.

"No."

I walk back to the counsel table and slam the document on its surface. "Still think this jury should believe you as a blood-safety exert, Dr. Kleinman?

Tom Asher told me about the FDA product recall of L.A. Red Cross blood. He even told me how to get the copy of the FDA inspector's report with a Freedom of Information Act request. He knows exactly where all the industry skeletons are buried. I make a mental note to call and thank him as Roslyn, Bill and I take the elevator downstairs.

The long trial days scrape of Bill's energy, starting at his face and extending downward. The straight line that used to define his shoulders slope further downward every time I see him. His arms look too heavy for him to bear. They hang limp over the sides of his wheelchair as Roslyn wheels him down the ramp that leads to the parking lot. As we help Bill into the blue handicapped van she rented, she tells me that she is going to take Bill and the boys back home to Florida. She matter-of-factly explains how they all need the structure and routine of home to cope with all that is happening as she collapses his wheelchair to stuff into the trunk. "The twins need to go back to school, Bill loves that couch . . ." she closes the trunk and abruptly turns around. She gives me a tight hug that I have to bend down to reciprocate.

"Just tell me when it's over," she says as she lets go.

I never see Roslyn cry. She just grazes her eye with the side of her palm before a tear dares to fall into the deepening lines of her face.

CHAPTER THIRTY-ONE

It seems like a long time ago when I hid between the quieter shelves of the mall bookstore and read about the CDC Atlanta meeting Randy Shilts' recounts in *And the Band Played On*. That meeting has become my life now—getting each member of that meeting to Hackensack in order to expose the truth: that the timeline and magnitude of the AIDS epidemic could have been drastically curbed if the blood bankers listened to the CDC. Corruption masqueraded as cautiousness, and what can be salvaged of its disastrous results are being salvaged under the dome of this musty New Jersey courthouse.

Today we have Dr. Herbert Perkins, director of San Francisco's Irwin Memorial Blood Center, on the witness stand. Irwin is the major blood supplier of blood products to all the Bay area hospitals, and Dr. Perkins held out against core testing donors for as long as possible. Even after the CDC reported the first infant infected with AIDS from Irwin's blood, he continued to deny transfusion AIDS. This will be the third time Dr. Perkins and Marc Conant will entangle over patient safety. The first time was right after Atlanta, when Marc Conant unsuccessfully led a group of physicians who were seeing their patients becoming infected from Irwin's blood in going public with their concern. The second time was in the Baby Osborn case, when Marc testified for the Osborn family and Perkins testified for the industry. Dr. Perkins' testimony caused the appellate court to reverse the jury verdict in the Osborn case, and that decision prevented all subsequent patient lawsuits in California.

As Matthews takes Dr. Perkins though his credentials from the witness stand, I doodle small images of pirate ships, geometrical boxes, and Flintstone characters in the corner of my legal pad. "Another Harvard degree on the witness stand," I think to myself as I fill in the shadows cast by Velma's stone necklace.

"Dr. Perkins, you served on the FDA's Blood Products Advisory Committee between 1982 and 1985?"

"Yes, I did."

Dr. Perkins has an olive complexion and hair that is thinning, oiled so that it sweeps over his crown like flipped parabolas. He straightens his posture every few minutes, maybe to look taller, and tries to connect with the jury by making eye contact, but his eyes keep wandering elsewhere. He explains how he stored donor core positive specimens, and when an AIDS test became available in 1985, he cross-matched them to see how many of the core positive specimens were also HIV positive.

"What were your findings, Dr. Perkins?"

The tip of my pencil is too worn to doodle so I put it down.

"My findings were that just thirty percent of the core positive specimens were also HIV positive. This means, if we had used the core test for AIDS, seventy percent of the blood we discarded was would not be HIV positive."

Even preventing thirty percent of this dreadful disease would have made it worth using, and the other seventy percent Dr. Perkins is referring to would have been exposed to hepatitis anyway. I am exasperated and tired of hearing this Alice in Wonderland logic from the blood bankers.

Matthews tries to convince the jury that the core test would have actually only have identified 30% of AIDS-positive blood donors, not 90%. "The other 70% would only identify donors with hepatitis," Dr. Perkins explains.

"Only." Everybody was so concerned with AIDS, that they seemed to forget hepatitis was a deadly disease as well.

Dr. Perkins testifies that if he had implemented core testing, the procedural flow would be close to halting because of overcrowding. "People would have come flocking to the blood banks just to be tested."

Matthews wraps it up neatly with the industry standard question. "Dr. Perkins, was it the standard of care to screen donors for AIDS when the plaintiff was transfused in August 1984?"

"No, Mr. Matthews. It was not the standard of care. In fact, it would have been more dangerous."

"Thank you, Dr. Perkins." Matthews sits down at counsel table. Dr. Perkins portrayed an endearingly clumsy, professorial manner with the jury. It is a job well done for the blood bankers.

"Mr. Baxter, cross-examination?" Judge Stark asks.

I can barely see the notes on my legal pad behind all the doodling, so I glance over it instead of trying to read directly from my notes like I usually do.

"Dr. Perkins, I have just a couple questions." His tweed jacket looks like screen that shows up on the screen when a television malfunctions.

"Dr. Perkins, what did you do with the hepatitis B core positive specimens in the pilot study?" Tom Asher explained to me that, like Dr. Kleinman, Dr. Perkins distributed the core positive blood from the specimens in his study directly to hospitals, marketing them as safe blood. This was the kind of blood that killed baby Osborn.

"It was a blind study." Dr. Perkins avoids answering my question.

"Did you use the blood from the core positive donors whose specimens you saved?" I rephrase.

"I was always in compliance with FDA regulations." In other words, there was no law against distributing the core positive units to patients from the blind study, even if all of it was identified as hepatitis or HIV-positive.

I approach Dr. Perkins with the April 1984 AABB News Brief that shows Irwin did, in fact, use core testing to screen out donors, even though Dr. Perkins claims it is ineffective. Since Irwin used the core positive blood from the specimens they saved in the pilot study, according to his own testimony, 30% of the released blood would have infected thousands of people with AIDS. This is consistent with the Grady internal memo, which states the double-benefit of core testing, as it rules out blood containing hepatitis and AIDS.

"Objection." Matthews jumps to his feet. "Your Honor, Mr. Baxter cannot use that because it goes to a subsequent action taken. Judge Van Tassel already ruled on this."

Judge Stark orders the jurors and Dr. Perkins out of the courtroom so we can argue it out. We both wait anxiously until the doors close behind them and begin arguing simultaneously.

"Judge, this is a cross-examination—"

"It is too prejudicial to allow into evidence—"

"Your Honor, Dr. Perkins just testified antibody is ineffective, when in, fact, he used it. This April 1984 NewsBrief goes directly to his credibility as a expert."

"I am going to allow it. Objection overruled." Judge Stark surprises us.

"It is reversible error!" Matthews practically hollers from the counsel table. He angrily agues that she does not have the right to be inconsistent with Judge Van Tassel's decision

"Sit down, Mr. Matthews!" Judge Stark blasts back. She orders to bailiff to bring the jurors and Dr. Perkins back into the courtroom. The tensions are nowhere near cool as they settle back into their seats. I am still in shock that Judge Stark allowed the document. Matthews is not wrong to be angry, but I am not going to let rules block evidence that so blatantly reveals the blood bankers culpability.

I place a blowup of the AABB's April 1984 *NewsBriefs* on the court easel before the jury. The headline reads "Irwin to Institute Anti-core Testing; New York Blood Center Rejects Concept." I turn the blowup so the jurors can read it.

"Dr. Perkins, do you recognize this AABB NewsBrief, dated April 1984, wherein Irwin announces it is going to begin core testing by May 1, 1984?

"Yes."

"Before the recess, you told this jury that core testing was ineffective. But, you began using it in May 1, 1984."

Dr. Perkins testifies that Irwin finally had to succumb to the public pressure imposed on him by Marc Conant and other physicians. "Stanford had begun testing donors, and it put competitive pressure on us to do something."

I read the AABB *NewsBrief* to the jury. "Irwin will begin anti-core testing no later than May 1. It is the feeling that Irwin needs to do more than it is doing." Irwin's announcement is not only inconsistent with Dr. Perkins testimony about core testing being ineffective, but it also demonstrates that despite using core testing to screen out contaminated blood, they released contaminated blood anyway. It is over for Dr. Perkins.

My strategy has evolved into short cross-examinations to attack the blood bankers credibility, rather than dispute the science with them. After all, their mistakes were not based in science as much as in common sense. At the height of an epidemic, rules, like viruses, shift and change and mutate; common sense is always the same, and common sense tells us to keep viruses at bay—not inject them directly into a human being's bloodstream. You don't need a degree from Harvard to know that.

CHAPTER THIRTY-TWO

Dr. Joseph Bove stands from the seventh row when Matthews calls him to the witness stand. I watch him walk down the courtroom isle with a confident stride, nodding to the jury. It is a mixed reaction from the jurors. Some jurors feign a smile back at him, while others are more serious. Dr. Bove seems to pause on the unsuspected reaction from the jury, but quickly suppresses his surprise by adjusting his jacket and clearing his throat. I do not think he realized how the jury has been hearing testimony about his internal memos for months before meeting him today. I have been daydreaming about taking down Dr. Bove since I first read about him in *And the Band Played On,* collecting fragments of all the things I could say that would really land a punch in his maddening confidence, but as I see him take the witness seat, the only feeling I have towards his confidence is envy. I am nervous because my desire to make a fool out of Dr. Bove is more passionate than what is appropriate for court.

"Please place one hand on the bible?" The bailiff asks holding the Bible before Dr. Bove. He places one hand above his head and the other on the bible, in a perfect right angle.

"Do you swear to tell the truth, the whole truth, so help you God?"

Dr. Bove is the strongest voice behind the blood bankers' decision to not test donors. "He is downright obstreperous," Don Francis told me, "the worst of the bunch in Atlanta."

"I do." Dr. Bove says with one hand on the bible. I cannot see his smile but I can hear it in his voice.

"Dr. Bove, you are the director of the Yale Medical Center Blood Bank?" Matthews begins direct examination.

"Yes." Dr. Bove is also a professor of transfusion medicine at Yale.

"And Dr. Bove, from time to time, you have been called upon by the Federal Food and Drug Administration to serve as an expert for the government?"

"Yes. When Dr. Dennis Donahue was forming the Federal Food and Drug Administration's Blood Products Advisory Committee, I was asked to serve on it."

"Dr. Bove, you were not compensated for serving on this committee?"

"No. It is voluntary. I considered it a personal duty to serve on the committee."

"Please tell the jury what the Blood Products Advisory Committee is?"

"I would be happy to." Dr. Bove leans in toward the jurors and explains the Blood Products Advisory Committee is an FDA committee of blood banking experts that makes recommendations for national blood policy. The committee evaluates donor screening, which included surrogate tests for AIDS from 1983 to 1985, and advises the FDA on what actions, if any, it should take.

"Dr. Bove, did there come a time when the Blood Products Advisory Committee considered the hepatitis B core antibody test as a surrogate test for donors at risk for transmitting AIDS?"

"Yes." Dr. Bove tells the jury. "The December 16-17, 1984 Blood Products Advisory Committee considered several surrogate tests, including core testing, but none were effective enough to implement. Too much good blood would have been discarded, which would have caused another national crisis: a blood shortage."

Matthews puts the December 10, 1982 CDC Morbidity and Mortality Weekly Report blowup on the easel. Where as Dr. Francis, Dr. Englemen and Dr. Conant had testified that this MMWR confirms the baby who contracts AIDS received it from an AIDS-positive blood donor, Dr. Bove refutes the link. "There are ten million transfusions a year. The CDC had a few isolated cases. This was not sufficient evidence."

"Dr. Bove, was there a consensus in the medical community then that AIDS was blood borne?"

"No. It was a hypothesis."

Matthew grabs the blowup of the industry's January 13, 1983 joint statement against laboratory testing and puts it on the easel. Bove testifies that it was a proper recommendation based upon the information they had at the time. He explains to the jury if they had used core testing, then it would have made blood more dangerous because high-risk people who want to be tested for AIDS would "flock" to blood banks and donate blood just to be tested for AIDS. It was the same thing Dr. Perkins said, but it sounded more convincing Dr. Bove's calm baritone.

Matthews puts Dr. Bove's January 24, 1983 memo to the AABB board on the easel and asks him to clarify what he meant in the internal memo to the AABB board.

Dr. Bove reads from the blowup. "We do not want anything we do to be interpreted by society or legal authorities as agreeing with the concept, still unproven, that AIDS is spread by blood." He turns to the jury and explains here is that the blood bankers did not want to add to the fear of transfusions when the risk is very small: one out of a million. "People would have put off their surgeries, refused transfusions, and placed their own lives at risk."

Mathews asks Dr. Bove whether the American Association of Blood Banks' recommendation against laboratory testing for blood donors was part of a conspiracy to delay testing. Dr. Bove emphatically denies this. "Once the FDA committee that considered core testing refused to endorse it, there was nothing we could do."

"Dr. Bove, are you saying that the FDA had the final word?"

"Yes."

"Thank you, Dr. Bove." Matthews sits down at the counsel table.

"Mr. Baxter, cross-examination?" Judge Stark asks.

"Yes, your honor." I walk to the easel and put Dr. Bove's December 1982 memo up. "Dr. Bove, I have just a couple of questions for you." A few jurors smile at this familiar statement now.

"In this December 1982 internal memo you wrote just a couple weeks before the Atlanta meeting, you say, 'AIDS continues to cause major problems in the blood collecting sector. My current best guess is that we are dealing with an infectious agent able to be spread by blood and blood products and that individuals who receive large quantities of factor concentrate are at increased risk.' Did I read your memo correctly, Dr. Bove?"

"If you mean, did you say the words—" Dr. Bove becomes cagey.

"Did I read your memo accurately?"

"You read the words, yes."

I take down Dr. Bove's December 1982 memo, and replace it with his January 24, 1983 memo. "Then in this January 24, 1983 memo, after another transfusion-AIDS case is reported by the CDC, you state, 'This increases the probability that AIDS may be spread by blood.' You go on to say, 'There is little doubt in my mind that additional transfusion-related cases and additional cases in patients with hemophilia will surface.' And it is in this context that you continue to write, 'The most we can do in this situation is buy time. We do not want anything we do now to be interpreted by society or by legal authorities as agreeing with the concept, as yet unproven, that AIDS can be spread by blood.' Did I read that accurately to the jury, Dr. Bove?"

"You read the words."

"And, Dr. Bove, by 'legal authorities,' did you mean legal and regulatory authorities, like the FDA?

"Yes."

"And, did you mean plaintiff lawyers, like me?"

"Yes."

I take down the January 24, 1983 memo from the easel and replace it with his March 29, 1983 memo. "And, in this memo, you note continuing pressure from the federal government and CDC to do something. You write, 'the next step on the horizon will be a request to institute mandatory screening of donor blood.' Then you go on, 'The evidence linking AIDS to transfusions is unconvincing.'" I stop reading off the memo and look at him. "Dr. Bove, what were you waiting for?"

"Objection." Matthews stands.

"How many deaths would be sufficient evidence?" I ignore the objection.

"Objection, your Honor."

"Sustained." Judge Stark hit her gavel.

"Dr. Bove, you testified that there are ten million transfusions a year?" "Yes."

I pull out the American Association of Blood Banks' own industry brochure that states the risk of contracting hepatitis from a transfusion is ten percent. I hand to Dr. Bove. "Dr. Bove, that AABB brochure says the risk of contracting hepatitis from a transfusion is ten percent?"

"Well, it depends on where." He becomes cagey again.

"Dr. Bove, I'm reading your numbers. Do you want to change them now?"

"It depends. It depends on where—"

"All right, how about, nine percent?"

"It's probably lower in some places."

"Eight? Will you give me eight percent?" The jury begins to laugh at the horse-trading between us.

"All right."

I go up to the court easel and use a large black marker to do the numbers for everyone in court to see. I draw a timeline beginning from 1982 to 1986. Judge Stark's ruling now allows me to cross-examine Dr. Bove about the subsequent use of antibody testing, so I take a quick second to internally relish in the fact I can draw a timeline.

"Dr. Bove, the hepatitis B core antibody test was implemented in 1986, right?"

"Yes, but for hepatitis B."

"If there are ten million transfusions a year, using your risk number, that comes out to 300,000 people per year infected with hepatitis from blood transfusions?"

"You're doing the numbers."

"Well, I'm using your numbers."

I write 300,000 in bold numbers, representing people over each year on the timeline at the easel. "Dr. Bove, 90 percent of these hepatitis cases are non-A, non-B hepatitis. That's 270,000 patients infected with hepatitis C each year?"

"You're doing the numbers."

"Dr. Bove, I am using your own numbers."

I circle the numbers with the black marker for the jury to see. "Now what percentage of hepatitis non-A, non-B cases are picked up by the hepatitis B core antibody test?"

"I'll agree to 30 percent."

"Dr. Bove, that's 90,000 cases of hepatitis C?"

I write 90,000 over each year from 1981 to 1986 on the timeline. "So use of the core antibody testing for AIDS would have prevented 90,000 cases of hepatitis C per year, plus reduces AIDS cases." I put the marker down and look at him. "What were you waiting for?"

I think about the hug Janet gave me the last time I saw her. "Dr. Bove, how many patients had to die?"

"Objection." Matthews angrily stands.

"Sustained." Judge Stark gently warns me.

"I'm finished, your Honor."

Dr. Bove, to this day, has no remorse about the blood bankers' decision against core testing. He insists the CDC's evidence was weak because its study population was too small to be meaningful following Atlanta, that using a surrogate test would mean discarding good blood and causing blood shortages. They'd be throwing the baby out with the bath water.

CHAPTER THIRTY-THREE

I watch the red digital numbers on the clock turn one at a time, all night long. It has been six weeks since the trial began, and though I feel exhaustion in my bones, sleep escapes me. At 4:10, I carefully get up, trying not to wake Patti.

"Honey, are you all right?" Patti mumbles, half asleep.

"Yes, go back to sleep. I'm just getting a drink of water." I head downstairs to the kitchen and pace around in a circle for a minute and Abby comes over to me. "Who is the one with the tail to chase?" I tell her as I give her a hug. I take all the notes out of my trial bag and lay them down on the kitchen counter, as I always do the night or morning before trial. I am so tired all the words look unintelligible, more like an army of ants than alphabetical letters. I reach into Patti's purse on the kitchen chair and take out her Valium prescription, break one tablet in half and dry swallow it. Abby lies back down on her bed in the corner and I sit beside her, petting her head until she closes her eyes.

I walk into Judge Stark's courtroom later than usual and Matthews is already set up at the counsel table. Standing with him is a handsome man of tall stature and eloquence in a dark suit. I recognize him immediately as Dr. Dennis Donohue, the retired chief of the Blood Products Division for the Federal Food and Drug Administration. He was appointed to head the Blood Products Advisory Committee by Dr. John Petricciani, the commissioner of the FDA between 1973-1985. Dr. Donohue and his boss, Dr. Petricciani, attended Atlanta as the FDA heads. Blood products, like the platelet that infected Bill, are regulated by the FDA as a biologic. Dr. Donohue was the top man with oversight of the blood industry, reporting directly to Dr. Petriccinni.

"Mr. Matthews, are you ready to proceed?" Judge Stark asks from the bench. I am waiting impatiently for the café coffee to kick in.

"Yes, your Honor." Matthews replies.

The cadence of footsteps shuffling into the jury box begins our final argument of the trial. The motions of our arguments feel almost operatic now. Dr. Donohue raises one hand, puts the other on the Bible and swears to tell the truth, so help him God. He really fit my image of what a top government official would look like, about 6' 2 and 200 lbs., with a self-assured smile tugging at his lips. He centers his shoulders and head on whoever he speaks to, looking them squarely in the eye, as though he is beyond reproach. Of course he is a dangerous witness—like the other blood bankers, confidence billows out of him like calm ocean waves.

"Dr. Donohue, you were the chairman of the Federal Food and Drug Administration's Blood Products Advisory Committee in 1983-1984?" Matthews asks.

"Yes. Dr. Petriccinni, commissioner of the FDA, came to me and asked me to create a new Blood Products Advisory Committee."

"And what is the purpose of the Blood Products Advisory Committee?

"The committee oversees national blood policy and makes recommendations to the commissioner of the FDA on policy."

"Did there come a time when the committee considered surrogate tests for donors at risk for AIDS?" Matthews is referring to the Blood Products Advisory Committee meeting on December 16-17, 1983.

"Yes. The committee looked at various possible tests, but none were promising enough to use."

"Did the committee consider the hepatitis B core antibody test as a surrogate test for AIDS?" Matthews moves closer to the jury.

"Yes, the committee was against it."

"Dr. Donohue, will you tell the jury why the committee was against it?"

False positives, of course. All the usual jargon about discarding good blood. It was as though the blood bankers' witnesses were soap opera stars, made to memorize lines as soon as they arrive on set. Except the witnesses never fail to look convincing. I don't know whether it is their well-tailored suits or sophisticated mannerisms or typical blood banker confidence, but they always seem to put my articulated disagreements with this "false positives" baloney back to square one.

"Dr. Donohue, so then even if the American Association of Blood Banks wanted to recommend core testing, they would have come to you first?" This question kicks me before the caffeine from the courthouse coffee does. This, I was not expecting.

"That's right. They would have had to come to me for permission, and I would have said no."

Almost spontaneously, Matthews follows with, "So it would have been against the law?"

"That's right."

"The buck stopped with you?" Matthews is having his way.

"That's right. The buck stopped with me."

I turn my face away from the jury so they do not see it turn white. The blood bankers just got away with jury nullification, which means they told the jury to ignore the evidence in the case. It is like when Johnny Cochran told the O.J. Simpson jury, "If the glove doesn't fit, you must acquit." Dr. Donohue just told the jury that no matter what the evidence showed in the case, to ignore it because he was in charge. The buck stopped with him.

After weeks of trials and years of fighting the case, the blood bankers' trade association is just too powerful to beat. They are the ones who have the political friends with clout, friends who willingly to throw themselves under the bus for them. It is one thing for the blood bankers to testify that they complied with FDA requirements. But, now, Dr. Donohue tells the jury that it would have been illegal for the blood bankers to do more without coming to him first.

Before I went through the security check this the morning, I noticed the image of the blindfolded woman holding the scales of justice engraved into the cement. The engraving was shallow, flattened over time. Justice is supposed to be blind, but I am not so sure.

"Mr. Baxter, cross-examination?" Judge Stark brings me into the moment. I met Dr. Donohue a few years earlier for his deposition in Seattle. He called Don Francis a paranoid hothead, so there is no use going into the Centers of Disease Control's admonition for the blood bankers and FDA to begin testing donors.

"Dr. Donohue, just a couple questions?"

He nods.

"You testified to this jury that as chairman of the Federal Food and Drug Administration's Blood Products Advisory, you did not endorse core antibody testing?"

"Yes."

Reading from my legal pad. "You said they would have had to come to you, and you would have said no."

"Yes."

"And, of course, you are under oath?" I ask facing the jurors.

"Yes."

"And, you want this jury to believe you?"

"Yes."

"Dr. Donohue, take a look at the court monitor, please?" Earlier, I slipped a video into it. I hit the "on" button of the court monitor set up on a metal table for everyone to see. We hear the opening theme music from the TV news magazine show *20/20*, the episode from July 1986. The host, Tom Jarriel, looking dapper and polished, interviews Dr. Dennis Donohue, speaking into the camera.

TOM JARRIEL

> *20/20* has been conducting its own investigation into how thousands of units of blood, contaminated with the AIDS virus, got into the national blood supply during the early-to-mid- eighties. I'm here with Dr. Dennis Donohue, formerly the highest-ranking FDA official, who oversaw the blood industry.

A younger Dennis Donohue sits in a chair across from Tom Jarriel.

TOM JARRIEL

> Dr. Donahue, our investigation shows that the hepatitis B core antibody test was a good surrogate test that detected people who were exposed to AIDS. Yet the FDA and the blood industry refused to use it.

DR. DONAHUE

Of course, I thought the core test should have been implemented.

TOM JARRIEL

What happened?

DR. DONAHUE

I was for it, but I couldn't get it through the committee. It was too heavily weighted with industry people.

TOM JARRIEL

That sounds almost clubbish.

DR. DONAHUE

It was clubbish, too clubbish.

I hit the pause button and freeze the frame with Dr. Donahue on the TV monitor for the jury.

"So, Dr. Donohue, my question is, which one of you should this jury believe?" I ask, facing the jury.

"Objection." Matthews tries to save him. The jurors look back and forth, between Dr. Donohue and me.

"Should the jury believe you in that *20/20* interview, or here, today, as a paid witness for the American Association of Blood Banks?"

It is the first time I catch a glimpse of emotion from a juror. Juror two turns and looks to juror one with an expression of disbelief. Juror one gestures back to her to restrain her reaction. Like I said, the jury may throw out all or any part of a witness' testimony based on credibility.

Tom Asher, a wealth of information, may have saved the trial with that video. He found it in a box and sent it to me by overnight Fed-Ex the day before Dr. Donohue testified.

CHAPTER THIRTY-FOUR

Matthews feigns emotion so well that even I'm caught off guard, watching from the audience. His voice cracks, he chokes up, then calms himself. "Ladies and Gentlemen, no one feels as badly about what happened to the plaintiff as I do."

Summation day reminds me of the scene from *To Kill a Mockingbird*, in which the courtroom is full and the tension in the air is robust. Law clerks all around the tri-state area take time off to come see the lawyers they've read and heard so much about over the past few months do closing statements. Courtney stays home from school to come to court. Matthews brings his family too. The courtroom is re-arranged, the counsel tables removed, and a podium set up toward the jury. I sit in the eight row, in awe of Matthews' speech. I do believe he is the paragon of all trial lawyers.

"But we didn't put AIDS into the blood, it was already there." Matthews reminds the jury how the blood bankers were always in compliance with the FDA regulations and did nothing wrong.

"Madonna. You all know her name. Madonna is a pop phenomenon. She is known all around the world. But when the plaintiff's transfusion occurred, no one had even heard of her." Matthews urges the jury not to judge his client based on what is known today about transfusion AIDS, but rather to place themselves back into 1984. He even grabs my blow-ups that I had neatly arranged to use, and goes through them one-by-one, offering alternative explanations.

I check the courtroom clock. Two exhausting hours have past since Matthews began, but he is nowhere near closing. In an articulate voice, he reminds the jury of all the witnesses who testified, one at a time. When comes to Dr. Donohue, he says: "You saw only an edited version of the *20/20* interview. You did not see the parts that were edited out and left lying on the cutting-room floor."

Though it has been two hours, everyone is mesmerized by Matthews. His oratory skills could probably rival those of ancient Roman dictators. He talks tirelessly until his voice begins to give out. It is a classic summation and precisely executed. He even ends with the classic defense scare tactic: "If you return a verdict for the plaintiff, Bill Snyder, then you will open the floodgates of litigation." Finally, with a hoarse voice, he croaks a thank you.

"Mr. Baxter, closing argument?" Judge Stark immediately moves on. I was hoping for a break after the hours of sitting, listening to Matthews. I make my way down the middle isle of the packed courtroom to the podium. Every single eye is on me: every law clerk, reporter, spectator, and Judge Stark. I can feel their gazes through my gabardine suit.

The day before, I practiced the closing on Patti and Courtney, who patiently sat in the kitchen chairs I lined up in the living room. I have it down to three legal pads and forty-five minutes. As I place my legal pads on the podium and look into the faces of the jurors, I notice deep exhaustion on their faces. Juror one looks aggravated, like he has had enough. I do not blame him. It has been months now, and Matthews just sucked the last energy from them. I flip the first page of my notes.

"Ladies and gentlemen—" It is no use. They are too tired to even listen to me. I did not expect this to happen. I put my legal pads aside, look back at them and begin again.

"Ladies and Gentlemen, everything you heard from Mr. Matthews over the last couple hours, forget it. Use your own memory of the evidence. You know the truth. Return a verdict for my client, Bill Snyder." There is a dead silence in the courtroom. Patti and Courtney look at me, puzzled. My closing argument was anticlimactic, but a sense of appreciation brought color back to the jurors' faces. Judge Stark is so surprised that she says something that's picked up in her microphone: "Well, certainly two different styles."

"Charging the Jury—Enter Quietly," reads the 18 x 10 sign that hangs across the outside of the courtroom doors. The case is out of the lawyers' hands now, and the judge is explaining the law to the jurors. Everyone knows the sign means do not enter, but if you must, be very quiet.

Inside the courtroom, Judge Stark reads the jury charge straight from her notes that she has prepared, with the input of the lawyers, to the jurors.

"Ladies and Gentlemen, in deciding the issue of negligence, you may consider what a reasonable and prudent person would have done based upon the state of knowledge at the time plaintiff, Bill Snyder, was transfused on August 26, 1984." This is the T.J. Hooper Case law that I fought for to determine the negligence of an industry. However, Judge Stark adds, "What the industry was doing may also be considered as evidence by you about what was reasonable at the time."

Judge Stark continues charging the jury on the law. "You may weigh the credibility of the witnesses you heard testify and accept or reject their testimony." When she's finished, Judge Stark has the bailiff put the names of the jurors into a cylindrical wooden box, the kind people might use for bingo games, and turns it around before taking out a name. Juror five has just been designated the alternative juror. This concerns me, because she is the only juror to have said "good morning" to me throughout the entire trial. The others avoided eye contact with me in the hallways and courtroom. As an alternative juror she does not get to deliberate on the case. In another last minute disappointment, the conservative-looking, *Wall Street Journal*-reading juror one is designated as the jury foreman. I feared this from the beginning of trial. His seniority made him a leader with the jury by default. Judge Stark finishes instructing the jury and the bailiff leads them to the jury room to deliberate the case. There is nothing to do now but wait for the verdict.

I anxiously pace the halls of the courthouse, retracing my steps to every quiet place I had found solitude over the last couple months. I go into the third floor men's room, open the window and look out over the court annex. I pace up to the fourth floor alcove to gaze out at the county jail annex. I go to the courthouse cafe to get coffee, even though I have no intention of drinking it. Matthews waits in the plush lawyers lounge, leaning back in leather wingback chairs with his entourage.

I should have aimed for a settlement, I think to myself above the loud, nervous tapping of my foot on the floor. "Take the money," is what I have always said. "You never know what a jury will do." It's the golden rule. But I broke the golden rule and am now plagued with doubt. If I had settled the case, then no one would ever know what happened. But if Matthews wins the case, it will be vindication for the blood bankers. They will not hesitate to keep boasting how nobody has ever won a transfusion AIDS lawsuit. Roslyn and Bill are in Florida, waiting for a phone call. Marc Conant, Ed Engleman and Don Francis are also waiting to hear from me. I decide to get out of the courthouse and wait in the quiet of my office.

The office looks like a tornado blew through it, with papers and exhibits everywhere. Weeks of unopened mail with rubber bands around them lay on the floor. I did not let anything but

Bill's case permeate my life for the last few weeks, almost like my mind does not know how to think about anything else. I stare at the the phone, mentally demanding it to ring so the bailiff can tell me the jury is back with a verdict, but it does not ring. I notice dust, dirt and food crumbs on the edges of the keys and wipe the phone down with toilet paper from the bathroom, hoping the phone will ring as a reward for finally cleaning up, but it remains comatose. I go home.

On the morning of June 24, 1994, the third day after closing arguments, the office phone rings. I had been anticipating and wishing for it so ardently that when it finally came, my hands had trouble reaching for it. On the forth ring I pick it up. It is the bailiff. "Mr. Baxter, the jury is back with a verdict and the judge wants counsel back in court." Crossing Hudson Street to the courthouse I think about how the key players from Atlanta came to Bill's trial, right here, to Hackensack. Urban renewal still has not happened, and the courthouse dome continues to be the only structure that towers over the city.

The doors of Judge Stark's chamber open, and the courtroom goes still. "Bailiff, bring the jury in." Judge Stark is especially officious and does not even say hello to the counsel.

I listen to the scuffling and stepping of the jurors walking into the jury box for the last time. I am too nervous to look up from the doodling on my legal pad for fear they have decided against me. All I can manage at the moment is to wait for the scuffling sounds to stop, so I know they are seated.

"Mr. Foreman, has the jury reached a verdict?" Judge Starks asks.

"Yes, your Honor." He stands and answers with a sense of the gravity of the outcome.

The bailiff takes the verdict sheet from juror one, and hands it to Judge Stark. She reads it with a complete poker face. Then the bailiff hands it back to juror one.

"How do you find?" Judge Stark asks the foreman.

"We the jury, as to the first count, find that the defendant, American Association of Blood Banks, was negligent by not recommending core antibody testing to screen donors." The jury foreman reads it from the verdict sheet.

I lift up my head yet to process what I have heard. I hang on for whatever comes next from the jury.

"How do you find as to count two?"

"We find, Your Honor, that the defendant American Association of Blood Banks' negligence did, in fact, cause the plaintiff, William Snyder, to become infected with AIDS."

There's a stir throughout the courtroom. Judge Stark throws a serious glance in its direction and it quiets down immediately.

"And what did you award the plaintiffs?" She asks.

"We have awarded the plaintiffs, William and Roslyn Snyder, the sum of $1.3 million dollars." I look up at juror one and he nods to me. I had been wrong about him all this time.

Judge Stark asks Matthews if he wants the jury polled. He says yes, so one-by-one jurors stand and publicly state how they voted. It amazed me that the jury verdict was unanimous.

"Ladies and Gentlemen, thank you for your service as jurors. You are hereby excused." Judge Stark releases the jury. As they stand, I look at them with gratitude and watch them leave, and they look equally thankful to be finally leaving.

Matthews turns to me with a surprising congratulatory handshake as commotion ripples through the courtroom. I make my way through the crowd to the hallway telephones to call Roslyn. "Thank God, it's over," she tells Bill. I call Patti, who makes celebratory dinner plans immediately. Don Francis and Ed Engleman congratulate me—they had been waiting for this much longer than I have. Marc Conant's entire office erupts into cheers.

The news of the jury's verdict flashes across the country in hours: "Jury finds blood bank group liable for HIV case spread by transfusion." *The Star-Ledger,* Friday, June 24, 1994: "Million for AIDS victim. Tainted-blood recipient gets an award from jury." *The Herald & News,* June 24, 1994: "Landmark verdict on HIV blood. Bergen jury decides trade group negligent," writes Bill Sanderson for *The Record,* June 24, 1994.

It is the first time the industry's trade and lobby association has been held accountable for their political and business practices that resulted in injuring a consumer of the industry's products. The verdict has wide reaching ramifications beyond Bill Snyder. Other trade associations fear it is a legal precedent that opens the door for consumer protection against them. Consumers, like gun shot victims, may hold them responsible for injuries linked to their political and business practices that up until now have been protected. Bill's verdict has just made inroads for consumers against the bastion of political action groups that have operated with immunity, until now.

The weekend following Bill's jury verdict, I sleep for days. Patti replaces the pillow covers of the pillows under my head while I am sleeping, but I hardly notice. The years of worrying, the insomnia and trial are finally over. My office and home telephone rings with calls from newspapers, radio and cable television reporters wanting to know more about case. I clip newspaper articles and proudly hang them in my office. I did it.

CHAPTER THIRTY-FIVE

The blood bankers appeal Bill's jury verdict in what is called *Snyder II*. I have laid everything on the line to fight Bill's case. It is still the only case in my office, and every time I think I won, it begins over again. Bill's case was filed on November 23, 1989. In the first pre-trial appeal decided on October 30, 1990, the New Jersey Appellate Court carved out Bill's right to sue the blood bankers. On July 31, 1991, the New Jersey Supreme Court affirmed Bill's right to sue the blood bankers' trade association and sent the case back to the trial court for discovery and trial. On June 24, 1994, the Hackensack jury found the trade association negligent for contaminating the blood supply and infecting Bill. Now, five years after beginning Bill's case, the blood bankers take it all back before the appellate courts, to 1989.

"Roslyn, how's Bill doing?" I call Roslyn from my office to break the news to her and Bill.

"He's tired all the time, but he still makes the boys lunches for them to take to school."

"How are you managing with the boys and everything?"

"Oh, I worry about the boys."

"You are a trooper, Roslyn."

"Yeah, well they can put that on my grave stone some day." Roslyn cackles.

"Roslyn, I have to tell you something." There is no easy way to tell her.

"Oh brother. What is it?" She gets more serious.

"The American Association of Blood Banks has filed an appeal from the jury verdict."

"Bill will never see a nickel of that money." The blood bankers posted a bond with the court for the amount of the jury verdict. It is returned to them if they win the appeal.

"They are saying they did not get a fair trial because of Judge Stark's trial ruling."

"But I thought they already had the appeals." Roslyn's cynicism about the system and life creeps back into her voice. "You mean they can throw out the whole case after all this time?"

"Don't lose faith, Roslyn."

"Whatever." I am no more tired and discouraged than she is.

On May 2, 1995, *Snyder II* is argued before the New Jersey Appellate Court. Judge Pressler once again presides over the argument.

Matthews stands at the podium arguing a litany of trial errors, any one of which requires tossing the verdict. He begins with reversible error, that Judge Stark should not have admitted into evidence the blood bankers' later use of the hepatitis B core antibody test in 1986, since it post dates Bill's transfusion. Then he moves on to the use of the *20/20* news video. "It was reversible error to have allowed the jury to see a *20/20* video interview that was edited. Pieces of Dr. Donohue's interview were left on the cutting room floor and the video did not accurately show what he said."

"Your Honors, the *20/20* video interview was a prior inconsistent statement by Dr. Donohue permitted for the purpose of impeaching his credibility," I argue back. Matthews continues to insist that since Judge Van Tassel had previously excluded the Red Cross memo, that it was reversible error for Judge Stark to later allow me to use it as evidence of conspiracy. Though Matthews says "reversible error" often enough that it sounds like the chorus to a very long song, these are worrisome arguments.

The most disconcerting argument Matthews makes, however, is for charitable immunity. He argues that the New Jersey Charitable Immunity Statute provides the AABB with a shield of immunity from patient lawsuits because it is a nonprofit trade association. This means that there never should have been a trial in the first place.

"The AABB is not 'charitable' because it charges fees for its services," I snap. I point out that through its lobbying efforts, the AABB has voluntarily intertwined itself to such a degree with state and federal governments that it has assumed a quasi-regulatory role.

Driving home, I cannot tell what is going to happen. The case can be tossed by the court on any single issue or remanded for an entirely new trial. Either way, it would be a disaster because Bill will not survive.

On June 5, 1995, Judge Pressler rattles the legal community once again by affirming Bill's verdict against the industry's trade association. The New Jersey Appellate Court's opinion is instantly carried across the country. Bill Sanderson is there all the way to the end. He does another front-page story: "Blood Bank Group Must Pay Award in Transfusion Suit," *The Record*, June 6, 1995. All the other newspapers followed with their own headlines. "Blood bank association told to pay in AIDS transfusion case," *The Star-Ledger*, June 6, 1995. "Blood bank's liability upheld in AIDS case," The *Herald and News*, June 6, 1995.

I have an advanced copy of the official public court opinion and call Roslyn as I promised. I read parts of the court's opinion to her over the phone.

"Judge Pressler, writing the opinion for the court, states, 'The evidence at this trial supports the jury's finding that the response was not only 'unnecessarily slow' but also that it was clearly imprudent and unreasonable, resulting in the unnecessary contamination of the blood supply.'"

"Wait, I want to bring the phone by Bill so he can hear too." Roslyn says. "All right, go ahead."

"Hello Bill. This is what it says about the Red Cross document." I read the Legalese in the report like it is a bedtime story. "'Finally, we are satisfied that the trial judge did not mistakenly exercise his discretion in admitting an American Red Cross memorandum written in February 1983 suggesting conspiratorial action between the Red Cross and the AABB in concealing from the public the import of the known AIDS data, its likely blood-transmissibility, and the risk of transfusion-AIDS.'" *Snyder v. American Association Of Blood Banks*, 48 N.J. Super 23, 47-46, (App. Div. 1995)

The official court opinion also deals with the admissions made by Dr. Bove on cross-examination about how hundreds of thousands of people got hepatitis B and AIDS as a result of the trade association's refusal to recommend testing earlier. The appellate court states, "Despite this concern, defendant's evidence shows that the core test is now routinely used as a surrogate test for non-A and non-B hepatitis. According to the defense figures, some 300,000 persons were infected with hepatitis up to the mid-1980s, of whom 90 percent, or 270,000, were infected with non-A, non-B hepatitis. Hepatitis B core antibody testing picks up about one-third of the donors with non-A, non-B hepatitis. Consequently, use of the core test as a surrogate for AIDS would also have resulted in preventing 90,000 cases of non-A, non-B hepatitis annually."

CHAPTER THIRTY-SIX

I am livid when I get the news that the AABB wants to challenge Bill's verdict yet again, this time with the New Jersey Supreme Court. This time, the AABB is joined by other trade associations—the American Association of Tissue Banks, the American Society of Association of Executives, and the American College of American Pathologists—and political groups. This time, they argue the case on First Amendment grounds.

The First Amendment protects freedom of speech, including the speech of lobbyists who influence the political process. They evoke the Noerr-Pennington doctrine, by which private entities are immune from liability under the antitrust laws for attempts to influence the passage or enforcement of laws. In other words, actions by trade associations and political action groups intended to influence government regulators is a form of protected speech under the United States Constitution.

The scope of Bill's case keeps getting bigger and bigger and never ending. Every time I collect a victory, the blood bankers come back with endless resources, more allies, and another appeal. Each time they stand on a different constitutional argument: First, the constitutional right to privacy forbid the disclosure of the donor's information in a civil lawsuit; then, Charitable Immunity for a quasi-governmental regulatory entity like their trade group and, now, their position against donor testing was constitutionally protected free speech. It is like being in a science fiction movie, where I zap the gigantic green creature with my gamma ray gun, but this only makes the monster grow five more arms, three more heads, and unimaginable amount of power.

Months later, while working on another round of supreme court briefs, I take a breather and walk from the office down Main Street. As I pass the drug display window at the corner of Mercer Street, I see the reflection of a man standing across the street. He looks tired, haggardly, as though cinderblocks are perched on his shoulders. I look for the real version of this raven-like man, but there is no one. I do a double take in the window reflection and realize it is me. I step closer to the stranger in the reflection, almost touching my nose to the window, still in disbelief. The skin under my eyes look like fallen curtains, falling into my cheeks and causing ripples in the rest of my face. I contort my face into a smile just to see if it does anything to give my face some personality, but it just makes more lines, indistinguishable from the rest.

Is this what it takes to standup for the injured? There are days when it feels so futile to keep trying that I avoid the office. I was naive to think I could make a difference against an industry powerful enough to get away with inadvertently killing its own consumers. My brief brushes with success in the case only makes the fall harder to get up from. Bill's case has been more than taking on the blood industry; it has been more than revenge for Janet. It has defined me, and if I lose now, I'd feel no more substantial than the smoke trailing behind jets over the New Jersey turnpike.

The day I graduated from the eighth grade at St. Brendan's, the nun told the class to enjoy our graduation day. "For some of you, it will be the last." Her eyes rested right on my forehead, like a sniper target. After our graduation ceremony, I walked past the crowd of families embracing or waiting to embrace their kin, took off my cap and grown, and threw them into a garbage can as I walked the four miles back home. I have filled my head with grandiose illusions of helping the powerless, but I know my motivations are in large part due to an obsession with proving myself to that nun, to all the people who barely noticed or cared about my failures. It is not my clients' lack of power that I fight for, but my own. The overachieving, grade-nosy students in my law school classes were right: the only way to be successful in law is to join that long line of gray suits and briefcases that work for corporations and insurance companies. In their defense, it would be nice to have a real job and be paid each week and not watch the clock's red digital numbers flip in the darkness all night long.

As the reflection in the window stares back at me, the sharp lines in my face softening into curves of resignation, an abrupt shift in attitude shocks them back into tautness. I hit pause on this dramatic scene I am filming of myself and chuckle. Sentimentality does not suit me. There is no way I will quit. It is not about the motivations that brought me where I am now, but who I want to be tomorrow. I turn away from the image in the window and walk back to the office.

On November 6, 1995, the New Jersey Supreme hears oral arguments. Roslyn waits for a phone call, optimistic because she has to be. The blood bankers' side of the courtroom is filled with lawyers, lobbyist representatives, and spectators. The rows behind me, on the respondent's side of the court, room are empty. A few heads turn as I open my litigation bag, take out my files and legal pads and set up at the respondent's counsel table. I place a small photo of Janet on the table where only I can see it.

As usual, Matthews persuasively argues that the blood bankers should not be penalized for simply exercising their First

Amendment right of free speech and being on the wrong side of a public debate. "There was no consensus about what should be done at the time." Matthews also grabs the court's attention with raising the charitable immunity issue again, before giving up the podium and sitting back down at the counsel table. It is very scary how you could hear a pin drop every time time Matthews takes a breath in between sentences. The attention he naturally commands is so rapt. Now it is my turn.

"The First Amendment does not protect speech in furtherance of conspiracy intended to mislead authorities about the risk of AIDS contaminated blood to avoid regulation." I argue for twenty minutes from the podium before that red light comes on.

"Thank you counsel. You will be notified of our decision." Chief Justice Wilentz ends the oral argument. The Justices begin to stand to leave the bench. As the scuffling of feet and friction of judicial robes begin to engulf the room, I interrupt the motions.

"Chief Justice Wilentz?"

I cannot budge from the podium. Everyone stops for a moment to look at me. The red light is conspicuously on.

"They shouldn't get away with this."

There is no doubt that I overstepped my boundaries, but I figure, after today, it's over. There are no more chances.

"Thank you, counsel," Chief Justice Wilentz says courteously. He could have blasted me for that outbreak, but he remains impartial.

That night, I call Roslyn from the office as promised. She and Bill were sitting, waiting for my take on the outcome of the Supreme Court argument.

"Roslyn, I'm sorry, but I can't tell how it may go this time."

On June 5, 1996, six months later, winter is gone and it is a warm summer morning. I wake up at sunrise, go down to the newspaper stand and cut open the bundle of newspapers. I grab copies of the *New York Times, the Record* and *Star Ledger* and leave a few bucks on the pile.

"Blood Bank Is Held Liable in AIDS Case," *The New York Times*, June 5, 1996 reports. "The New Jersey Supreme Court ruled today that the organization that oversees the safety of the nation's blood supply was negligent in the early 1980s for rejecting tougher screening tests for AIDS-contaminated blood."

"State's Top Court Holds Blood Bank Group Liable for HIV Testing in 80s," *The Star-Ledger* reports, "The powerful American Association of Blood Banks (AABB), a nonprofit organization that sets the standards used by nearly every single blood bank in the United States, can be held liable for failing to take more aggressive steps in the early 80s to safeguard the public from AIDS-tainted blood, New Jersey's top court said yesterday."

On June 4, 1996, more than seven years after beginning Bill's fight, the New Jersey Supreme Court affirms *Snyder II*. It is the news of the day. The supreme court clerk gave me a courtesy call that the court's opinion is going to be released the day before. I got up early to head for the newspaper stand.

In a six-one decision, Justice Garibaldi dissenting, the New Jersey Supreme Court holds: "Nor should the association enjoy immunity when they stubbornly reject persuasive evidence, *unreasonably prolong the debate*, and fail to inform their constituents of the threats to the public health. The record reveals that the AABB led the charge against surrogate testing... *A less favorable view suggests that the AABB resisted surrogate testing because it did not want to suffer the added inconvenience and costs of such testing.*"

The New Jersey Supreme Court is the highest and only governmental authority to officially find that the AABB's actions contaminated the blood supply. *The New York Times* reports, "Today's decision, written by Justice Pollack, said the Association of Blood Banks was financially liable because it breached its 'duty of care' to Mr. Snyder by rejecting the recommendations for tougher screening for their blood." *The Record* reports, "AIDS verdict upheld against blood-bank group: Lack of screening led to infection in '84." *The Record*, June 5, 1996.

The New Jersey Supreme Court rejected the AABB's argument that as a trade association and industry lobbyist their actions are protected under the First Amendment and Noerr-Pennington doctrine. The court held that the doctrine, which protects lobbyists' political and commercial activities as free speech, does not extend to Bill's personal injury case. Instead, the court stated, "The AABB's liability does not rest on its right to petition the government. The jury found that the AABB was negligent for failing to recommend that its member banks adopt surrogate testing, and not for the AABB's lobbying efforts or its participation on the FDA Blood Products Advisory Board. In brief, the Noerr-Pennington doctrine does not apply."

In a pair of jeans and an old sweatshirt, I look around the office for the last time. The pigeons are cooing and the ceiling light is flickering. I take the law school diploma off the wall, wrap it in brown paper and place it on top of the poster of the Golden Gate Bridge, folded into a quarter of its size. The office is packed into boxes.

The Trial Lawyers for Public Justice, Washington, D.C., nominated me for their Trial Lawyer of the Year Public Achievement Award. There I stood, blinded by the stage lights of a New York dinner club, shoulder to shoulder with the most prominent trial lawyers in America. I did not get the award, but it was an honor to be nominated for it. But, even this honor is not enough to keep me in a profession where you have to deal with the worst in people, day in and day out. The stage lights are blinding. I cannot see beyond them or pass the end of the stage, but I know Patti is out there, in the audience. It is a comforting

George T. Baxter, Esq.

feeling to know that no matter how uncertain the future will be, she is there.

The seven-year legal battle has come to an end, but there are no winners. Bill and Janet are dead, and I am irreparably weary. I look over the newspaper headlines sprawled over my desk as I pack them away and I think about that blindfolded woman holding the scales of justice over the courthouse doorway. All I know is that in a small Hackensack courtroom, Bill Snyder, a retired factory worker, got justice against the leaders of a billion-dollar-a-year industry, who manipulated the national blood policy to their own end and caused one of the largest public health disasters of all time. Let those symbols decorate our courtrooms as they wish.

I am on the way out the door, balancing a box filled with personal belongings in my hand, when the phone rings. I pause. Why did I forget to unplug and pack the phone? Should I answer it? I pick it up and it is a woman. "I am sorry, but you are about a week too late," I tell her. "I have closed my law practice." After years of fighting the system and befriending Bill and Janet to their last days, I can never sell out now and be a lawyer who argues for whatever side pays him. The experience has defined me, but as scary as it is, I have to search for my place elsewhere. Hopefully, I will find another way to make my life as meaningful as it felt from helping them.

The woman is insistent. She tells me how devastated she is over her twelve-year-old daughter, who was infected with AIDS from a blood transfusion. She read about me in the newspaper. Maybe this is where I belong now, at least for a little while longer. Not as someone in the system, but rather someone using it to fight for people who cannot do it on their own. I put the box down on the desk, scramble for a legal pad inside the box, and begin taking notes.

EPILOGUE

Seventeen years later, while writing this book, I googled Janet's husband, Kyle, and was surprised to find his name on Linked-in. It couldn't be him, I thought, because he must have died from AIDS. Every person who was alive back then knew somebody who died from AIDS. I sent an email to inquire whether he is same person who was married to Janet. He emailed me back and said, "Hello, George."

We decided to meet for dinner at the Stony Hill Inn in Hackensack. He brought Naomi, Christian and their families with him. Naomi was as old as Janet was when I knew her, with two children. She remembers the day Janet first got the news that she had AIDS, when her doctor informed her via telephone and she collapsed to the floor. Christian came with his wife and baby son. I told him how proud Janet was when he started to play the bagpipes. I gave Naomi and Christian a copy of Janet's video deposition. I never thought that when I stood by the video camera coaching Janet to tell her story that day in my office, we would be preserving it for her children to see when they grew up. Kyle remarried and is a happy grandfather. Janet's last name has been withheld, and the first names of her husband and children changed to protect their privacy. The name of Janet's hematologist Dr. Feldman has been change too. The two decades that have passed since Janet's death does little to separate her family from the pain of the ordeal of losing her.

Bill survived for a few more years before dying from AIDS-related illnesses in 1999. Roslyn passed away ten years later in Daytona Beach, Florida, on September 10, 2009, but not before writing a letter thanking me for standing by Bill and the family. It was a short note, as was Roslyn's way, on simple lined paper in blue ink. The twins are presumably institutionalized.

The evidence from Bill's trial fueled the United States Congressional Energy and Commerce Committee and the Oversight and Investigations Sub-Committee to launch its investigation into the blood industry and its federal regulators who allowed more than 29,000 people to be given AIDS-contaminated blood. The FDA stepped up blood bank inspections and began to enforce safety regulations. Tom Asher worked closely with the committee investigators and gave them the documents from Bill's case, which included the blood bankers' internal documents. Congressman John Dingell, a Democrat from Michigan, chaired the committee investigation. The committee hearings were live on C-Span.

I caught a shuttle from Newark to Washington, D.C. to watch Dr. Englemen testify before the committee. I also ordered the C-Span footage. Congressman Wayden asked to be recognized by the committee chairman, then placed his statement on the record. "Let this CDC study be entered into the record. The CDC estimates 29,000 people were infected with a unit of blood contaminated with the AIDS virus via blood transfusions."

Congress Bliley asked the big question. "Was there a conspiracy of silence between the blood industry and its government regulators? Did the blood industry refuse to use a test to detect people exposed to AIDS for economic reasons and allow tens of thousands of people to be transfused with blood contaminated with AIDS virus? I want Dr. Bove's memo introduced into the record." This is at C-SPAN NEWS FOOTAGE, BLOOD SUPPLY SAFETY INVESTIGATIONS, 22:06-22:08:30.

Questions are being raised by authorities around the world about the safety of American blood products. The sergeant from the Canadian Royal Mounted Police contacted me about the investigation they launched against the American Red Cross that exported AIDS-contaminated blood products into Canada. We talked on several occasions over the phone and he was very interested in the industry conspiracy that avoided the regulation proposed at the Blood Products Advisory Committee on December 16-17, 1983, that would have made them test for AIDS. I sent him the Red Cross documents that had turn up in Bill's case. I also sent him Dr. Bove's January 24, 1983 Report to the AABB board, and Dr. Cummings February 5, 1983 Red Cross memo. The Royal Canadian Mounted Police criminally charged the American Red Cross, Cutter Laboratories, and other American pharmaceutical executives with misrepresenting the risk associated and distributing AIDS-contaminated blood products. The blood bankers and pharmaceutical executives pled guilty.

In March 2012, Scotland's Penrose Inquiry ended its public hearings that included testimony as to the ways in which unsafe American blood products infected thousands of people in Scotland.

In February 2009, Lord Archer of Sandwell concluded a public parliamentary inquiry that found American blood products killed over two thousand of the U.K.'s hemophiliac population. Lord Archer described it as a "historic human tragedy."

France criminally charged three former cabinet members for distributing blood products contaminated with AIDS. Former Premier Laurent Fabius, former Social Affairs Minister Georgia Dufoix, and former Health Minister Edmond Herve were charged with manslaughter for their parts in the management of France's blood banking system in the 1980s.

In Japan, drug company executives were convicted and sent to jail for selling blood products that infected 18,000 people, a significantly smaller number of people than the 29,000 Americans infected in the United States.

The United States government and regulatory authorities, on the other hand, never held a single blood banker accountable for the thousands of people given AIDS-contaminated blood. Patients who were infected with AIDS expected to go away and die quietly, while the people responsible continued their lives unscathed. Today, the babies born in the early to mid-eighties who were infected as children by contaminated blood have been unable to get the political support for minimal compensation to help with their disabilities.

The blood bankers' refusal to take action after Atlanta resulted the largest single catastrophic event in the history of American health care. The American Red Cross, which controls about almost half of the nation's blood supply, continued to operate under a Federal Court order over its collection practices.

By 2003 the blood bankers rack up twenty-one million dollars in fines, despite promises to comply with federal safety procedures to ensure the safety of the nation's blood supply. In 2010, the FDA fined the American Red Cross another $9.6 million dollars for allowing potentially contaminated blood into the nation's blood supply, again. The FDA Commissioner has said that at this point the Congress needs to get involved.

What happened with the blood industry in the early to mid 1980's is the result of greed and a break down in regulation. Since then we have seen it again in Enron and Wall Street. Where there is a lack of oversight and regulation, or lack of accountability, there will be abuses of trust and power that are damaging to the public.

Judge Sylvia Pressler retired as the Presiding Judge of the New Jersey Superior Court Appellate Division in 2004. I met her daughter, who arranged for to meet her mom for lunch at Judge Pressler's home. Judge Pressler and I discussed Bill's case in retrospect and she said the smoking gun were the blood bankers' internal documents that persuaded her. Judge Pressler passed away on February 16, 2010. Judge Isabel Stark served twenty years as a judge and passed away on January 9, 2013.

Don Francis co-founded VaxGen, a bio-tech company in South San Francisco that undertook the herculean humanitarian effort to develop a world AIDS vaccine. Don invited me to join his company as the senior vice-president and general counsel. For a short time, I left my private law practice to become part of Don's team. Presently, Dr. Francis is the Executive Director of Global Solutions for Infectious Disease in South San Francisco.

Marc Conant retired from private practice, but decided he missed treating patients and reopened his practice. Today, he practices medicine in San Francisco. Presently, Marc is involved with finding better treatments for HIV and AIDS. He also founded the Conant Foundation, a charitable foundation for the research and education of AIDS. We have remained close friends since I first met him in San Francisco.

In March 2012, he was awarded the "Public Health Hero's Award" by the University of California—Berkeley School of Public Health. He sent me a personal invitation to attend the ceremony. Don Francis, a prior recipient of the "Hero's Award," presented the award to Marc.

Ed Engleman continues to safeguard the blood center at Stanford's blood center as its director. In April 2010, the FDA approved the first cancer vaccine based on Dr. Engleman's research. Years later, I met Ed Engleman for lunch at Stanford. He told me the reason he testified in Bill's case was to set the record straight about what really happened.

ACKNOWLEDGMENTS

Every Last Drop is a story that I had to tell and is my first book. I sat at my laptop and just wrote away, from beginning to end, and had pages of notes. Then, of course, the material had to be organized into chapters, rewritten and revised. There are several people I have to thank for their assistance and support during this long and challenging process. Michael Denneney, Stephen Pascal and Maggie Cadman who helped me to edit the early drafts of the book. Maggie Cadman is more than an editor; she became a friend who took a personal interest in this story.

Dr. Donald Francis was a good sport to reread several drafts of the manuscript and offer his page-by-page critiques. It is in Don's generous nature to lend a hand when he can. I am also grateful to Dr. Marcus Conant for providing his straightforward thoughts and useful feedback about the book.

Thank you to Denise Huang and Daniel Petraitis for help with initial cover design concepts. A heart felt thank you to Mary Stavropulos, who was my legal secretary during this time. So often Mary went without a paycheck so we could fight this case for the Bill and Roslyn Snyder.

My special thanks to Leslie Griffith, the celebrity, award-winning, San Francisco Bay Area investigative journalist and owner of Leslie Griffith Productions, for producing the incredible promotional trailer that you can view at www.youtube.com/watch?v=Wba6CD0U_V4. I met Leslie at the University of California School of Public Health Award ceremony for Marc Conant in 2011. Leslie produced and directed the six-minute video book promotion as a courtesy because she is so solidly committed to finding and revealing the truth. She even offered me the great advice, "Trust in your story," which I repeated to myself often.

Like many writers, I imposed on family members to read the early drafts and give their thoughts. I thank my daughter, Courtney, sisters, Rosalind and Virgina, and Mom. And, I thank Patti for being the wife who hung in their during the years that are portrayed in the story.

I saved for last, my special gratitude to Nikkitha Bakshani, a bright young woman out of Skidmore College with a talent for writing creative nonfiction. She got her hands around the story and helped to elevate it beyond what I could have done with it. She mentored and taught me writing techniques, offered suggestions and edited the book until it was ready for publication. She brought a sharp and fresh point of view to the storytelling that I am certain will make it more interesting for the readers.

Printed in Great Britain
by Amazon.co.uk, Ltd.,
Marston Gate.